Lucas

THE SUNSET YEARS

Lucas

THE SUNSET YEARS

PAUL CHEESERIGHT

JAMES
JAMES

© TRW Automotive Inc 2005
First published 2005
ISBN 1 904022 10 3

Edited by Susan Millership
Designed by Robin Farrow
Typeset in 9.25/13.5pt Helvetica Neue Condensed

Printed and bound by
Butler & Tanner Ltd, Frome, Somerset

Published by
James & James (Publishers) Ltd
Gordon House Business Centre
6 Lissenden Gardens, London NW5 1LX

Lucas History Group

Publication of *Lucas the Sunset Years* became possible when the following consortium of former Lucas executives agreed to support the project:

Lord Blyth, Dick Garner, Sir Anthony Gill, Brian Henderson, Reg Hennery, Bob Lucas, Bryan Mason, Sir Brian Pearse, Ken Strangward and Alan Watkins.

They described themselves as the Lucas History Group and, in addition to providing initial funding from their own resources, were able to secure further financial assistance from TRW Automotive (the successor company of TRW Inc) headed by John Plant, himself a former executive of the original Lucas company.

Armed with this financial support, four members of the consortium – Bob Lucas, Bryan Mason, Ken Strangward and Alan Watkins – agreed to bring together the financial and administrative strands of the project.

Assisted by Roy Middleton and his colleagues at TRW Benefit's Administration they then launched the sales programme which achieved sufficient advance orders to enable the publication contracts to be signed and *Lucas the Sunset Years* to take its place on our bookshelves.

Author's Acknowledgements

The idea for this book emerged in 1996, during the months after the merger of Lucas Industries with Varity Corporation to form Lucas Varity. For the tens of thousands of Lucas employees, past and present, there would be a memoir of a disappearing but honourable name from British industry. For me, immersion in Lucas affairs after several years of watching the company for the *Financial Times*, would be a valuable adjunct to research I was already doing.

Idea became project in 2000 as a result of a commission from TRW Inc, by then the owner of Lucas Varity. The commission was to take the history of Lucas Industries from the point where Harold Nockolds left off in his detailed two-volume work*, to celebrate the company's 1975 centenary, to the point where TRW assumed control in 1999.

TRW required a corporate history of about 50,000 words which, when coupled with Nockolds's books, would be complementary to its own history** written by Davis Dyer. It saw the Lucas commission as an addition to its archive. While it was happy to see the work published, it had no wish to become directly involved. So by 2001, there was a manuscript but no publishing plan, or, indeed, funds to support one.

After three years exploring various alternatives, publication became possible when Bryan Mason pulled together an informal consortium of former Lucas executives. They agreed to bear the initial costs of publication and to assist with the publication process itself.

All concerned with the publication are indebted to Bryan for his perseverance – without which the book would not have appeared – and to him, Dr Alan Watkins, Ken Strangward and Bob Lucas for their crucial advice on the text and choice of illustrations, as well as managing the onerous tasks of sales and distribution.

By this time I had become indebted to people across the Lucas spectrum. My research started with documents from the Lucas files held in the Shirley complex. There I met unflagging courtesy and cooperation, not least from Alan Bell who found me places to work and regaled me with old Lucas stories. At the Heritage Motor Centre, Gaydon, site of the Lucas archive, Alison Roper, the archivist, was patient and concerned.

The Lucas documents made the base of this book; contemporary comment from newspapers and stock market analyses formed a supplement. The Nockolds history provided the material for the first chapter. But feeling for the events described, the insights into the problems and solutions, the joys and the sorrows of the sunset years, came from a series of interviews with the Lucas participants.

Bob Dale, Tony Gill, Tony Gilroy, David Hymas, Ken Maciver, Bryan Mason, Roy Middleton, John Parnaby, Brian Pearse, Victor Rice, George Simpson, Hugh Spottiswoode, Frank Turner, Alan Watkins and Jeffrey Wilkinson were among those who gave me time and reminiscence, comment and insight, a taste of corporate life and generous hospitality. I thank them unreservedly.

When I had drafted the history, various former executives helped me to iron out creases of uncertainty while leaving me to make my own judgments. Outside the group, Sir Geoffrey Owen at the London School of Economics and Professor Roger Sugden at Birmingham Business School not only offered encouragement but also perceptive suggestions.

Hamish MacGibbon at James & James nurtured the project with great patience and imaginative flexibility, while Susan Millership and Robin Farrow applied huge reserves of energy, tact and skill to bring it to fruition. Throughout all the twists and turns of the last five years, Hazel Duffy, my wife, never wavered in her support, cheerfully accepting, to paraphrase Clarissa Eden, diesel injectors, caliper brakes and the like all over the drawing room carpet; the manuscript belongs to her as well.

PC August 2005

* Harold Nockolds. *Lucas, the first hundred years, Volume 1: The King of the Road, Volume 2: The Successors.* Newton Abbott: David & Charles, 1976.
** Davis Dyer. *TRW, Pioneering Technology + Innovation since 1900.* Boston, Mass: Harvard Business School Press, 1998.

Contents

LUCAS LAMPS

British Made

LONDON
BIRMINGHAM
MANCHESTER
DUBLIN
NEWCASTLE ON TYNE

We make LIGHT of our Labour.

The First Century

Joseph Lucas started business on the streets, trading door-to-door. The foundation for a major British industrial group with extensive international interests was a cask full of paraffin in a basket on wheels.

Trundling around with a basket did not come from free choice. Joseph Lucas, trained as an electroplater, had no work but he did have a family. He had the courage to recognise that he and Emily, his wife, had started to lose their grip as they looked for solace in alcohol. Joseph gave up drinking in the late 1850s. Emily did not.

By his mid-20s, Joseph Lucas would not have been picked off the streets of Birmingham as a potential tycoon; rather, he looked like a permanent petty tradesman with too many responsibilities. But he had the advantage of a rudimentary education: at a time when half his contemporaries would have been illiterate, he could read and write and was numerate. For Nockolds, that decision to start trading and stop drinking meant that 'Joseph Lucas was cast in the true Birmingham mould of independence.' Certainly the local conditions encouraged the independence. Birmingham grew rapidly in the nineteenth century not as a home for large factories in the style of Manchester but as a centre of diversity. It was a city of small business.

By 1860 Lucas had extended his range of wares to household items such as buckets, shovels and chamber pots and to more commercial items such as boiler fillers and small cylinders. Ten years later he started to make the items he wanted to sell, starting with shovels and expanding into other domestic utensils. Gradually he drifted towards lamps. What set him on the route which led to an international group was the 'Tom Bowling', a ship's lamp named after a character in an eighteenth century sea shanty. The 'Tom Bowling' actually belonged to Isaac Sherwood, another small Birmingham manufacturer. Lucas used to sell the lamp for him but, finding it was much admired by its users, he thought it would be a good idea to make it himself. So he bought the lamp from Sherwood. With his friend, George Thomas, who became both the first Lucas

Joseph Lucas.

Facing page: Early bicycle lamp advertisement. Lucas developed its first bicycle lamp in 1878, mainstay of their business until the era of the motor car.

9

Tom Bowling oil lamp patented by Joseph Lucas in 1875.

CAV-Bosch was a joint company formed by Lucas and Robert Bosch between the wars. Staff about to leave on an outing in 1933.

foreman and the son-in-law of Joseph, he found a workshop, called it 'The Tom Bowling Lamp Works' and hired five men. Soon he had changed the design of the 'Tom Bowling' to make it more portable, so that if one part broke it could be individually replaced. Lucas applied for, and received, his first patent. He would not have known it, but the grant of the patent in August 1875 marked the decisive first step in the formation of the Lucas commercial dynasty.

Those were difficult times. What became known as the Great Depression had started: manufacturers had constantly to contend with falling prices and profits were hard to make. Probably the gloomy economic context of the last quarter of the nineteenth century meant little to Joseph Lucas. Like any proprietor of a small business, the constant grind gave little opportunity to worry about the wider circumstances. The fact that he had either to deal with or escape from an alcoholic wife created a separate burden.

His refuge from home was a suitcase. He spent his time on the road searching for orders. His energetic selling, leaving Harry, his eldest son, in charge at the Birmingham factory, was one factor behind the survival of the company. A second was the energy with which Lucas, father and son, both improved their existing products, responding to the market as it would now be seen, and sought new products for his factory to make. The company was successful to the extent that the orderbook constantly enlarged, but, characteristically for a small company, this created its own financing problems. Finding enough working capital was a constant preoccupation, especially for Harry; cashflow was in continual crisis. Harry was a master of the post-dated cheque. But there was a

third factor behind the survival of the young company.

Lucas found the bicycle and the bicycle found Lucas. Cycling and Lucas spread together. By the time Joseph Lucas died in 1902, cycling neared its peak as a national pastime. By then the business of Joseph Lucas Ltd was devoted to making cycle lamps, bells, valves, inflators and other accessories. The shift of Lucas into the bicycle trade came with the 1878 introduction of its first cycle lamp, grandly called 'King of the Road'. It proved an inspired expansion. The new and expanding market provided an antidote to the Great Depression as bicycles in the 1880s and 1890s became a practical craze.

Certainly bicycles gave Lucas the commercial impetus to its first sales in the US, a public listing and the construction of a new factory at Great King Street. By the turn of the century Lucas, father and son, had become prosperous businessmen, their company an attraction for investors; their first public offering was comfortably over-subscribed.

As his father grew older, Harry took more and more practical control. The business he gradually took over had been stamped with his father's hallmark. Joseph Lucas, holding the general view that the British working population was wasteful, had a strict regime for the factory; eating on the shopfloor could mean the sack, and alcohol could not be tolerated. At the same time, he played the benevolent patriarch; he knew all his employees personally and was ready with a guinea at a time of need. With variations, this attitude towards employees of 'you do the best for us and we'll look after you' prevailed into the 1960s. Hence the later establishment of a savings bank, a share ownership scheme, a benevolent fund and, most importantly, a pension scheme.

If the bicycle made Joseph, then the internal combustion engine made Harry. It was a small step from making cycle components to motor components. Indeed, from 1902, the company had for sale items such as lighting sets, horns, pumps and lubrication kits, marketed under the ponderous name of *Motoralities* to run alongside *Cyclealities*. Technical innovations followed quickly as the company sought to keep pace with the new and rapidly expanding motor industry. Electric lights followed dynamo lights, and a complete lighting system for a vehicle was in place by 1914. Electric starters came to the market a year previously. But a turning point for Lucas was the acquisition in 1914 of Britain's only magneto maker, Thomson-Bennett, because this opened up the supply of ignition equipment to all parts of the economy using engines. It meant also that Lucas could move into the market gap left by the withdrawal, because of World War I, of Robert Bosch, the German manufacturer which had supplied 98% of the British market.

The War left Lucas stronger. It managed a higher level of business, not only of products with which it was familiar – signalling lamps, batteries, dynamos, self-starters

Left, Mr Shaw, Sports Organiser, right, Harry Lucas.

Peter Bennett and Oliver Lucas at the Lucas Sports Day, 1935.

Silver Jubilee decorations at Lucas
Head Office and Works, 1935.

for tanks and aircraft – but also simpler articles such as shell covers and rings. Profits at the end of the War were 80% higher than at the beginning; sales multiplied 3.5 times; the payroll increased from 600 to 4,000 people.

The War also marked the emergence of Oliver Lucas, Harry's energetic and technically alert son, as a significant force in the management and an obvious successor to his father, who, from 1919 onwards, took a smaller role. Oliver, with Peter Bennett, the teetotal Sunday-school-teaching entrepreneur, who had arrived with Thomson-Bennett, became joint managing directors in 1923, settling the leadership of the group, as it turned out, for the next 28 years. In 1922 Bertram Waring, the first qualified accountant to join the company, started his career with Lucas not knowing whether he would stay or not. He did, climbing the hierarchy and retiring as chairman in 1969.

Oliver Lucas and Peter Bennett manoeuvred the business to become the virtual monopoly supplier of lighting, starting and ignition equipment to the British motor industry. They pushed direct sales into markets from Europe to the Far East. Lucas already had most of the Morris custom tied up. When, in a delicate three-way negotiation, it acquired two rival companies, CA Vandervell and Rotax, it bought as well all the Austin and Daimler custom. Vandervell later became the CAV diesel equipment business, Rotax the base of Lucas Aerospace.

What Oliver Lucas and Peter Bennett wanted was high-volume production at the lowest price. They believed expansion would best be secured by acquisitions and the use of other people's technology – making products under licence. Transactions followed at a dizzy rate and on an international basis. During the 1920s British Lighting and Ignition came from Vickers, and Lucas bought Rist of Lowestoft, the future wiring business and Powell & Hanmer, an old cycling trade rival. In Europe it reached a patent exchange agreement with Robert Bosch of Germany: later this was extended in a complex series of arrangements resulting in a joint company, CAV-Bosch, opening the way to Lucas obtaining access to Bosch diesel-injection technology, where it was ahead of Lucas. At the same time the two groups offered each other exchange of design and manufacturing rights and carefully parcelled the world up between them for manufacturing and sales. In the Americas, which Oliver Lucas made a point of touring every year for information, the company bought manufacturing rights for electric horns from Sparks' Withington of the US and chassis lubricating systems from Auto-Research of Canada. In the early 1930s, Lucas and Bendix of the US agreed on joint manufacture of brakes for motor cars and starter motors for aircraft.

While lighting, starting and ignition equipment made up most of the contract business with motor manufacturers, Lucas during that decade branched out. Making wing mirrors, door handles, instrument panels, shock absorbers, electric windscreen wipers and other products led critics to talk of the company's monopolistic grip on the domestic motor industry.

Between 1920 and 1939, when World War II started, Lucas sales increased sevenfold to over £9m and profits rose sixfold to over £350,000. The number of people it employed rose from 3,000 to 20,000. As Lucas switched to war production, numbers on the payroll climbed – 31,000 in 1941, 40,000 in 1945, spread over 33 factories. The biggest of these was what had become the industrial behemoth at Great King Street, Birmingham.

The War acted as a technical spur. The effective end of the cooperation with Bosch meant CAV had to develop its own diesel-injection equipment; the demands of the war machine led to new developments like a rotating gun turret. But the most significant work was on Frank Whittle's new jet aircraft where Lucas had responsibility for combustion equipment and the fuel system. Like other engineering companies, Lucas switched production facilities to the making of arms and ammunition, but its usual lines of equipment were inevitably in high demand: Rotax, for example, produced a third of all the magnetos and three quarters of all starters used by British aircraft during the War. Significantly for later years, Lucas acquired Girling, which it designated as its main brakes business. Abrupt termination of government contracts hit production across the group, forcing heavy spending on additional and replacement machinery to bring business back on a peacetime track. In fact, during the five years after the War, sales more than doubled to £41m.

Oliver Lucas, from the third and last generation of the family to control the business, died in 1948. But he lived on in spirit: those who came into control had all worked closely with him and been influenced by him. Bertram Waring took his place as joint managing director with Peter Bennett, who was also the chairman. Kenneth Corley, a former personal assistant of Oliver Lucas and a future chairman, became a director.

The big commercial and technical issue for Lucas in the years after the War was to organise the standardisation of equipment, to limit the variety of component types. Common standards in the motor industry would allow component manufacturers to begin

Rotating gun turrets and parts for the first jet aircraft were among new challenges thrown up by World War II.

Gas turbine incorporating Lucas designed and manufactured fuel and combustion equipment. Lucas was involved with combustion research and fabrication from the earliest days of jet engines in the 1940s.

emulation of US companies with their long production runs. By the mid-1950s, productivity, quality and output of standard products had tripled.

In other respects, companies in the group signalled their future. Girling fitted its first disc brakes and produced a new line of shock absorbers. CAV, now accepted in its own right as a maker of diesel-injection equipment, put a new distributor pump on the market and started a joint venture for manufacture in France called Roto-Diesel. It followed this by buying into Condiesel of Spain.

Waring, chairman since 1951, understood perfectly the significance of the foundation of the European Economic Community in 1958 and set up a committee to examine the possibilities for Lucas. The chairman was Bernard Scott, another alumnus from Oliver Lucas's stable of bright young men, and, like Corley, a future chairman. The CAV venture in France was the first result, the start of a series of investments from which Lucas would emerge as a European manufacturer. The European expansion was a natural, and vital, trend for a group which had a position of such strength in the domestic market that it had been examined by the Monopolies Commission in 1960.

Lucas Electrical in the early 1970s supplied around 70% of the electrical equipment used by British motor manufacturers. CAV, helped by takeovers of companies such as Bryce Berger and Simms, was the world's biggest manufacturer of multi-cylinder diesel-injection equipment. Rotax became the focus of UK aircraft component manufacture, encouraged by the government to buy a series of smaller companies. By 1975 brakes of Girling origin had been fitted on one of every three cars made around the world. All of this provided a strong base for the provision of spares and services across the world. Indeed, the group had grown to such an extent that when Corley succeeded Waring in 1969 he had to streamline an organisation of 19 independent UK companies. By the 1970s Lucas employed about 80,000 people, forcing Scott, Corley's successor, into further reorganisation.

Bernard Scott took over in 1974. He faced international economic turbulence and the worst domestic recession since the Great Depression of the early 1930s. The Lucas reputation for harmonious industrial relations had frayed since unofficial strikes started in 1968. Political, economic and social instability marked the mid-1970s. Rising sales, dividends and wages could not be taken for granted.

Bertram Waring and HM Queen Elizabeth II visiting Great King Street in the 1950s.

One of the best known Lucas products – the Battery. This polypropylene cased Pacemaker Battery, developed in 1969, subsequently won the Queen's Award for Technology.

16

Mixed Fortunes

Lucas Industries started its second century during 1975 in circumstances as trying as Joseph Lucas found when he began the first. Just as during the last two decades of the nineteenth century British manufacturers worried about their productivity compared with American and German competitors, so, a hundred years further on some industrialists wondered whether they could compete at all. Increases in oil and commodity prices, after the first Arab oil price shocks of 1973, put pressure on costs. By June 1975, UK basic hourly wage rates ran 32% higher than a year before and national inflation hit an annual rate of 26%.

The fortunes of Lucas mirrored the national experience. Profits, which had been rising from the start of the decade, slipped in the year to July 1974 and the return on capital slipped with them. By July 1976, recovery was evident, everything looked more cheerful and pre-tax profits for the year to July 1977 at £76.8m were the highest of the 1970s. Indeed, in those calmer years after the upsets of the oil crisis, Lucas felt confident enough to raise new capital of £42.7m in May 1976, so that, with a new £100m investment programme, it could expand more quickly.

The Lucas share price had been rising in fits and starts: from a humble 35p on 6 January 1975 to a dizzy 338p on 14 September 1977, respectively the low and high points of the decade. If not exactly a darling of the stock exchange, Lucas demanded some respect from the brokers. Savory Milln, for example, put it among 20 shares which it had identified as likely to do well: companies which are improving efficiency, strongly placed financially and well represented overseas.

Freshly dressed in a livery of green with a new logo – the white diagonal stripe broken in a v-shape so that the two parts of the stripe seemed destined to come together as neatly and inevitably as Lucas systems fitted into vehicles and aircraft across the world – the group's progress in the early part of its second century seemed assured. But for

A new company logo, *below*, replaced the much-loved Lucas lion in 1975.

Facing page, Bernard Scott, centre, talking to William Dyoedwd Jones at Cwmbran; Eugene Hale, the factory manager, right, 1975.

every set of numbers which looked promising, there was another set which looked menacing, for every favourable circumstance an unfriendly counterweight.

'We had given ourselves a new corporate identity which had successfully taken hold across the world' recorded the minutes of a May 1976 meeting of management and representatives of the employees. The new logo could help to define not so much a 'new corporate identity' as a recognisable corporate identity for those who worked in the group. By the mid-1970s Lucas had spread so far with so many different names that new branding might help to create coherence out of a string of autonomous units, associated largely by common ownership but lacking much unity of commercial approach.

The group's own definition of itself was 'a leading world manufacturer of electrical, hydraulic and mechanical equipment used by internal combustion, diesel and gas turbine engines, road and rail vehicles, ships and aircraft. It also manufactures a wide range of industrial products.' By 1978 it had slipped 'electronic' into the description of its equipment.

The generality covered at this time eight sets of manufacturers, along with distribution and service companies. Lucas Electrical provided the UK motor manufacturers with about 75% of their electrical and electronic equipment: it got engines going, wiped windscreens, blew horns, provided the lights and the switchgear for any sort of vehicle. Lucas CAV made diesel-engine fuel-injection equipment. Lucas Girling was a brakes manufacturer, selling not only in the car and commercial vehicle markets but also to the railways. Rists Wires and Cables provided cables and harnesses to the motor, defence and telecommunications industries. Lucas Batteries sold its products for use in all sorts of vehicles, not to speak of caravans and lawnmowers. Lucas Aerospace had three main divisions: engine management, making fuel control systems; fabrications and actuation, with a range of products from thrust reversers to ice protection systems to flying controls; and electrical, dealing with equipment such as generating systems and constant speed drives. Lucas Defence Systems aimed to gather technology from the group's operating companies and apply it to defence projects. Finally, SMEC acted as an industrial holding company for an array of subsidiaries engaged in, for example, electronic components, timers and switches, ceramic capacitors, measuring gear, fluid power and electronic machine tool drives.

The centre of gravity remained in the UK where, in the second half of the 1970s, there were 45 major manufacturing sites and 60 of lesser importance. By the end of the decade Lucas had over 69,000 employees in the UK and more than 18,000 in overseas subsidiaries. Associated companies employed a further 21,000 people in Europe, Australia, Brazil, India, Iran, Mexico, South Africa and the US.

Myer Goldstone, group General Manager of Lucas Industries Australia, 'turns the first sod' while Derek Ward, centre, General Manager of Lucas Parts and Service Division, and John Sargeant, Property Manager study plans for the new Lucas Parts and Service National Headquaters, Mordialloc, Melbourne.

From the earliest days Lucas had an international outlook. It looked first towards Europe and by the start of its second century had built a significant presence. In France, Girling and Rists had manufacturing plants; CAV worked through a 67% holding of RotoDiesel; Electrical had started the lengthy saga of establishing a presence through Ducellier; Aerospace operated through Thomson-Lucas, a joint venture company. In Germany, Girling Bremsen represented the brakes business. Joint venture companies established Lucas in Italy and Spain; Fausto Carello made lights and Condiesel was the CAV arm. There were distribution companies from Sweden to Switzerland, from Germany to Greece.

Outside Europe, Lucas scattered across the continents, manufacturing in Australia and New Zealand, Argentina and Brazil, Japan and Korea, India and Bangladesh, the

Caribbean and, of course, the US. Partnerships spread from Afghanistan to Trinidad. Everywhere, there were distribution companies.

If there was a problem, it was that there was too much activity in the countries of the old British Empire and not enough in developed and the faster growing developing economies. Indeed, in 1978, as sales approached £1bn a year, the Lucas board warned shareholders and employees alike, 'There seems little prospect that a manufacturing company the size of Lucas, based primarily in the UK, can continue to compete successfully unless it becomes a fully international organisation, designing, making and selling in all the major countries associated with the transport industry.' That meant an even greater concentration on Europe and a build-up in the Americas.

A board and, underneath it, an executive were in charge of meeting this aspiration. The board was a mixture of non-executive and functional directors; it did not have on it the chief of any operating company. The executive brought together the functional directors and managers of the main operating companies. These directors and managers overlapped in two interdependent groups: one under the chairman and concerned with strategy, the second under the group managing director and concerned with operations. Bernard (Sir Bernard from 1979) Scott, as the executive chairman, held this structure together. He was the dominant personality of the two tiers.

Scott is a rarity among the Lucas leaders of the last two generations. Executives who came after him or who had recollections of him had no ill to say of him. 'He was the best person I've known at Lucas,' said Tony Gill, a later chairman knighted as Sir Anthony. He had natural commercial flair and marketing skill, honed by the experience of a career solely in Lucas, apart from military service in World War II. Steeped in Lucas, for he had first arrived as a 16-year old in 1931, Scott managed at the same time to avoid the insularity and complacency of some of his contemporaries: indeed, as non-executive chairman of Lloyds Bank International, he had to have a wide outlook. So he had a clear sense of where and why Lucas had to fit into the scheme of international business.

By the time he reached the apex of his Lucas career, he had managed to straddle the divide between head office man and line manager. Oliver Lucas, the third-generation Lucas to run the group had spotted his talent and made him his third personal assistant. (The second had been Sir Kenneth Corley, eventually Scott's predecessor as chairman and chief executive.) In 1959 Scott had become general manager of CAV and set it on a path of expansion. Later he became Corley's understudy before his own turn at the top.

Scott's task was to pick up the pace, which had perceptibly slowed at Lucas by the end of the 1960s. Gill saw him as a good manager with a keen sense of what needed

Godfrey Messervy, centre, holding a model of Concorde, with Lucas Export Prize winners, left to right, Ray Weldon, Gail Turner, Barry Chittock, who won the 1st prize, a trip to New York on Concorde, and Ronald Betteridge, March 1978.

to be done to catch up. Scott had a toughness, visible in his eyes which turned from blue to grey if he faced a challenge to his authority. At the same time, he had sufficient humility to back away from a position if somebody could convince him of a better course. In the habit of those days, he did not encourage informality. Gill worked with him for 20 years and never called him Bernard.

Scott continued where Corley had left off in seeking to give the group a more intellectually rigorous leadership; changing the board so that it would question and support rather than rubber-stamp, making it necessary to be more than a chum of the chairman to have a directorship. He encouraged the autonomy of the managers of the different businesses, although they had limited freedom to undertake capital expenditure; spending over £100,000 needed executive approval until 1978 when the figure went up to £250,000.

In what had become a pattern of executive behaviour at Lucas, Scott made provision for the succession. He had helped to nurse the career of Godfrey Messervy, his successor and the man he made group managing director. Like Oliver Lucas, he was a good talent spotter, opening the way for Gill and for other senior executives such as Jeffrey Wilkinson and James Blyth.

The flowering of the Lucas dynasty started to fade with Scott. He was the last chief executive to have worked closely with the Lucas family. In this respect, as in others, he made a bridge between the old and the new. Under Scott, the notion of a company run

Shaftmoor Lane, a 'state of the art' factory, became a hot bed of militant industrial activity. It was eventually sold to Magnetti-Marelli.

by a patriarch clucking over an appreciative workforce disappeared. Scott had liberal views of the role of a company in the community and ready acceptance of a mutual dependence of employer and employee which went beyond the exchange of money for work. Under Scott, Lucas embraced the reality that the future would not be British – it would be international or nothing.

In 1977 the UK government, employers and trades unions busily debated concepts and methods of industrial democracy, a vague phrase which usually meant adjusting corporate systems of control or finding a way of giving labour greater influence over capital. In Scott's view, it would be a mistake to try and impose from above what must grow upwards from the grassroots. He told workforce representatives during April that 'Lucas had to develop greater and fuller commitment of all employees in the affairs of the company.'

For Lucas and its peers in the UK automotive and aerospace industries, the problem of arranging the interests of employers and employees so that all moved towards a mutually accepted goal hung over all other questions. Not everywhere but in many plants, managers had ceased to manage, shopfloor workers had split into sections; factory life was an unceasing negotiation where the only certainty remained uncertainty. National agreements could mean little in the face of local preoccupations; often there had been a surrender of power from national trades union leadership to local unionists and shop stewards active on the factory floor. Observing all this, continental Europeans called the UK 'the sick man of Europe'. Concern about industrial relations lay under the commercial worries of Lucas management; the need to raise productivity and quality not only to conserve business with existing customers but to attract new customers.

Yet the uncertainties at Lucas proved less pervasive than in many parts of British manufacturing. Historically, Lucas had been seen domestically as a reliable employer. It had eschewed the practice in other parts of the motor industry where employees had been recruited and laid off whenever a company wanted. 'Lucas prided itself on offering permanent employment,' recalled Bryan Mason, who worked on personnel matters from 1960 and became group director (personnel) in 1980. 'So we expected a greater degree of loyalty than that given to the auto manufacturers.' Although that loyalty dissipated in the industrial friction of the 1970s, residual goodwill made the plight of Lucas less difficult than it might have been.

For all that, Lucas factories became more difficult to run at precisely the time when they needed the greatest flexibility to meet changing market needs. Generally, the greater the degree of strife, the lower sank the quality of supervision. People who might have been expected to seek advance no longer wished to become foremen and charge-hands, feeling they could not rely on the support of management. Often it was easier for managers to give in to a demand, to back away from an exercise of authority, simply to keep production moving.

Among the Lucas motor component plants, the two most unstable were the CAV fuel pump factory at Fazakerley in Liverpool and Electrical's dynamo and starter factory known as Branch Works 3 at Shaftmoor Lane, Birmingham. In the 1970s, Liverpool had become a byword for industrial antagonism. Recalcitrance – management called it 'local bloodymindedness' – spilled over into the Fazakerley workforce; it had been recruited when CAV relocated a plant there in response to the urging of the UK government, anxious for business to create job opportunities on Merseyside. Disharmony made the plant vulnerable; diesel-engine manufacturers could easily shift orders to another supplier since Fazakerley had never been a monopoly supplier. But that is exactly what Branch Works 3 had become. 'By the early 1970s, it had become the single supplier of starters to the British motor industry. If industrial mayhem was your game, Branch Works 3 was a good place to concentrate,' Mason noted. Even then, the just-in-time system of deliveries operated, meaning that the plant held no stocks as a buffer against breaks in production. So, said Mason, 'it was vulnerable to an opportunist strike, it was always on a knife edge.'

Lucas Aerospace meanwhile dealt with problems of a different hue. A disparate collection of companies, all hurt by the collapse in 1971 of their main customer, Rolls-Royce, and pulled together under government aegis in the interests of creating commercial power through consolidation, faced continuing reorganisation and, inevitably, reduced employment. The quantity of orders fell back in the years after the 1973 energy crisis, putting further pressure on jobs. Out of resistance to job losses sprang the Lucas Aerospace Combine Committee of shop stewards from 17 factories. Quickly they realised that, to influence the affairs of Lucas, they would have to see the retention of jobs in a wider context than simple resistance to management plans. They would have to devise wholly different ways of running the group. To that extent, the Combine threatened traditional forms of company management; its existence met Scott's dictum on the needs for a grassroots movement in favour of industrial democracy, but, of course, his thoughts on industrial democracy did not involve handing over the company to workers' control.

The Combine had its heyday in the mid-1970s, a period of intellectual ferment around the likely future of British industry – could the sick man of Europe recover? Hilary Wainwright and Dave Elliott, sympathetic historians of the movement, saw the Combine

Personnel and industrial relations leaders throughout the company's history.

Alec Nicol

Ron March

Bryan Mason

John Williams, General Manager,
Lucas Aerospace.

as 'not only a new trade unionism, but a new politics, a politics not only for people but also of and by the people.' In 1976 the Combine produced its Plan which, in essence, tried to show how Lucas Aerospace could use the extensive skills of its workforce to shift away from the production of components for the defence industry to a range of equipment designed to meet social needs: kidney machines, heat pumps, alternative energy, airships and so on. It caught the imagination of Tony Benn, the secretary of state for industry, who in his diary commented on the Combine leaders: 'I was very impressed by Mike Cooley and Ernie Scarbrow. I think Mike Cooley is an International Socialist and Ernie is a Communist and by God they have produced some excellent stuff – it just shows what the shopfloor is capable of.' But Benn was soon moved on himself. Other members of the Labour government remained cool to the Combine.

Limited discussions between Combine members and Lucas executives took place. Management, however, saw the Combine's suggestions as impractical and nothing much more than an irrelevant nuisance. It had no intention of changing the orientation of Aerospace and reasserted its view that 'the only way to secure jobs in the market economy is to manufacture the products which the company is best at producing effi- ciently and profitably.' The Labour party challenged this view. At its annual conference in 1978, delegates passed a resolution applauding the Combine's plan and telling the government to implement it. In truth there was little the government could do, but Gerald Kaufman, the minister of state for industry, convened a meeting of Combine offi- cials, union leaders and the management. At this meeting, the management, by agreeing to set up a working party with the unions, shuffled the problem away from attention and gave Kaufman enough to placate Labour party conference delegates.

There, in effect, the matter rested: death by committee. The Combine gradually came apart, the victim of its own internal contradictions and the changing external envi- ronment. Its membership was an unlikely mixture: idealists of the political left who wanted to change the world, disgruntled engineers frustrated in their work, malcontents angry at the company or the unions or both, traditional unionists worried about jobs, political agitators searching for causes. Had it been propelled by the larger trade unions, the Combine might have fared better. Even then its life probably would have been limited; the coming recession changed priorities from company control to company survival. As it was, the Combine showed up the fevered atmosphere at the start of the second Lucas century, illustrating how industrial relations crossed into politics, how business had ceased to be the preserve of business. The effect, recorded in the group board minutes of January 1979, was 'the appalling decline in manufacturing effec- tiveness caused by the nation's industrial troubles.'

Supplier performance Award presented by Bill Davis of Boeing Vertol to the workforce at Hemel Hempstead, October 1981.

In general terms, the Labour government's twin statutory policy of restraining wage and price increases worked to bring down inflation in 1976–78 and to revive corporate fortunes, but this did not rule out particular rivalries inside factories. Executives at Lucas developed a variety of techniques and habits to avoid and to calm unrest. As trades union leaders ceded power to the local level and individual shop stewards moved into the key negotiating positions on the shopfloor, Lucas plant managers found themselves dealing directly with industrial relations. To take pressure off them, Mason remembered,

> We invented a raft of people – personnel officers – and put them into the factory. The shop stewards could raise a problem but work must carry on. This lifted problems off the factory floor into an adjacent room to reach an accommodation. It worked. But it was a poor substitute for doing it properly. We knew 50 to 60% of the difficulties were imaginary, the product of an over-sensitive group looking for complaints.

Alongside this approach, management and unions worked out a whole series of procedures, of hoops to take a problem through, designed to elongate the opportunities for reaching agreement and shorten the possibilities of a strike.

Different managers had different approaches. At Electrical, Wilkinson found in 1974 a lack of direction:

> My first job was to break the company up into manageable units – there were 30 people on the executive. I broke it down to starters and alternators, lighting and so on. And then

I broke down the factories into small units. I put people on to the shopfloor and over-managed the factories.

Recirculating Ballscrews, Lucas Aerospace, Hemel Hempstead – subject of an industrial dispute in 1975.

For Gill, at CAV, there was no choice but to take on the shop stewards in the plants at Finchley and Acton, west London. At Acton, he said, 'The shop steward was dedicated to the cause of getting industry into the hands of the workers. This chap was paid by the company as a full-time shop steward. He was playing havoc. I couldn't avoid getting involved; the logic was that if this chap is full-time, you need somebody full-time beating him.' Gill plucked an executive from the personnel department, 'took him out of normal personnel work and assigned him full-time to anticipate, make plans to combat what was going on. We knew we had to outguess this guy. It was resolved in a focussed way.'

Alan Watkins took over responsibility for the electrical division of Aerospace in 1975. His approach to a workforce, unsettled by both internal rationalisation and the external industrial climate, was order and organisation. At Bradford, he found nobody in charge so he put in a site boss. At Hemel Hempstead, his base, he found his relations with shop stewards changed when they realised he was not a hatchet man, in and out after cutting back the workforce. He gave up the thought of compulsory layoffs in favour of voluntary redundancies, got the shop stewards involved in producing a graph of volume in relation to sales price and won more change and less strife. He associated plants with specific products and made each site a profit centre. 'Each site had something to go for,' he said. But implementation had to be delayed while the Combine drama played out.

In spite of all the attention lavished on industrial relations, Lucas had a sharp setback in summer 1977 when the toolmakers went on strike for ten weeks. Their action surprised Wilkinson: 'I went off on holiday. I came back home and there was a contractor in the garden. "When are they going back then?" he asked me. Nobody had told me they'd come out.' The toolmakers wanted staff status. The annual pay talks had broken down on the issue of more pay and the nature of steps to be taken to reach staff status. The management negotiator had followed instructions not to give way to new demands; the toolmakers walked out.

At first Wilkinson had strong support within the region's motor industry, and, in any case, the Lucas management thought the toolmakers would settle in the third week.

I found that this was a Midlands thing. Harold Musgrave (then running the BL plant at Longbridge) said, 'Stand firm'. They all rang – 'Don't give in'. The board said, 'Stand firm'. After three to four weeks, the phone started to go – 'When are you going to settle?' After six weeks the phone was silent. It was almost like being a pariah.

Opening of the Hemel Hempstead
Sports and Social Club Bar,
October 1981.

The toolmakers proved themselves to be a powerful organisation of skilled men, disciplined and organised. At this point, Wilkinson was joined by Ron March, the group personnel director; talks in pubs and smoke-filled rooms started with the national leadership of the toolmakers' union, the Amalgamated Union of Engineering Workers. A settlement patched together, the toolmakers returned to work on 12 September.

Looking back, Mason sees the strike as 'an example of how such action can produce uneconomic demands and get them met. What they wanted was unwarranted.' A month after the return to work, Scott told the board that 'the rough conditions being experienced were largely as expected, that other companies were having similar industrial relations problems.' But for Lucas management, that did not compensate for the financial impact of the strike. Electrical's production, during August, had fallen to 15% of the planned output. In that month, the first of the Lucas financial year, the group made a loss of £4.68m, compared with a planned profit of £0.3m; the shortfall at Electrical was £3.8m. Group figures never quite recovered that year. Scott had estimated, immediately after the strike, that it would cost £11m in profits. 'Experience has shown that the effect was worse than this, together with some continuing damage due to orders switched to competitors and not regained,' he told shareholders and employees when he announced that pre-tax profits for 1976–78 had fallen to £73.1m from £76.8m the year before. Lucas fortunes were starting to slide.

Prospects at home seemed uncertain at best. Domestic car manufacturers faced the same industrial difficulties as Lucas itself. Their share of the British car market had been slipping. Imports consistently took around half of local sales. In the aerospace sector, government policy on defence purchases lacked consistency and the local civil market remained tiny compared with the US and Europe. But, even if Lucas set aside all of these transient factors, it still had to look overseas.

   A company of its size could not ignore the fundamental numbers: it had 69% of its manufacturing in a country which had 1% of the world's population and 4% of its vehicles. The UK market was simply not large enough to support a group whose future lay always in the development of high-technology products. On top of that the motor industry had started to change fast. Scott drew attention to three factors:

1. The development of what is essentially a single world market for vehicles.
2. More competitive pressures from Third World manufacturers forcing everyone in manufacturing industry to use the most efficient locations.
3. A real shortage of skills in the UK, especially when compared with our European partners, making the most effective deployment of those skills all the more important.

Coming to terms with these factors became the underlying theme of the next years of Lucas activity as the group worked with renewed urgency to reduce dependence on the UK market. If it could export reliably from the UK, well and good. If it needed a manufacturing presence elsewhere, it could establish one, usually by joint venture or acquisition. Ideally, it would run its UK and overseas manufacturing in tandem. Before recession overtook it, Lucas tried to lift its presence in Europe and the US.

   The single issue which kept the board occupied for a year with meeting after meeting from mid-1978, concerned Ducellier, an associate company, part of the Lucas Electrical network and the biggest electrical equipment manufacturer in France. From 1962, Ducellier had been owned in partnership, 40% by Lucas and 60% by DBA, a consortium company made up of the original Ducellier, Bendix and Air Equipement but where the effective player was Bendix, the French unit of the US components group. In August 1977, following talks with Bendix, Wilkinson sought and obtained a sanction from the Lucas board to raise the Lucas shareholding by nine percentage points to 49% and extend licensing agreements for another ten years. The cost would be £2.85m, but, Wilkinson told the board, 'Over the ten years, total revenue from profits and royalties will range between £21.5m and £25m.' So far, so good.

Wilkinson, though, was caught unawares when Scott negotiated with Bill Agee, the Bendix chief, to buy the remaining 51% of Ducellier for $26m. In his anxiety to pull off a deal, Scott misread the political subtleties of investing in France. At this time, the French government sought to plan economic development. It encouraged inward investment but on French terms, where French companies were pushed to compete on the continental stage. The French government had nothing against Lucas as such, but it could not be expected to be overly sympathetic to Lucas interests if these interfered with the policy of fostering a national components industry which would both support local manufacturers such as Citroën, Peugeot and Renault and would compete with groups such as Robert Bosch. If, then, Scott wanted to control Ducellier, he would have helped himself had he prepared the ground in government and official circles. But he did not: he acted as he would have done at home and publicised his agreement with Agee. 'This was Mistake Number One,' judged Wilkinson.

By the summer of 1978, politics, the law and commercial opportunism had trapped the Lucas bid. Scott, although his wife was French, did not speak French, so Wilkinson, fluent in the language, handled the negotiations. To help him on the French side, he had Jean-Maxime Lévêque, a senior banker and Lucas non-executive director, who, in the tradition of the French intellectual elite, switched easily between government and commerce. Wilkinson could easily obtain support from the British government; during this period Lucas had a cosy relationship with the Labour government and, as Gill remembered, 'Nobody in Lucas needed to do more than pick up the phone to get an appointment.'

In August Bendix gave Lucas 30 days to get the matter settled, an ultimatum promptly rejected. But, by this time, Lucas had a rival. Ferodo, the French company later known as Valeo, had been holding secret talks with Bendix about buying control of Ducellier. Huffily, Scott told the board of 'his feeling that the manoeuvrings of Ferodo and Bendix were not what one would expect from two such prominent companies.' But Ferodo and Bendix had not acted independently. Behind Ferodo lay the French government. It became clear – indeed, President Giscard d'Estaing stated as much – that the government wanted control of Ducellier to remain in France; the government also wanted to ensure that French car manufacturers had a variety of sources for their components. If it fended off the Lucas attempt to control Ducellier, then a French solution had to be found.

At this stage the Lucas board was alert to the possibility of compromise but not yet in any mood for it. The British government had become involved; both James Callaghan, the prime minister, and Eric Varley, the industry secretary, pushed the Lucas case in

French government circles, although not robustly enough for Sir Anthony Part, a Lucas non-executive director who had been a senior civil servant. Lucas itself decided to fight the threat of Ferodo in the French courts. It based its case on the rules controlling rights and liabilities in a partnership. In short, it argued that Bendix could not dispose of its stake without Lucas approval.

Lévêque thought that Lucas had a good chance of winning the case but he told the board that if it did, if the judgment went against Ferodo, then Ferodo 'would look to Lucas to help them from a face-saving point of view' and, he suggested, 'Ferodo were anxious to improve their bargaining position and to reach a satisfactory agreement with Lucas.' Godfrey Messervy felt that Ferodo needed Lucas because its own technology was stagnant but, he asserted, 'Lucas was not going to give away its know-how.' Given the French government's policy, as Lévêque saw it, 'of pushing Ferodo into as advantageous position as possible with a view to making it a major component manufacturer,' then a little help from Lucas might not go amiss; if not Lucas, then Bosch, but that raised for the French a series of other problems. So, behind the legal dispute, Lucas faced considerable pressure to compromise.

Lucas won the legal case, but the matter did not end there. The French government still withheld approval of Lucas taking control of Ducellier. 'It didn't say Yes, it didn't say No,' recalled Wilkinson. 'It said, go and sort it out with Ferodo.' Which is what Wilkinson had to do. Eventually the two companies agreed on joint control, a deal which was, said Wilkinson, 'really for partition'. Each had 49%, the balancing 2% of the shareholding went into the care of a French bank, and Lucas would hold management responsibility for five years.

At one level, Lucas had not advanced from its position of 1977. At another, a new possibility opened up; 'There could be further opportunities for cooperation in Brazil and Spain,' Wilkinson told the board at its final discussion on the subject, thinking of what he had discussed with Scott three years before. This was how Lucas might lead *un grand groupe*, a combination of component companies to rival Bosch. But the board was only too happy to see the end of the matter. Wearied by the tortuous progress, it asked that 'the saga of the Ducellier negotiations be fully recorded.' It never has been.

By contrast, expansion in the freewheeling economy of the US appeared simple. Americans knew little of Lucas, but that was hardly surprising. In 1978–79 Lucas made sales in the US of about one sixth of the value it made in Europe. Although, towards the end of the 1970s, the prospects for the US economy looked gloomy, Lucas internal reports made clear that 'temporary considerations must not deflect us from our determination to become a significant manufacturer in this most industrialised of countries.'

In 1977–78, for its industrial arm, Lucas bought small US companies to strengthen its distribution network, not least in the fluid power sector. It acquired a stake in Siliconix, a growing California manufacturer of semiconductor devices, which, apart from its capability in process controls, offered what Lucas executives in the US saw as 'an attractive technological investment in engine control electronics.' In mid-1979, Girling had started to expand its engineering facilities in the US; it wanted to support its direct export business, having stuck its foot in the pond and secured a brakes contract with Ford and a clutch-actuation equipment contract with American Motors. But the big prize looked as if it would be in fuel-injection equipment for diesel engines.

Gill first proposed, and the Lucas board agreed in February 1977, to set up CAV in the US with modest engineering, testing and assembly facilities. One purpose was obvious: to remain a world player in diesel equipment, CAV needed a direct presence in a major growth area: 'US customers are unlikely to use CAV FIE [fuel-injection equipment] unless we have an operation in the USA.' The second immediate purpose was defensive: to maintain its business with Perkins, the diesel-engine maker at that time starting a new plant in Canton, Ohio, and threatening extensive use of local produced components: 'If CAV do not set up in the USA we can expect to lose the majority of the Perkins Canton business.' That would be 48,000 pump and injector packs, Gill reminded the board. Construction of a plant at Greenville, South Carolina, started in 1978; it would be one of the centres for the great fuel-injector adventure of the 1980s, when diesel looked as if it could drive Lucas out of recession.

Meanwhile, Lucas had been chasing the expansion of the international motor industry. The group presence grew in Brazil with the purchase of a lighting company, a build-up of braking business and the accelerating production of diesel pumps and injectors. Construction of a nozzles factory started in Korea. New service facilities opened in Australia.

In spite of the gathering pace of activity around the world, Lucas remained a predominantly European group. In 1977, the UK and Europe took 80.6% of sales; the following year they took 80.2%, although half of the work carried out by Lucas factories in the UK ended up overseas, either provided directly or as part of another company's product. Of the £105m spent on factories by the group, £88m went in to UK plants.

Sir Bernard Scott explaining a technical detail to HM Queen Elizabeth II at the Royal Smithfield Show, right, Douglas Walker, Chairman of the Show's Joint Committee, Earls Court, December 1971.

3 2

The Operations, 70s Style

The clumsily titled Joint Production Consultative Committee started during the 1940s, when management and workers came together to talk about output for the national war effort. The habit of talking continued and, until the committee expired at the end of the 1970s, the management used it to percolate news down to the workforce, and the workforce used it to convey upwards grievances and shopfloor information. The management took it seriously enough for Bernard Scott or Godfrey Messervy to act as chairman of the meetings. Some of the impressions they, or their colleagues, imparted made it seem as if, more than 20 years after World War II, they still felt the company remained on a war footing, with issues of quality, finance and staffing.

Lucas was at odds with too many customers for the management to feel comfortable. Dealing with the automotive business, largely that of Lucas Electrical, Geoff Claydon told the committee in August 1976 that British Leyland 'had identified that half the failures on their vehicles involved electrical equipment.' At a headlamp factory in Cannock, Staffordshire, 3.95% of everything made had to be scrapped. For the first time in ten years, Lucas appeared on the list of Ford's ten worst suppliers because it had been delivering products with wrong, missing or loose components. Claydon worried about the US 'where new technology products such as electronic ignition and petrol injection had shown particularly high failure rates, leading to loss of customer confidence.' Over a year later, he reported that some plants had still only received temporary approval from BL and Vauxhall, both of whom wanted more systematic and expensive testing of the products they bought. Still, the position improved between 1976 and 1977: 'We had made good progress in sending the right parts to the right customer at the right price.'

On the Aerospace side of Lucas, in 1976 Messervy complained to the committee that a contract for engine control units with Rolls-Royce, the aero engine maker, was in serious jeopardy because the plants could not deliver on time. Later he related how 'customers at the Paris Air Show had pointed out that if the company could not deliver

Facing page: Michael Foot, leader of the Labour Party and MP for Ebbw Vale accompanied by Mrs Anne James, Mayor of Torfaen on a visit to Girling, Pontypool.

on time during a slump, then there was little likelihood of it being able to do so during an upsurge'.

While these expressions of worry concerned only two of the group's businesses, the effect of such visible failings dented the reputation of the whole group and therefore became a matter of continuing central concern. Scott – and, indeed, his successors – may have wanted the different businesses to assume more autonomy, but the centre had to grapple with matters which had significance across the group. Clearly quality and, in the broad sweep, amiable customer relations, were one such. Another was finance.

Understandably enough, in the second half of the 1970s, financial demands tended to run ahead of the ability to meet them. In the UK, of course, a company had to run to stand still, at least until the period of falling inflation. The effect of currency fluctuations and domestic inflation, in any case, worked against the competitiveness of British companies and Lucas could not escape that. From 1976–77, the trend in UK profits went down steadily, compensated in part by the equally steady rise in overseas profits, but the numbers of the former were much higher than those of the latter. Lucas lost ground in some UK markets because it could not increase its sales revenue by a higher percentage than the rate of inflation. The group's internal calculations, measuring output against the total of hours worked, showed that, in 1977–78, only Batteries and Rists of the UK businesses were more productive than they had been in 1973–74.

Meeting the group's financial criterion of a 25% return on capital employed became more of an aspiration than an expectation. Isolated activities exceeded the target, but the best result for the group as a whole was 19% in the financial year to July 1977. As the group managed its finances cautiously, Messervy's complaint to employees after the announcement of the 1977–78 results, 'We are extremely short of money to spend on the re-equipment of our factories,' had an air of inevitability about it. Scott disliked taking out loans but knew it had to be done, telling representatives of the workforce that they 'were a means of putting money in other people's pockets, and for this reason were always taken out grudgingly.' Shortage of money held spending back, but Lucas still managed in 1977–78 to spend over £105m on its factories. The group traditionally and strongly held the view that its future could only be assured by research into, and development of, new products and on this it spent, that year, £35m. This was a modest 3.6% of sales, but more than four times the amount paid to shareholders in dividends. On a group basis, this would have been about three-quarters of the relative spending of Bosch, the great German rival, but given that some of the Lucas spending went on aerospace research and development (R&D), probably Bosch had a considerably higher automotive R&D bill than Lucas.

A third central concern for Lucas, tightly linked both to organising higher productivity and strongly related to the search for new products, remained throughout the second half of the 1970s: the recruitment and retention of scientists, engineers and technicians. Reports submitted to Lucas Group Services, the headquarters company offering support for the operating companies, show a discouraging position in the mid-1970s. John Armstrong, the veteran chief education and training officer, complained in January 1976 that training was at its lowest ebb for 20 years and that facilities were simply not suitable to meet new needs. Within months, as the group made its financial recovery, the central research department declared that its rundown had stopped and 'recruiting was now on hand, with the aim of restoring staffing to a viable level.' For the managers dealing with staffing at the grassroots, there could never be enough people or enough adequate facilities; they would always be handicapped by what they saw as parsimony at the centre. In 1978, while Bert Evetts, the group manufacturing director, told the Group Services board about the shortage of skilled engineers, Scott told the shareholders about 'the healthy upward trend in our reception of young people into the company' and noted that 'with over 1600 apprentices of all kinds under training throughout the group in the UK, our overall intake levels are twice as high as they were four or five years ago – three times as high in the case of graduates.'

Queen's Award for Technology, Aerospace, Netherton, 1977.

At the end of the 1970s, Lucas had over 3,700 people in the UK and more than 870 overseas engaged on R&D. In the UK, this was slightly fewer than the number in 1972–73. The build-up of R&D staff abroad was the new element. That reflected the Lucas world view. Joe Righton, the group technical director, told the board how

Joe Righton, first General Manager of Lucas Aerospace, later Group Technical Director and Vice Chairman, received his CBE in 1977.

> the decline of the British motor industry not only reduced the local engineering 'pull' on us, but also means that the design authority tends to move to USA or Europe, using non-British standards. This is being, and can only be, simply overcome by using Lucas local overseas expertise, and those companies without that resource will have more difficulty.

Against the background of Messervy's worries about cash, Righton wanted the group to be paying the top salaries to engineers to keep them wandering away to France, Germany and the US. He wanted them engaged on what they were good at, and for them to be sure that 'to get (pay) increases, they do not have to be managers.' Infusing the board's sense of priorities, he reminded directors that 'good equipment helps to hold and attract good engineers, and is more important than elaborate buildings. Improving this situation is a priority.'

Righton had in mind the international technical position of the group:

Visit to Cwmbran and Pontypool, late 1970s, left to right, Jock Blackstock, personnel director; his wife, Vanessa; Mrs Scanlon; Hugh Scanlon, General Secretary of the AEU (later Lord Scanlon) and Ken Strangward.

We have a technical lead on lightweight braking systems, IDI diesel-engine injectors, some lighting and electric vehicles in the automotive field. Our strengths in the aircraft field are in digital engine controls, electric generators, small electric actuators and main engine fuel pumps. Against this, we are behind in automotive engine management, largely due to lack of customers (although we could have a basic world patent), car rotary diesel pumps, small starters and batteries and, in the aircraft field, small gas turbines and flying controls.

Nearly 28% of Lucas's sales to the automotive industry came from Electrical in 1977–78. So, of all the main operating businesses, it most obviously held the key to the financial performance of the group; it could propel the performance or pull it back. It propelled in 1976–77 and in 1977–78, as it recovered from the toolmakers' strike. Wilkinson told the board its output levels 'were the highest consistently achieved for many years.' But then Electrical started to hit trouble.

Internally, electricians had disputes with the management; pay disagreements, often for minor amounts, were commonplace as the national disciplines of the government's pay policy broke down. Externally, strikes at British Leyland and Ford put the Lucas plants on short-time working. Indeed, in the second half of the 1970s, as British Leyland's fortunes continued to slide, Lucas executives found themselves asking what would happen if the state-financed carmarker disappeared. Electrical's 'market position in the UK is heavily overshadowed by the uncertain future of Leyland, which still accounts for half of our original equipment sales' said a report to the board. At any rate, there seemed little prospect that British vehicle production would increase.

But Electrical faced not only a hostile commercial environment but changing demands from the motor manufacturers. Tony Gill explained that

Ken Strangward presenting the Directors Suggestion Award to John Cunningham, who worked at Cwmbran and was a local government councillor and trustee director of the Girling (Cwmbran) Trust. Left to right, Ivor Stroud, John Cunningham, Bert Heirene, Ken Strangward, Windsor Probyn and Mel Picton, 1981.

> Lucas was in the business of producing limited lines of products in volume: high volume, low variety. But the change was to high variety and lower volumes. This played havoc with productivity – there's a problem with machines, you need more flexible labour practices. Moving from the old idea of one-person-one-job to multi-skills is a dramatic cultural change.

Nowhere in the Lucas group would the change be more acutely felt than at Electrical. The only way to offset declining UK sales would be overseas and Wilkinson mounted, as he reported to the board, 'vigorous pursuit of European business and the development of new overseas licensing opportunities.'

At this stage Electrical exemplified Righton's concern: the pursuit 'placed strains on our heavily loaded engineering resources.' Sales by overseas subsidiaries and associated companies by 1979 were about half of those in the UK, where the biggest single contributor was not electronics and systems or starters and generators or lighting but parts and service.

The brakes business of Lucas Girling had trodden, towards the end of the 1970s, many of the paths on which Electrical wanted to travel. Arguably it was and would remain the most consistently successful of the Lucas businesses. Manufacturing subsidiaries in France and Germany made profits, although sales margins remained under constant threat; Girling provided nearly a quarter of all the drum and disc brakes used on French cars. In the more lucrative European trucks business, where Girling had a relationship with all the manufacturers, it had to accept lower prices than it wanted simply to secure new contracts. In Japan the company consolidated its influence with the introduction of the new Colette caliper. Much of its business came from licensing and about half of all Japanese cars and motorcycles used brakes originally designed by Girling.

In the UK, however, Girling faced the same problems as Electrical from disruptions at British Leyland and Ford. It was dangerously exposed, although not quite so much as Electrical, because the two car manufacturers absorbed 40% of its UK original equipment sales. Girling, anyway, had to deal with industrial problems of its own, especially at plants in Bromborough on Merseyside and Cwmbran and Pontypool in Wales.

The future of Massey Ferguson, the tractor manufacturer, and Perkins, its diesel-engine subsidiary, the one trapped in a financial struggle, the other losing ground in the marketplace, remained the danger area for CAV. Although dependence had been reduced, the two in late 1978 accounted for 16% of all CAV sales. Demand for diesel equipment in the agricultural, industrial and marine sectors had weakened, but continued strong in the car and light van markets.

Trade Union organised march to oppose the closure of Lucas Girling brake factory at Bromborough, Cheshire. Negotiations eventually compromised with the cessation of autobrake manufacture and concentration on railway brakes only. Within a year Bromborough operations were transformed into arguably the most profitable within the group – labour relations were exemplary.

CAV factory opening in Korea, 1979. Sir Bernard Scott with, left, Reg Hennery, Manufacturing Director of CAV who managed the project and David Hymas, centre.

CAV factory, La Rochelle, France.

Although restricted by the lack of a British diesel-engined car – a strong domestic market would have given the group greater economies of scale – Lucas directors pinned high hopes on an international expansion of CAV and backed that with an investment programme: the new plants at Greenville, South Carolina, and its twin at Ipswich, Suffolk, the venture in South Korea, expansion of plants at La Rochelle, France, and on the Medway in Kent, and an increased stake in Condiesel. A tangible reward was a new contract with Volkswagen and greater sales to Sofim and Fiat to complement sales to Citroën and Peugeot.

For all that, Bob Lucas – no relation of the founding family – installed as general manager in 1978, told the board of his worry: 'The current level of capital expenditure is so low, particularly in replacement plant.' Earlier Bert Evetts warned that 66% of CAV plant was more than ten years old and Bill Shield, the group finance director, had told the CAV board that the business needed a return on capital of 22% before it could afford to spend on plant replacement the amount set aside for depreciation. In the second half of the 1970s, the return was never higher than 17%. Evetts, echoing Joe Righton's strictures about engineers, worried about the failure to raise productivity; he put this down to the dilution of the production engineering effort in expansion projects, both at home and overseas. Raising productivity, in his view, must take priority over any more overloading of the production engineers.

CAV, whatever the reservations, looked for expansion. In contrast, the Batteries business looked for survival. Alan Watkins, who cut executive teeth there, explained that 'the batteries industry had almost destroyed itself'. Elimination of technical faults lengthened battery life. Lucas sold both to the original equipment manufacturers and to the aftermarket, where batteries were sold via agents to garages and then to motorists. But new tyre and battery specialists changed the cosy structure of pricing by providing a more direct and lower priced service to motorists. With excess capacity and lower prices in a shrinking market, 'there was a recipe for a harder time', recalled Watkins.

The time turned out harder than it might have been. An industrial dispute in autumn 1976 deprived Lucas aftermarket outlets of their winter stocks; a year later the toolmakers' strike, followed by further disruption in November, again stopped deliveries for the winter season; a year after that, in 1978, domestic disputes cost 200,000 batteries between August and November. With other manufacturers far ahead in the development of new, low-maintenance batteries, the Lucas position at home looked weak. While 13 overseas operations, on the whole, contributed modest profits, they could not compensate for domestic failure. In any event, the price of lead doubled between August 1978 and March 1979 and lead made up 30% of total costs.

From 1978, Bob Dale had the task of coming to terms with the whirlpool of technical, industrial and market problems. He saw higher productivity as the only way towards maintaining a profitable business; there was little likelihood of price increases running ahead of cost increases. By 1979 he had begun to think that Lucas might extricate itself from the business. To obtain the necessary productivity demanded heavy investment which could not be justified. 'Alternative plans are therefore being considered,' he warned the board.

Less menacing, Lucas Batteries in this period devoted considerable energy, helped by a £2.2m subsidy for three years from the Department of Industry, to developing an electric vehicle. It did not want to make the vehicle, but it did want to provide the power system and controls. In 1978–79, it commissioned 35 Bedford one-tonne vans which went out on trials in London, Paris, Vienna and the US. Even the British royal family had one. The company thought it had an international technical lead in electric vehicle development, a relief after falling behind in the basic business.

Electric vehicle developed by Lucas Batteries.

So different from Batteries, Rists, the wiring business, ran ahead of profit forecasts in the late 1970s. It even managed continuity of production in the disrupted winter of 1978–79 by judicious flexibility in working hours and advance accumulation of components. But it worried about the future of British Leyland, Ford and Chrysler, its main customers, and sought to offset future loss of orders by extending the role of its Calais plant in the French car industry and developing specialist applications: computer harnesses for IBM, black box controls for the Tornado, the European fighter aircraft, and tank harnesses for the defence industry.

All of the companies dealing with the motor industry leaned on the bolster of spare parts sales in the aftermarket to push up revenue. In September 1975 the first board meeting of Lucas World Service, designed to bring together the service organisations of the individual companies, asked Glyn Stiley, the general manager, to produce financial objectives which would recognise the group aim to double profits in four years.

Stiley had a hard slog. By 1978, far from luxuriating in higher profits, he had to contend with losses. Bill Shield, the group finance director, acerbically reminded the World Service board that the service business had traditionally generated cash; it was shocking that companies should be forecasting consumption of cash. Stiley had been pushed from the inside and buffeted from the outside. Too many channels of communication between the operating companies and their overseas subsidiaries produced uncoordinated pricing; Electrical and Batteries failed with supplies; disappointing performance reduced funds for capital expenditure; warranty claims in the US remained a major anxiety. Other component manufacturers had been just as attracted to the profits of servicing as Lucas, so competition became more severe; British Leyland, through Unipart, had become an aggressive competitor. Lucas had to fight to hold market share. There were no easy profits from service.

In total, sales of vehicle equipment made up more than 81% of Lucas's turnover. A further 7.75% of Lucas turnover in 1977–78 came from industrial products, made in companies under the umbrella of SMEC. By summer 1979, SMEC had absorbed Lucas Defence Systems, which became one of three divisions, the others being Electronics and Hydraulics. The odd collection of Defence companies had 'For Sale' signs on them: G&E Bradley, which serviced electronics equipment and had produced, before orders dried up, kidney machines; Premier Precision, a sub-contract machining company suffering from under-investment; Horstman, whose fortunes were linked to making turret gearboxes on tanks being sold to Iran; Technical Services (Egypt) which provided support for the Egyptian Army.

Bob Lucas receiving the Design Council Award for the Microjectors designed by Peter Howes from HRH the Duke of Edinburgh.

SMEC made modest profits, but consistently at a level beneath its planned commitment. Low consumer demand hurt the timer and capacitor business for televisions and washing machines, but, in the late 1970s, the type of measurement instruments and electronic components made for industrial switchgear held firm. Hydraulic systems business was patchy at best.

Purchase of a 25% stake in Siliconix, the US maker of semiconductor devices in the process control industry, for $6.1m and subsequent top-up buying of shares for $1.6m in 1978 and 1979 presaged the 1980s drive into the US market. Cash shortages prevented an immediate extension of the acquisitions programme, directed at electronic components and fluid power.

Aircraft equipment, from Lucas Aerospace, provided the remainder of turnover in the 1977–78 financial year. Aerospace managers had spent nearly a decade trying to make sense of a medley of companies pulled together under government auspices with the aim of creating a significant international grouping. Aerospace in the 1970s always needed, and always was, restructuring its operations.

James Blyth, credited by colleagues with a remarkably receptive and clear mind, swept in as general manager in late 1977, immediately reminding the board that 'Lucas Aerospace is failing to meet its margin commitment by a considerable measure in every operating division.' In a trenchant summary of the problems he would address, he noted:

> The total business demonstrates an unfortunate combination of two classic effects. From
> its acquisition and amalgamation phase, it retains a duplication of resources . . . From its

retrenchment phase, it has acquired bad labour relations, an ageing skilled workforce, a surfeit of older, mediocre managers and an almost universally depressed morale.

Too much business focussed on UK and Europe, Blyth said. Rolls-Royce was too important a customer. 'We have no significant North American presence.' Market forecasting had been poor. Development work had been project – rather than product-related: 'with a few notable exceptions we have been developing "me-too" products for markets which already have surplus capacity.' Internally, the management structure had been 'too functionally oriented', making effective communication and delegation difficult. 'We have, by default, permitted our [shop] stewards to become much too dominant.' In short, all was not well in the largest aircraft equipment company outside the US.

James Blyth, appointed Director and General Manager of Lucas Aerospace, 1977.

Part of the reorganisation involved the closure of an old Engine Systems factory in Liverpool and the construction of a new plant, and the same process for the Electrical Division in Bradford. Only then, Blyth calculated, could the divisions make profits. But there were delays as the company held talks with the workforce, the Confederation of Shipbuilding and Engineering Unions and the Department of Industry. The upside of the delay was the provision of Department of Industry funds for the new Bradford and Huyton factories: 'very advantageous for us,' commented Blyth.

By the end of the 1970s, the airlines had started ordering aircraft again. Although the Tornado project moved in fits and starts, a sales drive in the US had started to produce defence orders. 'The market for many of our products is in cyclical upswing,' Blyth reported, 'but unless we can slim ourselves sufficiently to enjoy good returns during this period, we will be unable to manage our way through the inevitable subsequent downturn.' With that comment, Blyth wrote the plot for Aerospace over the next years.

New Department of Trade and Industry funded Aerospace factory, Bradford, opened by HRH the Duke of Edinburgh in 1984.

Traumatic Recession

The pain of recession became acute in the final quarter of Lucas's 1979–80 financial year, the early summer months of May, June and July. Another energy crisis set off international inflationary pressures and turned into an economic slowdown. Everybody felt it. As General Motors announced its highest quarterly loss, British and continental car manufacturers went on to short-time working. Around 400,000 new cars, equivalent to nearly a third of annual car production, hung around awaiting buyers in the UK. For Lucas, international economic troubles capped a troubled year.

'The rhythm of production was mostly noted by its absence,' declared Bert Evetts during November 1980, in his manufacturing report to the board.

> The first quarter was disrupted by the regrettable CSEU-Engineering Employers Federation dispute in the national scene; the following quarter saw the factories trying to operate recovery programmes and, at the same time, satisfy the understandable but nevertheless intense customer pressures for priority. A task further compounded in the next quarter by the many extraordinary measures taken in the factories to keep production going during the national steel industry dispute – the worst effects of which were felt in many factories during the last quarter when some stocks were depleted. On top of all this, from January through to the present day, reducing demands in the vehicle equipment companies have been, and still are, the order of the day.

Profits before tax, on a gentle slide since 1976–77, now fell sharply to £41m, from £70.7m in 1978–79, as UK companies lost money in the second half. Yet commentators responded with some relief. 'The results were not so bad as the £30m or less which market analysts had been predicting, and helped by a maintained dividend of 11p a share net, the shares jumped 17p to 186p,' reported *The Times* newspaper. Noting 'retrenchment' as the overriding theme of Lucas's report, the *Observer* thought Lucas

Facing page, US Navy award to Lucas Aerospace, Bradford, for delivering the four thousandth Harpoon actuator, September 1985.

'is tackling them (problems) with resolve and determination'. The *Financial Times* remained detached:

> Lucas has shown its ability to generate big profits in the upward part of a cycle when rising demand impacts on a slimmed down cost base. But this is not a normal cycle and it must be realised that Lucas is being forced into an expensive shift in capacity overseas and into aerospace.

Overseas figures, in fact, prevented the annual figures from being lower, not least Girling's operations in France and Germany, CAV's business in Spain and Brazil and Electrical's plants in Argentina, India and Brazil. The trouble, rather, lay in the UK where Electrical had a thumping loss of £16.25m, compared with a forecast profit of £3.5m. Batteries made a bigger loss than expected. The other businesses made profits but well adrift of what proved to be optimistic forecasts. More than £5m had to be set aside to cover the cost of 3,000 redundancies at Electrical.

But the worst was yet to come. In financial terms, the lowest point came between August 1980 and January 1981, the first half of the Lucas 1980–81 financial year. In March, the group published a pre-tax loss of £25.4m (the internal working numbers came out worse). The figure scratched the psyche of a company which had been accustomed to making profits and probably could not quite understand why it should stop doing so. The first reaction was to see the loss as a hiccup, uncomfortable but short-lived. The board considered the figures on 26 March and the minutes recorded

> the chairman's belief that the loss result was the first ever to be reported to shareholders in the company's history and this was a serious matter though he did not feel this was necessarily an argument for reducing or passing a dividend . . . Lucas had always maintained its dividends in the past and having regard to the not unreasonable prospects lying ahead it was his view we should maintain the interim dividend.

The stock market lived in hope too: the shares rose 4p to 177p, pushing the *Financial Times* to make the observation that 'the stock market will shrug aside almost any company setback so long as there is some kind of hope that recovery is on the way.' The *Daily Mail* classified the shares as 'a bet on the speed of the economic upturn and a gamble on the final dividend.'

The front-line financial figures would never be as dramatically awful again. Indeed, the group managed a small profit in the second half so that the final published pre-tax

loss for 1980–81 was £21.4m. The board maintained the dividend at 11p a share, just as the market had hoped, but there was a loss of 38.6p a share. 'All the automotive companies were in deep trouble,' wrote David Shackley in his annual assessment for the directors of the Lucas state of affairs. What silver lining could be found came from the turnaround which Blyth had masterminded at Aerospace. 'The contrasting fortunes of the automotive and aerospace business is a remarkable feature of the year and the timing of this major contribution (£17m of profits) from Lucas Aerospace could hardly have been better from the group's point of view,' Shackley commented.

The group's expectation of 'the not unreasonable prospects' did not arrive in the 1980–81 second half. Indeed, Shackley warned the board, 'We enter 1981–82 with a weak sales demand and no real evidence of upturn.' The path between the quest for survival and profitable expansion would prove long and painful, more fraught with difficulty than the board imagined in March 1981. But Lucas did not stand alone.

Recession, tight money and a high exchange rate pushed British manufacturing into a traumatic period of adjustment. This would not only result in widespread changes of practice and technique but would also cut it back in size, reduce its role in the national mix of wealth creation and break the economic back of local communities. GKN, a peer company of Lucas, later called 1980 'the year when GKN's financial fortunes reached their lowest point since the 1930s'. But Lucas did not prove to be so damaged in its habitual lines of business that recession forced it to abandon them. It would not have to re-invent itself as GKN eventually did, or, indeed, as smaller companies such as W.

Godfrey Messervy with, left, HRH
The Duke of Kent and Society of
Motor Manufacturers and Traders
President Sir Barrie Heath, right, at
the National Exhibition Centre,
October 1978.

Canning and Concentric also did. Recession forced Lucas to trim the edges, to question verities long since taken for granted and to do better what it had been doing or had started to do.

The world changed, industry changed and, fortuitously, leadership of Lucas changed. After 49 years at Lucas, Bernard Scott retired and, in seamless succession, Godfrey Messervy took over as chairman and chief executive on 1 April 1980. He had been groomed: on the board since 1972, group managing director for six years and deputy chairman for a year. He reached the apex of his career just in time to take responsibility for the group's declining fortunes. He preached continuity. The *Evening Mail* of Birmingham interviewed him shortly before he formally took the top post: 'he stressed he would not be making any radical changes in the way the company had been run by Sir Bernard Scott.' In fact, he would make changes and he had changes forced upon him, but he could not have been called, and would not have seen himself, as a great innovator.

Messervy spent his professional life at Lucas, joining after service as a paratrooper in World War II and two years at Cambridge University where he did not complete a degree in engineering. Instead he went to CAV as a production trainee and started his rise through the ranks. Coming from a Midlands motor family, joining Lucas would not have been a hard decision for an aspiring engineer. His membership of the Lucas family deepened when he married the niece of Sir Bertram Waring, chairman for 18 years until 1970.

Some of Messervy's subordinates still wondered, 20 years after his accession, how he managed to surface at the top. Although he promised continuity, his style was quite different from that of Scott. Much less of a driver, he encouraged the executive to take more responsibility; 'He exerted less authority than Scott who was conscious of the fact that he was better than most of those around him,' Tony Gill remembered. Messervy, a social man with a genuine interest in engineering, had an easy rapport with customers, not least Roger Smith, the chief of General Motors, with whom he went hunting and fishing. 'His strength was at the external interface, not at the internal hard grind,' Bob Dale believed.

He was content to let those responsible to him get on with the work. David Hymas worked for him at CAV: 'One of the things I had to do was to write all his board reports. He never used to change them very much.' By all accounts he lacked the flair of Scott, but perhaps that did not matter when he took over. In effect, he had a war of attrition to wage. He looked the man for the job in the sense that, as Gill mentioned, 'He was

Lucas Service Conference, 1980. Left to right, Tony Lane, Jacksonville, Florida Distribution Center Manager; Ed Swedelson, Englewood, New Jersey Distribution Center Manager; Peter Murray, LINC Marketing Staff; Shusake Iwase, Lucas East West; John Setchfield, LINC Management Staff and Robin Biggins, Los Angeles, California, Distribution Center Manager.

correct in his behaviour but he was rather too willing to provide what was expected of him; he would always be seen as a good fit for the job.'

Just over three weeks after he took over, Messervy made Gill and Jeffrey Wilkinson joint managing directors. This formalised an arrangement which Scott had started in the interests of creative tension; both of them had been divisional managing directors with Messervy in between them and Scott. Messervy's decision to continue with the arrangement did not satisfy either and it made uneasy colleagues just underneath them in the hierarchy. 'The organisation set up was almost designed for rivalry,' commented Dale. Gill and Wilkinson could scarcely avoid getting in each other's way; at best, the structure was unusual.

At the operational level there was separation of powers: Gill had responsibility for CAV, Girling and Aerospace; Wilkinson had responsibility for Electrical, Batteries, Rists, World Service and Industrial. But at a functional level the responsibilities of one crossed into the domain of the other: in Gill's sphere, Messervy placed engineering and manufacturing – the technical side of Lucas; in that of Wilkinson, he placed marketing, public relations and finance – the commercial side.

The group presented Gill and Wilkinson as a dream team, men of roughly the same age imbued with the spirit of Lucas but bringing to their joint task different skills from different backgrounds. In public the two conveyed unity. But in private they found harmony difficult. Their sharpest disagreements probably came in the chairman's committee where the two joined with Messervy to steer the group. Messervy found them difficult to control. He was not the sort of man who was capable of banging heads together; his approach was too laid back. Really he wanted Gill and Wilkinson simply to get on with running the group while he could tilt the tiller a little this way and a little that, as it appeared necessary. Probably Messervy was not as clever as either. Certainly

Lucas CAV signing an Anglo-
American agreement to develop a
micro-processor controlled diesel
fuel injection system.
Left to right, E. B. (Bunty) Wootten,
President Lucas Industries Inc.,
Trevor O. Jones, TRW Automotive
Worldwide and Bob Lucas, Lucas
CAV, 1980.

he appeared reluctant to grasp long-term issues, although he had the conviction to see through the immediate reconstruction of the group and deal with recession and its fallout.

The division of portfolios between Gill and Wilkinson reflected their backgrounds. Gill trained as an engineer and his first jobs were as an engineer. He entered the group in 1960, when CAV bought Bryce Berger, where he had risen to deputy managing director, and he spent all his subsequent Lucas career at CAV until he became a divisional managing director. Wilkinson, on the other hand, had been a Lucas graduate apprentice and his first job in the group was administrator at Batteries. He had worked in Electrical and he, too, had spent time at CAV. Frustrated by the promotion prospects in the late 1960s, he left Lucas for Simon Engineering. Scott lured him back, originally intending to place him in charge of a diversification programme. But first, Scott wanted a survey of troubled Electrical. Wilkinson did that and, in 1974, agreed to become the Electrical company doctor.

Gill was an engineer who became a manager and who, working away from the main currents of Lucas politics in Birmingham, felt like an outsider. Wilkinson, though, was a manager who had to come to terms with engineering. Well acquainted with the ebb and flow of Birmingham politics, he was the insider. Given his background, Gill almost inevitably saw Electrical, historically the centre of the group and sometimes treated like a head office toy, as a commodity business, either a generator of cash to be invested in diesel and other technologically interesting parts of the group or a drag on the group's future prospects. Because both Scott and Messervy had been chiefs of CAV before him, he had an historical tide behind him in favour of investment in diesel. Wilkinson had a less detached view of Electrical; making electrical equipment was what the group did, it was what it knew about, the gathering speed of electronics advance added a new dimension, but to survive and prosper Electrical had to be bigger, it had to invest in expansion and for that it needed to look to Europe.

Both Gill and Wilkinson recognised that, sooner or later, one of them would have to go. Meanwhile, at the apex of the group, at the starting point for dealing with the biggest series of commercial and industrial upsets since World War II, division reigned. Messervy, however, tried to inject new energy at the top of the group by bringing through a new generation of senior executives. During the 1980–81 year, old stalwarts departed: Joe Righton who had joined Lucas in 1936, Bert Evetts who had come in 1933, Glyn Stiley who began in 1948 and Charles Davidson, the group commercial director, recruited in 1949.

Messervy, carrying on where Scott had left off, made certain that the group opened up to new ideas and independent analysis of its position by having on the board a majority of non-executive directors; the only executive directors were Messervy himself, Gill, Wilkinson and Bill Shield. Functional directors he kept at the level underneath, the Executive. Bob Dale, then running World Service, Bryan Mason and Tony Jarrett, the group director of product technology, came on to the Executive, joining the chiefs of the bigger operating companies and functional directors. But James Blyth left at the high point of his Aerospace success; the UK government asked for his services and he went on secondment for five years to run the arms sales business of the Ministry of Defence, never to return to Lucas.

In the interests of simplicity, Messervy scrapped Scott's scheme of dividing the Executive into policy and operations. The new streamlined version covered both. It looked out to a battered industrial landscape.

British politics changed in May 1979, when the Labour government of James Callaghan gave way to the Conservative government of Margaret Thatcher. The change came as a relief to the board, a return on its investment of £18,000 a year, rising to £20,000 in 1978–79, the subscription it paid each year to the Conservative party after a perfunctory annual discussion about the advisability of such spending. It paid the money, believing that it would help to offset trades union contributions to the Labour party and that the Conservatives would master inflation. On the second belief, the Lucas board turned out to be grievously wrong, at least initially; Thatcher and Sir Geoffrey Howe, her chancellor of the exchequer, managed to push inflation up before they brought it down.

Short memories and political mythology have it that, as soon as Thatcher came to power, the trades unions retreated and industrial relations changed overnight. That is not quite the case. Indeed, three months after the change of government, group

Without Ted Warwick and Lucas CAV's concealed lighting and batteries the world would have been denied fairy-tale glimpses of the Royal Wedding, 1981.

companies endured, what Messervy later called in a report to the board, 'the most costly dispute in Lucas history.' This was the national engineering dispute, starting in August, during which CSEU members staged a series of two day strikes each week and put in place an overtime ban. The CSEU pressed the Engineering Employers' Federation (EEF), representing companies of the sector, for a shorter working week and additional benefits, like longer holidays. With negotiations taking place at industry level, Lucas remained a spectator, but in support of EEF resistance to the union demands. Lucas employees seemed none too keen on the dispute: the board in September noted 'the cooperation the company was receiving from its striking employees and the company's distaste, nevertheless, for having to support actions which in the short term were damaging to its own people'.

The strike knocked Lucas sideways. It reduced production schedules to meaningless pieces of paper. The manufacturing programme in September for signal and headlamps was 769,200; the output was 416,751 or 54%. For caliper brakes, the programme was 230,000, the output 111,000 or 49%. And so the list went on for all of the UK factories except those of Rists and SMEC. The dispute ended on 4 October. The EEF gave way without consulting member firms, Mason recalled. Apparently it tried to send a telex message to Evetts, but he never received it. At any rate, the episode infuriated Lucas, which felt left in the dark; it promptly considered withdrawing its membership. 'This was the end of the EEF as a serious player in the industrial relations ritual,' Mason observed. Lucas was on its own. It certainly felt like that when the board looked at the numbers.

The factories started normal working on 11 October and, Messervy reported, 'We lost 13 working days through the dispute, but the real effect was much greater due to the overtime ban which had such a serious impact on our factory processes and on start-up efficiency. The cost of the dispute to Lucas will probably amount to some £60m in sales and £25m profit.' Without productivity improvements Lucas expected the shorter working week and extra benefits to add up to 7% on manual payroll costs.

For Lucas, the engineering dispute proved to be the nadir of its industrial relations. There would be further disputes and arguments across the UK factories running into the mid-1980s, but never again would there be disruption on such a wide scale, an extra cost of such proportions or a profit loss of such magnitude. Recession and the redundancies which accompanied it shifted the internal balance of power in Lucas away from unions and shop stewards back towards the management. From 1980, the problem for management was not placating the workforce, so that output might continue, but organising it in a way which created unity of purpose around the best processes, so that output might rise in quantity and quality. For the workforce the main problem became survival; with national unemployment over two million and rising, and manufacturing industry in turmoil, hanging on to a job became the major preoccupation.

Recession changed the atmosphere. It exposed companies in all their vulnerability; the erosion of productivity and the loss of competitiveness in the 1970s left costs hopelessly high on international markets. With sterling strong on the foreign exchanges and the government showing no taste for intervention, there would be no relief by devaluation. For Thatcher and Howe, exposing industry to the rigours of the market was a virtue in itself. Thus exposed, Mason explained, 'All Lucas management effort went into reducing cost – all the excesses and malpractices were exposed and attacked.'

Shackley set out for the board in October 1981 the scale of the change. Over the two years 1979–80 and 1980–81, Electrical lost 30% of its employees, CAV 17%, Girling 30%, Batteries 31%, World Service 26%, SMEC 34% and Rists 24%. Overwhelmingly the job losses took place in the UK. Only Aerospace stood aside, major cutbacks having taken place throughout the 1970s, although further cuts came later when its markets turned down too. By the end of the 1980–81 financial year the UK payroll stood at 53,728 compared with 63,995 a year before, while worldwide Lucas employed 72,735

CAV's Microjectors were exported to General Motors for use in their Oldsmobile Tornado.

people against 82,705 a year before. Messervy set out the size of the cuts for the directors at a meeting in October 1981: 'During the past 18 months, 62 establishments closed down, some 13,700 redundancies and over 1m square feet of space disposed of.' Cutbacks on this scale were commonplace in British industry; indeed, some in the City of London complained that Lucas had not acted quickly enough.

In his annual personnel report, presented to the board in August 1981, Mason observed that 'the change in outlook and confidence among our employees in most factories and offices brought about by the present business climate, has been dramatic.' Two months later, Shackley noted how 'the vast majority of redundancies have been accomplished by voluntary means without serious opposition from unions.' In part, that lack of opposition reflected the changed balance of power. But it also reflected much greater efforts of communication within the individual companies, the sort of communication which Scott had preached in the 1970s and which Messervy had acknowledged as essential when he took over. 'We have carried out the most intensive programmes of self-scrutiny,' Mason reported.

> General managers in all companies set out the critical positions of their businesses followed by detailed discussions led by managers at all levels. The thoroughness of this approach, coupled with the inescapable facts, have produced a period, which is continuing, where disputes have been few and during which we have announced an even more limited review of pay from July 1981.

Here, then, for the management came the opportunity to reorganise the factories, introduce more flexible systems of manufacture and, money permitting, bring in new technology. But Mason warned that managers would have to be sensitive, not to behave in ways which 'can easily replace the 1930s as the store of examples of management malpractice from which our trade union representatives will draw for years to come.'

Looking at the operational numbers, Lucas managers knew of the gap between the performance of their factories and those of international peer companies. As a group, Lucas recorded in 1980 sales of £13,800 for each employee. But the comparable figure for Bosch was £21,600, for Bendix £24,600 and for Nippondenso £47,800. As well, Lucas tied up more money in holding stocks; its stocks constituted 27.3% of sales compared with Bosch at 16.2%, Bendix at 23.2% and Nippondenso at 7.2%.

The trial for the Lucas automotive companies was twofold. First, they operated in depressed markets and all contended with lower sales. In 1980–81 sales at Electrical

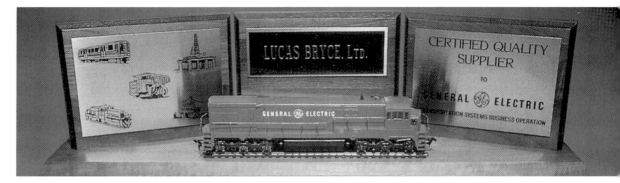

finished the year down 17% on the already weak 1979–80. Those at CAV finished 7.6% lower, those at Batteries 20.7%, those at World Service 6.4%, and those at Rists 11.7%. But Girling was worst affected: sales down 24.0%. All of that contrasted with Aerospace where sales rose by no less than 42.4%, giving it, exceptionally, a higher value of sales than any other operating company in the group. Nevertheless, the sales of the UK companies turned out to be 23% less than their forecasts, scattering hopes that recession would be short-lived. Managers in the automotive companies knew there would be no immediate relief from a higher value of sales. This brought up the second part of their trial.

The lower the sales and the less the profit, the more diminished the ability of managers in the operating subsidiaries to finance the investment necessary to bring in new machinery and new practices, the better to compete internationally. The responsibility of financing rising demands for both working and investment capital fell more heavily on the parsimonious group treasury. If the treasury was cautious it was simply because the group was using cash faster than it expected. Shield reported to the board at the end of the 1980–1 financial year that Lucas's net overdraft was £164.25m compared with its forecast of £127.25m, and that the group had used up £75.25m of cash during the year, although it had held back capital spending to £56m after forecasting spending of £81.5m. Interest payments more than doubled during 1980–81 and gearing rose, on the published figures, to 23% from 14.35% in July 1980, modest ratios by late twentieth century standards but alarming for a group as conservatively financed as Lucas had been.

Some preparation for coping with financial strain had been made as recession approached. Wilkinson remembered how 'Shield and I agreed that, any time he was approached with a bank facility, he'd take it. We built up more than £50m of credit lines.' As the pressures built up, 'Gill and I made a habit of talking to the banks, got them

World Class Supplier Award presented to Lucas Bryce by US General Electric Corporation, 1986.

Bob Lucas, Alan Blew, Peter
Howes and Roger Mugford at
Buckingham Palace after receiving
the MacRobert Award, November
1981.

in on the act, got them to identify with the problems. And the two main banks – Lloyds
and Midland – we saw regularly so we ensured they knew what we were doing.'

Although recession cast dark shadows, Lucas had its own patches of light.
Engineering Today, the weekly specialising in industry affairs, reported in October 1980
on the Motor Show, the annual showcase for motor manufacturers and their suppliers:

> There are more new models and new ideas from the British motor industry than for a long
> time . . . yet a higher percentage of workers are on short-time and more manufacturers
> are laying off workers than at any period since the 1930s. More than ever, the Motor Show
> is a brave piece of tinsel, erected to hide the ravaged face of the industry . . . Among those
> putting a brave face on domestic crisis is Lucas, which, fresh from losing 3,000 workers
> has new products ranging from a diesel injector pump to its MF-3 maintenance-free
> battery on show.

During the worst of the recession, indeed, Lucas companies did not stop new developments, nor did they stop introducing new products. CAV captured what Gill called 'the
mood of the time' and invested accordingly. 'Because diesel cars were so economic and
were thought to be low polluters, because diesels had taken over on trucks and buses,
they were thought to be the big thing of the future,' he explained. RotoDiesel and
Condiesel introduced the DPC pump, which eventually captured most of the French
market. Pushed by demand from General Motors, production of the microjector, the
miniature electronic fuel injector, built up quickly at Ipswich and Greenville; at its peak
Greenville made $750,000 profit a month, Gill recalled.

Representatives of Lucas CAV with the Queen's Award for Technology, left to right, John Holloway, quality foreman; Brenda Marczell, setter; Mike Lait, development engineer, all from Ipswich and Harry Warren, development engineer, Sudbury.

Apart from the introduction of its new battery, which quickly improved the company's share of the replacement market, Batteries pooled its electric vehicle expertise into a joint venture with Chloride, the other British company making a significant contribution to the new technology. The Department of Industry brokered the marriage as a price for continued subsidy, a grant of £600,000 a year to the project. Lucas had management control of the new company, Lucas Chloride Electric Vehicle Systems while the Department of Industry met 50% of the net costs, Lucas 30% and Chloride 20%.

Girling sought to maintain a technological edge in the marketplace by refining car drum brakes and introducing a new commercial vehicle brake package incorporating Skidchek, its anti-skid system. Rists developed a ring main wiring system for buses, replacing hundreds of wires with just three and started to think about making it applicable to cars.

For Electrical, meanwhile, Wilkinson pursued the idea of the Grand Groupe, the international alliance to compete with Bosch. Since February 1980, secret talks and studies had been taking place, examining the idea of pulling together parts of the electrical equipment businesses of Lucas itself, of Ducellier, the joint-venture company owned by Lucas and Valeo after the protracted legal and commercial arguments of 1978–79, and of Paris-Rhône, a subsidiary of Valeo. Hence the title Lucas gave it: the LDP project. This demanded a reorganisation of manufacturing in five product areas: starters, alternators, lighting, small motors and electronics.

By summer 1981, movement on the industrial side had been such as to set off detailed financial discussions but Wilkinson had to tell the Lucas board that 'cash for the project was the main problem . . . the French government were looking to Lucas

Margaret Loft receiving the Queen's Award for Export from Sir Joshua Rowley, 1981.

whereas the Lucas objective was for the money to be raised in France.' Still, the French government seemed to be prepared for Lucas to control the project; for Wilkinson, following the arguments only two years before about Ducellier, this was one plus. Another was the support of the French motor manufacturers. At the same time a financing gap of about £20m emerged between Lucas and Valeo regarding how much Lucas would pay to bring Paris-Rhône into the combination. Then, following elections in France and the decision of the French ministry of industry to have a study made of the state of the electrical equipment industry, progress towards a combination started to drag. In November, though, Wilkinson still hoped that in a couple of months he would be able to make definite proposals to the board. Optimism stretched far enough for the fruition of LDP to be written into group strategic planning.

The harsh business conditions forced Lucas to give more attention to group strategy. Until 1979 it had simply brought together the expressed aspirations of the operating subsidiaries, synthesised them into one document and called it a strategy. Now it wanted a group strategy 'against which future achievements would be monitored.' Initial board discussions threw up as many problems as resolutions, but they began to touch the themes which would recur over the remaining years of independent existence.

There was the basic problem that, as the board minutes put it, 'We were short of cash but long in opportunities.' Obviously this pointed to the wisdom of moving from less profitable to more profitable areas and of giving more rigorous thought on how to select investment. It opened up consideration of partnerships. The board started to address the desirability of reducing dependence on the automotive industry and as Lévêque put it, 'a handful of vehicle assemblers'. But directors accepted that the major growth opportunities were diesel fuel-injection equipment, particularly in the US, automotive electrics and industrial control electronics. Strangely, the first board document on strategy made no mention of braking systems. Directors questioned whether it would be realistic to finance 80% of spending needs from internal sources. They found that over the next five or six years there could be a £200m gap between financial needs and financial resources.

When the board debated strategy in October 1981, financial questions loomed largest. In essence, the directors tried to sort through the issues so that the group would have room to manoeuvre. A staff paper noted that the operating companies had been mainly directing their energies to survival and that consequential financial constraints inhibited development. So board thinking turned towards the means of raising cash.

Lord Rootes, the industry veteran and former chief of the eponymous motor group who had been on the Lucas board since 1973, suggested 'mergers and collaboration with others could be the solution even if we did not have a majority holding'. Other directors echoed that thinking: John Hull, a merchant banker by background, 'could not see how the funding gap could be solved without Lucas becoming part of a larger group and establishment in a major world market'. Both were more prescient than they would have appreciated at the time. Messervy worried about the stock price. He spoke, the meeting minutes recorded, 'of the need to be properly competitive in the financial market if the money we were likely to need was to be obtained by way of a rights issue; the alternative was to restrict some of our trading arrangements or sell off assets or promote mergers, partnerships and so on.'

The discussions proved to be harbingers of change. Survival first, remodelling and hard choices afterwards as four questions, posed in the board papers, found answers. 'Can we raise the funds to support all the proposed strategies (of the operating companies) at the time they are required . . . if so, should we do so? If we cannot raise the funds until the present business is restored to better financial health, which combination of strategies would achieve this most quickly? If we can only raise funds by divestment, which strategy do we sacrifice? If we wish to secure a substantial reduction in our automotive business simultaneously, it may involve at least one major divestment.' There lay the furrows of Lucas history for the 1980s – with a warning from Hull:

> There was little room for manoeuvre and there could be discomfort if things went wrong; the key was to improve profitability and return on capital, and switch capital to areas where it could be put to better use; as matters stood we had not got the financial base we needed.

Lucas result makes a very clear message...

Lucas soars

Second-half profit lifts Lucas gloom

Lucas comes out of surgery

Lucas delights City with its turnabout to £4 million profit

Lucas delights with dramatic final upturn

Confident Lucas staunches losses

Lucas recovers shares soar in second half

...s say losses are over

A toast to pensioners as Lucas holds dividend

How we hit the headlines on November 10.

Above, Newspaper comments, November 1981. *Right,* Lucas CAV's revolutionary MicroNova.

Lengthy Convalescence

'Lucas comes out of the surgery' ran the *Financial Times* headline over a Lex financial commentary on 10 November 1981. What the headline writer did not know and what the company did not expect was that the post-operative treatment would have to be so extensive. As the market mulled over the 1980–81 results and the share price rose 15% in a day to 198p, Lex thought Lucas would be capable of £50m pre-tax profits in 1981–82. The Lucas board, too, scented recovery, which was why it rode over losses and maintained the dividend. In the event Lex was too optimistic by £30m and three years premature; Lucas had entered a painful two years that gnawed at its finances and sapped its confidence. In April 1983, according to board minutes, Godfrey Messervy said, 'We were at the tactical stage of getting fit; until then we had few options and were restricted to following the path we were on.' He meant, and neither the board nor senior management disagreed, that Lucas had to organise higher productivity and to generate more cash. The changes of 1979–81, the responses to the shocks of international recession and national deflation, had turned from an end in themselves to a beginning.

The numbers told the story. To be sure, profits returned in 1981–82 to reach £20.2m before tax, the same sort of figures which had been recorded in the early 1970s, but only a fraction of the value given the amount of inflation over the decade. That prompted the board to acknowledge the unthinkable: the dividend had to be cut. So it was, from the 11p which had held since 1978–79, to 8.6p. But the trouble did not stop there as, with management trying to overhaul the business in the most trying conditions, Lucas published pre-tax profits for 1982–83 at just above the break-even point, £2.1m, and acknowledged a loss for every share of 13.5p. By then the main Lucas markets really had started to recover and the group could see the recession behind it.

Lucas in the recession years faced the difficulty that it could not manufacture its way out of difficulty. Its internal sales forecasts proved consistently too optimistic. In the early part of the recession, Aerospace effectively had carried the group's figures, but

DX160 and DX95 – the first
entirely new popular car lamps
from Lucas for ten years, 1983.

then suddenly demand from Rolls-Royce fell away, by over one third in 1982–83, and the UK government slowed down its plans for the purchase of Tornado fighter aircraft. All of that left the position of Aerospace as miserable, for a short time, as that of the automotive companies. Again, in the first part of the recession, the demand for car diesel equipment had been firm but that fell away too. Although, overall, the fall in vehicle production between 1979 and 1983 was not dramatic in western Europe, it was 16% in the UK and 27% in the US, with the lowest point coming in 1982. David Shackley summed it up for the board in his 1983 assessment of the state of affairs:

> Income from automotive sales is now 15.5% lower than it was four years ago at the start
> of the recession. In order for the value of that income to have been sustained it should
> have been increased by 27%. By implication, therefore, the fall in volume of sales is
> somewhere near 35%.

Deprived of help from the markets, the attempt by Lucas and other British engineering companies to re-balance spending and revenue inevitably involved cost reduction. Even though a heavy immediate charge on the profit and loss account, the quickest and most obvious cut was in the number of jobs; simply the group had too many people in the UK for the amount of sales available. Before the recession, in July 1978, it had 69,631 UK employees. Coming out of recession, in July 1983, it had 47,111. The payroll had been cut by nearly one third. But the cruel reality emerged that, at least for the moment, all of these cuts did little more than hold the position. Production costs remained high; the group's indices showed payroll productivity in Electrical, CAV, Girling and Aerospace at a lower level in 1982–83 than when the indices had been started in 1973–74. Indeed, of these major companies only Electrical recorded an increase in productivity during 1982–83. Productivity had been caught painfully between falling volume and rising wages. 'Since July 1979,' Shackley noted, 'the cumulative addition to pay has amounted to 46% – and no company has achieved people reductions to that extent. The payroll is therefore higher than it was before the reduction commenced.' As employees left, so the factories closed. Messervy told shareholders and employees:

> To recognise the much lower output levels at which profit break-even must be assured,
> we have, as part of our on-going programme, closed 35 UK manufacturing and distribution
> units – almost 2m square feet of space. Total redundancy and closure costs during the
> three years (1980–83) amount to more than £56m.

In the UK, before the recession, Lucas had 45 major manufacturing sites, as it called them, and 60 smaller units.

With the impact of recession softening in 1983, Lucas presented to the world a moderately cheerful face. Messervy's message to shareholders did not disguise that 'much remains to be done' but he could pepper his annual commentary with encouragement: 'signs of economic recovery . . . good results from the overseas operations . . . programmes to restore profitability . . . personal involvement by employees in quality . . . new products to grasp new markets . . . successful fulfilment of our plans will bring a sharp improvement.' But the public face hid management and board worry about money.

The value of shareholders' funds had been dropping since 1978. By the end of the 1982–83 financial year the drop had been sharp to the point of danger. Commenting on the accounts at a board meeting, Ernst & Whinney, the auditors, warned, 'covenants on some borrowings specified that net shareholders' funds should not go below £400m. At July 31 1983, they were £420.6m, but the covenant to Morgan Grenfell excluded some £10m of plant revaluation, reducing the figure to some £410m.' Bill Shield, at one of his last board meetings before retirement, when, in April 1983, directors met to discuss strategy, charted the rise in borrowings from £67m in 1978 to more than £200m in 1983, exceeding the limit laid down by the group's finance and audit committee and taking gearing measured by borrowings as a percentage of shareholders' funds to 55%. Lucas, in short, had been breaching its own internal disciplines and slipping near to breaching its external obligations.

The minutes record Shield as reporting:

> Over the five years there had been persistent high usage of cash and decline in profit. Some £536m had been expended on fixed assets and research and development over the five years and City financial analysts asked when we would show a return on this investment. The release of cash through reduction of stocks was a priority task. The group had used up readily available resources and funds had now become more restricted, so that very strict control on cash was essential.

In fact, when Bob Brown, Shield's successor as finance director, presented the 1982–3 figures, he could point to the best ratio of stocks to sales for five years. In gross figures, they had come down by £30m during the year to £389m, a total which, to give it some perspective at the time Brown disclosed the figure to the board, was £179m more than the value put on the whole group by the stock market. But the glimmers of good

The Lucas Aerospace Fordhouses factory received a double Queen's Award in 1982; one for Technology for the Reheat Nozzle and Thrust reverser actuation System (fitted to the Turbo Union RB 199 engines of Tornado all-weather combat aircraft), the other for a 275% increase in exports.

CAV's inline pumps made in 3, 4, 6, 8 and 12 cylinder versions.

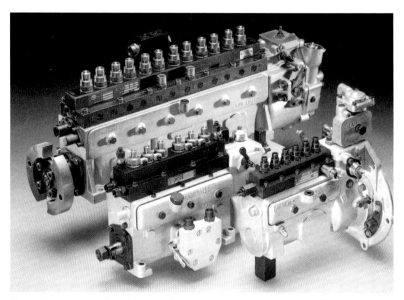

financial news, in spite of the continuing and heavy losses on the UK operations of Electrical, CAV and Girling, came 'in respect of cash performances; every company had responded with cash generation of £55m in June and July and a cash generation of £15.9m in the year.'

The recession and the consequential losses in the group's UK companies turned the forward looking perceptions of the early 1970s into the blindingly obvious pressures of the 1980s: a group of Lucas's size could not rely on the domestic market, it had to be international or nothing. Even in the darkest days of the economic gloom, Lucas looked outwards, especially to the US and Europe. Financing the vision contributed, of course, to Shield's financial concerns.

Cash shortage or not, Lucas companies spread out. In the early 1980s they found the funds to climb out of the US dilemma posed by Girling when it sought board sanction to start a brakes factory in Cincinnati. Derek Whitaker, the general manager, pointed out that Girling's US competitors – Bendix, Teves, Rockwell, Delco and others – manufactured on both sides of the Atlantic. Girling did not have a US manufacturing presence; this damaged credibility with US customers, affected the ability to support European customers in their US operations and weakened any attempt to head off Japanese companies holding Girling licences from supplying Lucas-designed products in the US. Whitaker told the board:

We have come to know, that US customers are generally reluctant to source volume business offshore and yet there is a frustrating circularity about establishing a new venture, particularly in a mature market. Without an established presence, one lacks the credibility, compared with established rivals, to gain business; but without business one lacks the justification for establishing the presence.

Credibility, fanned by the umbrella company in the US, Lucas Industries Inc (LINC), gained substance as sales grew, reaching towards $200m at the end of the 1982–83 financial year, with about half of that coming from Lucas plants in North America. Cincinnati came on stream at the end of that period, meeting a contract to supply Ford with drum brakes for medium-sized trucks.

The plan originally had been to meet the Ford contract through a joint venture company to be set up with Dayton-Walther, an Ohio company still largely owned by the third generation of the founding Walther family; heads of agreement had been signed, Ford thought the joint venture a good idea. But financial problems overtook Dayton-Walther as it too found itself short of cash. It pulled out of the agreement, leaving Girling with a contract which it knew it had to honour. Ford could not be left in a bind. At that stage in Ford's manufacturing programme, it would have been difficult to find an alternative supplier. 'Even more fundamental are the worldwide implications and possible repercussions upon Lucas Girling and the group's business with Ford, which involves an annual turnover in excess of £100m,' Whitaker informed the board. The initial spending in Cincinnati was an investment of £3m with borrowing of £2.9m spread over two years.

Spending in Cincinnati proved to be modest compared with Greenville, South Carolina, the Lucas plant which carried so many of the group's hopes for the diesel business. The original purpose for opening Greenville had soon become irrelevant: Perkins abandoned its diesel-engine plans for Canton, Ohio. But a much bigger opportunity soon emerged from the demands of General Motors (GM) for CAV's tiny fuel injector for diesel cars, the microjector.

This device, which came off the drawing board of Peter Howes at CAV in Acton, west London, in 1955, had been sitting on a shelf for over ten years waiting for manufacturing capability and technology to catch up with it. Its time came when, in 1977, GM acknowledged two factors: first, the design would match emissions legislation coming into force in 1980 and, second, it was the only device available which, in a converted petrol engine, would fit into the space of a spark plug. The microjector could reduce weight, cost and fuel consumption in a diesel engine. At that stage, as the industry in general addressed problems of fuel economy, GM had heady views on the prospects of diesel

CAV's Electronically Programmed Injection Control (EPIC)

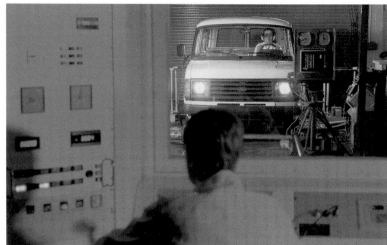

Below, DPS fuel injection pump, *right,* being tested in a complete vehicle dynamometer at the CAV's Gillingham Research Centre.

expansion in the US car market. So did Lucas. 'We were going with the established wisdom of the time,' Tony Gill recalled. 'The CAV expansion was driven by the notion that diesel cars were the coming thing.'

Trial production of the microjector took place at Sudbury, Suffolk, but when Oldsmobile at GM wanted a supply of 1.36m injectors a year for five years from July 1979, Lucas bought another factory at nearby Ipswich and equipped it as a showcase plant. This initial investment cost £8.4m in the expectation that it would be generating cash of £6.6m a year by 1980–81. It started swimmingly. The plant produced deliveries on time of reliable quality, more than the in-house GM plant, using Lucas designs, could manage. Then, when Oldsmobile decided it wanted more, it turned again to CAV, rejecting offers from Stanadyne and Bosch. Hardly had full-scale production begun at Ipswich than in, October 1979, Bob Lucas was back to the board with a request for £25.2m to build a new facility at Greenville to make initially 1.68m injectors a year and to increase Ipswich output by over 70%. It seemed the sky would be the limit; the microjector could be used by other GM brands, each set would probably be replaced at least once in a vehicle's life and the factory at Greenville would be on a site ready 'for further expansion there to meet even greater future demand for microjectors in the North American market.' The project would have yearly sales of nearly £23m to generate cash of just under £8.5m by 1983–84.

Confident, cheerful, and with an antidote to recession, Lucas started work at Greenville. Reservations were brushed aside. The *Economist*, reporting in November 1980, on the industry's competition for diesel advantage, calculated that production of

ROTAX

ELECTRICAL EQUIPMENT for AIRCRAFT

Lucas Aerospace grew from Rotax, and CAV, Lucas's diesel engine business, developed from C. A. Vandervell. Girling became the company's main brakes business. Lucas bought Rotax and CAV in 1926, Girling in 1943.

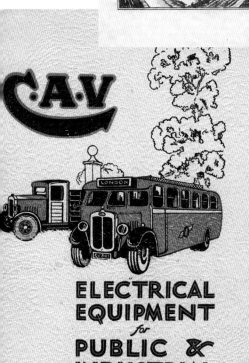

C.A.V

ELECTRICAL EQUIPMENT for PUBLIC & INDUSTRIAL ROAD VEHICLES

BRAKES · DAMPERS · CHASSIS ENGINEERING

it's continued
racing
successes that
keep

GIRLING

THE BEST BRAKES IN THE WORLD

— WAY OUT AHEAD →

GIRLING LTD
KINGS ROAD · TYSELEY
BIRMINGHAM 11

Seeing is Believing

A big step forward in blackout motoring safety and reduction of eyestrain and driving fatigue is made with the new Lucas Headlamp Mask, the result of extensive research and development.

The new mask has the well-known and exclusive Lucas Rim Fitting which directly replaces the existing lamp front, without need of modification.

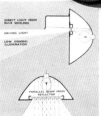

BETTER LIGHTING THAN EVER BEFORE

yet complies with official limitations.

Lighting Distribution superior to anything previously available—obtained by combination of a correctly designed, permanent asymmetric glass diffuser with a forward projecting cowl.

Remarkable spread, evenness of field and excellence of cut-off.

Upward obscuration better than so far available, source of light completely hidden from in front—vitally important for air raid safety and preventing dazzle.

No deterioration of light. Waterproof and dustproof light aperture, cleaned with a single stroke.

Lucas quality, finish and durability.

DIRECT LIGHT FROM BULB SHIELDED

DRIVING LIGHT

LOW GENERAL ILLUMINATION

PARALLEL BEAM FROM REFLECTOR

BEAM SPREAD EVENLY BY FLUTED GLASS

IMPORTANT:

This mask complies fu... with the Lighting (Restr... tions) Order, 1940, Pa... 17, and each one is test... photometrically befo... leaving our factory. Wh... used in combination wi... a clean reflector and ... standard bulb not excee... ing 36 watts at rated vo... age, it will be found to gi... no more than the specifi... 2.5 foot candles at 10 fee...

With the New LUCAS HEADLAMP MASK

Right, The Lucas Headlamp Mask , 'a big step forward in Blackout safety', Second World War civilian precaution against enemy aircraft.

Below, Lucas fuel pumps were fitted to the first operational jet aircraft in 1942 and to the Comet, the world's first jet airliner, 1949.

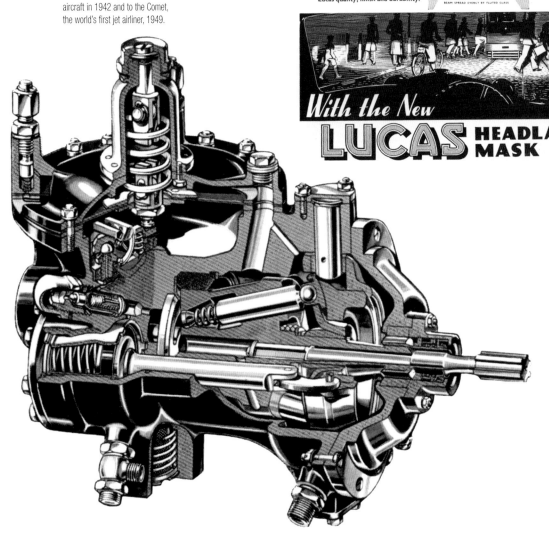

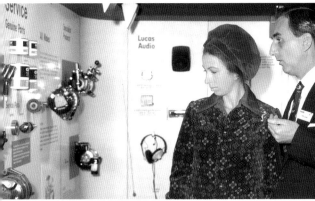

Above, Bob Lucas discussing Lucas products with HRH Princess Anne at the British Motor Show, 1978.

Below, George Frankl, Chief Engineer of Lucas Diesel Systems, receiving the Queen's Award for Technology from Deputy-Lieutenant George Bodin for the development of the Electronic Unit Injector, *inset,* in 1996.

Above, Reg Hennery, Manufacturing Director of CAV, retired after 46 years with Lucas in 1985. Reg, right, with Dr Tony Jarrett, Group Technical Director at the celebration, Syon Park, London, December 1985.

Below, Girling brake system components, *from top,* front disc brake calipers – Colette; self-levelling suspension; lightweight booster and compact master cylinder and stop control systems.

A new identity for Lucas

During the last 100 years Lucas has grown from a small Birmingham workshop into a major international trading group. Today Lucas Industries employs 90,000 people, generates annual sales of nearly £600m and comprises more than 200 separately identified subsidiaries or associated companies throughout the world

To be known as a large company was at one time thought to be a liability and many subsidiaries were encouraged to develop their own identities and play down their links with Lucas. Today, however, in order to meet changed national and international trading conditions the strength of Lucas will be enhanced if each company contributes to a united public image. A new Lucas corporate identity has therefore been developed, in association with Pentagram Design Partnership, and a programme is now under way that will give a dynamic dimension to our company and proclaim its status as a major international enterprise

In the past Lucas subsidiaries developed individual trade marks and symbols, most of which showed no link with the parent company. The Lucas lion was perhaps the most familiar, but it was seldom used by companies such as Girling, CAV or Bryce

All companies will be unified under the Lucas banner and market sector names will highlight areas of special activity. Automotive companies will be linked by the single word Lucas, and headquarters activities will be identified by the words Lucas Industries. A special alphabet has been designed for use with all corporate, market sector, brand and product names

The new symbol takes the form of a diagonal band with an L-shaped cut which is flexible in application and will lead to easy recognition. It is exclusive to the company and has been registered in every country in the world. The corporate colour is green

Famous brand names such as CAV, Girling and Bryce will be retained. The promotion of these long established names will derive new impetus in sales literature and packaging material through the controlled use of colour and the Lucas diagonal

Stationery for all Lucas companies throughout the world will conform to a single design. The market sector name and the Lucas diagonal will appear on all letterheads

Individual companies such as Girling and CAV will continue to trade under their own company names but the Lucas connection will be clearly indicated by the market sector name and the diagonal. News releases will give special emphasis to brand names and brand colours

Facing page, Lucas presented a united front with a new set of clearly connected liveries, 1975.

Above left, Sir Bernard Scott, right, at CAV factory opening in Korea, 1979.

Above right: Chairman Tony Gill hosting Long Service Awards.

Below: Geoffrey Messervy, Lucas Chairman, during evaluation of a motorcycle fitted with SCS at Fen End test track, 1982.

Above, Steve Deeming calibrating the fuel metering unit of a IAE 2500 engine to power an A320 aircraft.

Below, Girling Symposium, 1985, led by Girling Directors: Hans Hoenick, Brian Edwards, John Raper and Peter Hibberd, seated in the centre of the front row.

Facing page: from a 1970s Lucas brochure: inset, early examples of lighting and ignition equipment engineered by Lucas companies, compared with, main picture, a modern Lucas headlamp and electronic distributor.

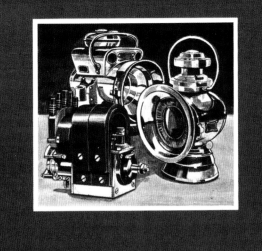

Lucas Aerospace supplied a Digital
Fuel Control sytsem for the Rolls
Royce RB211 524G aircraft
engine. This ensured optimum
engine performance and eased
pilot workload.

Lucas supplied wing slat and flap
actuation systems and tailplane
controls for the A300 Airbus; first
of a series of civil aeroplanes to
challenge, and by the end of the
1990s, overtake Boeing.

Prime Minister Margaret Thatcher
at Lucas Aerospace Bradford
factory, February1987.

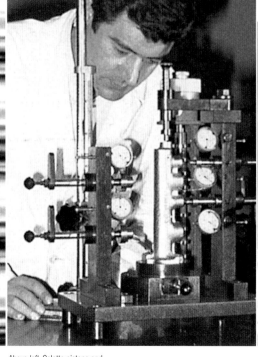

Above left, Colette pistons and, *right,* inspection of master cylinders, both at Girling España, Pamplona, Spain.

Philip Robbins, Service Manager at Lucas Services UK, Warwick, working on a Clayson 8080 combine harvester.

Gordon Barber testing an environmentally protected connector in a cold plunge test at Rists, Newcastle.

Carol Austin assembling a Maestro instrument pack at Lucas Electrical's Electronic and System's factory, Ystradgynlais.

Below, the Lucas EUI Concord Road team, left to right, Malcolm Lambert, Jim Newman, Dalip Dissanayake, Lukbir Panesar, George Frankl, Rob Gravestock, Adam Cox, Mike Davison, Lester McCalla, and Steve Barton, 1995.

Right, Ron Sharp, Chief Engineer, Electrical Systems, left, and Jim Fursland, Principal Engineer, Development, both of Lucas Aerospace's Power Systems Division examine a Compact Constant Frequency Generator after Test. This unit was used on Nimrod Airborne Early Warning aircraft.

Below, Foyer of the Lucas Group Research Centre, established in 1965 at Solihull, with a staff of 200 engaged in interdisciplinary research into electronics, mechanical and electrical engineering, materials and manufacturing processes.

Major investment in 1995 at Girling, Bouzonville in France, led to dramatic increases in productivity. *Left*, surface treatment (plating) of disc brake parts, and *right*, simultaneous assembly of both left and right brakes.

The MacRobert Gold Medal awarded to Lucas CAV for the design, development and manufacture of the Microjector, 1981. These injectors were exported to General Motors for their Oldsmobile Tornado.

Rover 3500 fitted with specially developed Lucas dual reflector headlamps, 1976.

Lucas Sports 1977

Below: Lucas Christmas Parties.

Above, Past and present Lucas
Board members, June 1987.

Below, Chairman's Garden Party
for ladies with 10 years service.
Operating Company Directors
waited on table.

THE LUCAS PLAN

A NEW TRADE UNIONISM IN THE MAKING?

Hilary Wainwright & Dave Elliott

ALLISON & BUSBY

Above, 'Lucas sisters': eight of seventeen members of one family who worked for Lucas over the years.

The Lucas Plan tells the story of Lucas Aerospace workers fight to defend their jobs and their plan to convert the company's resources from military to civilian products.

Right, The Royal Show sponsored by Lucas, 1986.

Lucas

Reflections

injection systems would require a dollar of investment for every dollar of yearly sales; without a big shift to diesel cars some companies would find themselves stuck with expensive and worthless plants. A month later, according to the board minutes, Rootes gave expression to 'thoughts about the possibility of the US public ceasing to accept the diesel-engine car.' But, in the knowledge that compensation would follow any cancellation, that the contract provided for price reviews, that, as Messervy put it, 'This order offered by Oldsmobile was the largest ever offered to Lucas,' that the project could run for ten years and help pump development, the bold advance seemed the obvious choice. For all that, David Hymas, the CAV finance director who later went to the US to run treasury operations for the group, believed the advance cost more than it should have done: 'The factory at Greenville was built extravagantly – the foundations would have lasted 100 years. It was over-engineered. There was brand new machinery. People from the US trained in Ipswich. There was a huge start-up cost.'

With the builders still at Greenville, GM came again to Lucas, this time for pumps. Its letter of intent, from Oldsmobile's director of purchases, said 'A decision has been made to purchase from Lucas CAV V-6 diesel fuel pumps to support a 1982 model year program of approximately 800/day beginning November 1 1981.' The first deliveries would be mechanically controlled DPA pumps; electronic controls would be incorporated in 1984 and the pumps would then be superseded by the fully electronically controlled EPIC pump, with which Lucas hoped to lead the market. CAV planned to make most of the components at its Medway plant in Kent and assemble them at Greenville. GM had given the group another opportunity to enlarge its US presence. Bob Lucas went to the board again, looking for cash in 1980–81 of £8.8m, although after that the venture would become self-financing and CAV would sort that out from its own resources. The capital expenditure required for Greenville came to £4.6m.

But the demands for money did not stop there. In April 1981 Bob Lucas was persuading the board to provide a further £5.36m to top up the Greenville costs. He expected that by 1982–83 the combined activities for GM would stop using cash and start making it. By 1983–84 he anticipated sales just short of £70m, a 5.2% return on sales and a 19% return on capital.

The middle months of 1981 proved a high point, a period when events on the ground matched the expectations, when CAV's investment programme, far more ambitious than its own cash could sustain, seemed to have found its own justification. The US diesel equipment market looked like a beacon for a bruised company; commenting on the overall 1980–81 CAV figures for the subsidiary's board, Hymas talked of 'a very difficult year with sales in real terms at their lowest level since 1973–74 and margin the worst

Eddie Weaver, an electrical engineer at Lucas Aerospace, Coventry. He completed 25 years service in 1976, received the BEM in 1981 and was Lord Mayor of Coventry, 1982/3.

British MCV 80 'Warrior' armoured
fighting vehicles and Challenger
tanks use Lucas CAV fuel injection
and electronic control
management systems in their Rolls
Royce engines.

ever'. Against that background, managers could find some solace that, in early 1981, the first microjector of local manufacture came out of Greenville. Oldsmobile's schedules for Greenville and Ipswich built up to 350,000 microjectors a month.

They proved to be halcyon days. Quickly the bottom fell out of the market. In October Greenville and Ipswich ran close to full capacity. In November, Oldsmobile scaled down its production schedule to 150,000 microjectors, less than half the level of the month before. It delayed the introduction of the V-6 diesel engine, slapping down the aspirations for pump sales. A tentative letter of intent from the joint venture diesel-engine company of Cummins and Case could not compensate for that. Lucas swallowed the bitter pill of foiled expectation. Greenville had just started to make a profit, four months ahead of schedule. Microjector operations in September and October had been making profits of £750,000 a month.

Lucas had done everything right to find everything wrong. It had responded accurately to the demands of the world's biggest car manufacturer, a valuable friend by any standards; it had invested; it had delivered; it had been reliable. But what Rootes had feared came to pass. The price of petrol dropped, so that US consumers, never anyway weaned on diesel, could see no advantage in branching out into the purchase of an unusual sort of car. At the same time as sentiment for diesel faded, Oldsmobile met technical problems. 'The Oldsmobile engine worked well but was not strong enough to withstand diesel pressures. It started to have crankshaft failures. The secondhand value of diesel Oldsmobiles dropped dramatically. Its popularity dropped. GM cut and run,' Gill remembered. Lucas lay high and dry with that expensive factory The *Economist* had mentioned.

But not hopelessly so. The cancellation clauses of the contracts with GM came into play. Gill said,

> We were paid for what had been done but that didn't include the opportunity costs – what other products could have been developed? Messervy and Roger Smith had this close relationship. GM remembered how much they pressurised and remembered that by compensating as much as we asked for. We came out of it not too badly.

Compensation came quickly: £6.5m in Lucas's 1981–82 financial year and £17m in 1982–83. It all made the 1981 plaudits – Queen's Award for Exports, Queen's Award for Technology, self-congratulatory claims of 'triumph' – look an anachronistic curiosity. For all that, the microjector adventure overshadowed at the time all other Lucas forms of penetration in the US market: the steady march of orders for Aerospace, the buying and

selling of companies by Lucas Industrial Systems, the replacement name for SMEC. It had been a bold dash for growth, one of two which dominated the recession years.

The second dash, although as time and discussion went on it seemed more like a plod, was the equally bold European venture in consolidation and rationalisation which Lucas executives called LDP, short for Lucas-Ducellier-Paris Rhône, and which had been discussed as far back as February 1980. During summer 1982, the need for decisions on whether to form a new group or find another way of resolving the difficulties of Lucas Electrical, Valeo and Ducellier took on greater urgency. Banks demanded an equity injection to ease the gearing of Ducellier. Jeffrey Wilkinson had been thwarted in his hope of having the whole matter settled by early 1982. His problem had been pushing everybody involved to execute what they had previously agreed. He set this out for the board in a paper he wrote in September 1982.

> Lucas has the necessary size, experience and financial strength to operate the new group and to make it capable of sustaining itself in future years. Valeo accepted this and in March 1981 signed a protocol that it was prepared to drop out of rotating machines and to sell its Paris-Rhône subsidiary to Lucas. Since that time, however, we have encountered a vacillating and prevaricating attitude on the part of both Valeo and the French Ministry of Industry.

Wilkinson, though, remained ready to cope with the frustrations if only because he did not want to contemplate the alternative.

> Without LDP, or an alternative industrial grouping, our UK rotating machinery would be unviable and its rundown and eventual closure would have to be faced. This would lead to a dramatic restructuring of Lucas Electrical since those parts which would survive could only do so by contraction or through some form of external partnerships. The overseas operations of Lucas Electrical would be in difficulties without continued central support.

But negotiations to bring about LDP had a slippery quality. When Lucas thought a conclusion might be within grasp, it would slide away. Partly this arose because Lucas held firmer in its aims than its putative French partners. Indeed, by the time Wilkinson was setting out the position for the board during autumn 1982 and in the months which followed, Lucas would be forced to look for new forms of combination because Valeo had changed its corporate mind. Discussions on money between Lucas and Valeo had

Press conference announcing the merger of the Lucas and Smiths Industries instrumentation businesses. Left to right, Keith Wills, Jeffrey Wilkinson and Roger Hurn.

Above, Keith Wills of Lucas Electronics became Chairman and CEO of the new company. *Below*, Marcus Berrisford of Smiths Industries became General Manager.

in any case stalled because Valeo placed a far higher – extortionate in Wilkinson's view – value on Paris-Rhône than Lucas. Further, the new combination would soak up capital expenditure of £115m over five years, roughly half of which would be in the UK. In London, the Department of Industry had indicated that a grant of £20m could be available, but, in Paris, the French government had made it clear that any support other than that normally available would not be forthcoming unless the group had majority French ownership. Of course, the financial questions could be settled if the will existed, but that will on Valeo's side seemed to evaporate when it acquired the alternator plant owned by Motorola at the French town of Angers and backed away from its previously expressed intention of withdrawing from the rotating machinery business.

Wilkinson believed these changes had four effects:

> Firstly it means that Valeo's shareholding in any new company will be substantial. Secondly, Valeo will now aspire to manage at least some of the new business. Thirdly, the French authorities can more readily oppose any unpopular features of a Lucas plan if there is disagreement between Lucas and Valeo. Finally, Lucas will now have to agree the detail of any restructuring with Valeo in a way that was not necessary when the latter was prepared to sell its business.

In other words, Wilkinson's big vision of a second significant European components group controlled by Lucas had clouded.

Lucas and Valeo remained partners in Ducellier. From the start, Ducellier had rewarded Lucas with a consistent stream of dividends and royalties. More than that, it provided Lucas with direct access to the French vehicle market; should it surrender its stake the way would be open to Valeo to form, not a European components group, but a French combination powerful enough to keep Lucas at a distance from a growing market. So the Lucas directors had little choice but to accept the demands of the worried pool of Ducellier's bankers: they wanted an equity injection of FFrs50m, of which the Lucas share would be the equivalent of £2.1m, to bolster Ducellier's precarious finances. If the capital injection did not come, then credit lines would not be renewed. Lucas construed the bankers' move 'as an attempt to force a resolution among the partners and the French government'.

Certainly that worked to the extent that talks resumed, but for a reorganisation of the businesses on different lines from those Lucas first proposed. Keith Wills, general manager of Electrical and working to Wilkinson, reported to the board in March 1983 that

Many of London's double-decker buses use Lucas CAV fuel injection equipment, heavy duty starters, alternators and transmission control systems.

> agreement had virtually now been reached with Valeo whereby Lucas would own 100% of the electronics, ignition and lighting business and rationalise with the UK business. Valeo would own 100% of the starter and alternator business and rationalise with their business in France . . . Ducellier would become a finance company [holding the fixed assets of the partnership and renting them to the two operating companies]. It was hoped to agree with the bankers to divide the borrowing into three: capital one third, one-third to be long-term loans at a more favourable interest rate and one third to be short-term loans.

So far, so good – and better still in July when IDICA, the French government's agency for developing the automotive components industry, Renault and Peugeot accepted the plan, with the carmakers evidently ready to negotiate prices and rolling long-term contracts. But snags emerged: the carmakers put some business elsewhere, pushing up Ducellier's losses and forcing short-time working. Nevertheless, although the bankers had their differences about financing the new scheme, by the end of 1983 the only outstanding issues were future arrangements for the aftermarket, remanufacturing and electronics technology. Settlement again seemed within reach.

For Wilkinson, however, the aim of strengthening Lucas in Europe went further than the talks with Valeo. He envisaged tighter links with Ducellier and associations with Marelli and Motorola in engine electronics and, as Wills told the board in February 1983, the vehicle for building a European presence could be a new company, Lucas Electrical – Electronics and Systems.

The new company would be an 80-20 joint venture with Smiths Industries. The Smiths instrumentation business, with assets worth just under £12m, would come into the fold of Lucas Electrical, which would put into the joint venture nearly £29m worth of assets. The idea for this had not come from Lucas; it had come from the UK government, keen at the time on supporting both electronics and consolidation in the components industry, with the inducement of a £25m financial package of grants and loans, interest-free for five years.

Internal discussion about absorbing the Smiths business appears to have been more limited than would normally have been the case for a venture of this magnitude. Indeed, when the board considered the question on 27 February, it spent most of its time considering finances; there is no record of debate about the strategic and industrial justification of the government's seduction by subsidy. The question of whether Lucas would gain in technology rather than in capacity seemed to have passed by the board although Jean-Maxime Lévêque 'asked if the number of employees were too high relative to sales'. Wills's paper held out the prospect of cost efficiency and better use of the Great King Street factory in Birmingham; it would place the company in a better position to move the customer base away from the UK to Europe. The financial calculations suggested the new company would make pre-tax profits in 1985–86 of £12.2m and a return on capital of 18.2%. Messervy concluded that 'even with a loan, it [the project] contained a fair amount of promise'.

Wilkinson, as it turned out, would not be at Lucas to see whether his hopes would be realised or Messervy's faith justified. In fact, he would have been bitterly disappointed at the outcome both of the joint venture with Smiths and of the broader European plan involving Valeo and Ducellier.

By mid-1983, after four years of battering in poor markets and monotonous repetition of financial setbacks, the Lucas leadership had lost its swagger to the point where Hull found it necessary to remind fellow directors that 'our objective was survival as an independent business'. But the board had not lost its sense of proportion. It had not looked for, and did not contemplate, a flashy initiative to seduce the stock market and put tinsel on its prospects. If anything, the experience of severe recession posed fundamental questions to the board and senior management about the nature of the group, what it could do and when it might do it.

Such questions crystallised in a seminal board meeting, held appropriately enough, not in the smart Mayfair offices of London but at a factory site in Shaftmoor Lane, Birmingham, on 28 April.

Lister engines that power all
Britain's unmanned light buoys
rely on Lucas CAV injection pumps
and injectors.

Discussion whirled around cash and how to generate it. The directors approached the sale of assets cautiously; Shield noted that 'if we sold off a company at a significant level below book value, it would put us into serious trouble with the bankers'. Most loans carried with them provisions relating the level of indebtedness to the net worth of the business. Anyway 'there were weaknesses in all three vehicle equipment companies in the UK. None were saleable in their present state. They had excess capacity for the market and we were faced with putting all three companies in order.' Rootes, believing 'we had got to look at something of a major nature', asked whether it would be possible to sell off half of Aerospace. This aroused little enthusiasm: 'It was a business we should build up,' argued Shield; 'It had made progress in productivity,' said Messervy; 'It was seen as synonymous with high technology,' said Gill, adding, almost to clinch the argument, that it 'could generate cash over the next five years'.

Unable to spy any easy money, the directors had little option but to fall back on the objective of improving financial performance so that diversification – 30% of business outside the automotive and aerospace industries – might take place later. This implied that where the group spent, it had to be sure the funds would create long-term growth. It meant that efforts to increase productivity must continue; Messervy predicted a further 10,000 job losses in the UK as 'manning levels were significantly worse than international competitors even after all the action that had been taken'. It meant too that Lucas would have to look at each business and decide in which to invest, bearing in mind earlier assessments of where the best growth opportunities might occur.

At the Shaftmoor Lane meeting, the directors had before them a list, drawn up by Alan Gaves, a group strategist, of peripheral businesses, the sale of which would not damage the group. It included battery and electrical companies in the UK and Commonwealth, service companies in Europe, a marine business, diverse industrial companies and the electric vehicle project, which, in total, might realise over £18m. He also identified

Lucas CAV pumps are used in a wide variety of marine diesels.

sports grounds, service properties, land and farms which might fetch about £8m. In similar vein, Gaves identified possible sales where there might be minor, but acceptable, damage to the group; these were largely service companies across the world. He created another category of businesses where sale would be possible but undesirable; the majority of these were industrial companies, some of recent acquisition. At any rate, higher financial performance involved trimming around the edges of the group but Gaves remained confident that 'the majority of our businesses are capable of being turned round'.

The turnaround itself could create problems. With a low market price – around 160p in April 1983 – the directors thought an improving Lucas could be vulnerable to a bid. They instructed the preparation of a defence strategy which could be put into operation rapidly. Looking back, Wilkinson thought an approach unlikely: 'We were perceived to be a disparate group difficult to manage; we had a significant amount of defence business; and the pension fund had a big holding.' (The holding was over 17% of the equity at this time.) But at Shaftmoor Lane, directors opened the possibility that a predator might want to cherrypick Aerospace.

The minutes of that meeting carry a passage made intriguing by knowledge of later events. During the debate about selling Aerospace, Gill said:

> He would be against selling part of Lucas Aerospace but it was possible. TRW recognised the complementary nature of the Lucas and TRW businesses. They had expressed interest in Lucas and Lucas Aerospace in particular . . . Lucas Aerospace talked about being stronger in the USA but unfortunately would not be able to obtain the cash to achieve it. Possibly the route to achieving this strength was by association with another company . . . Mr Gill commented that an acquiror could buy Lucas Aerospace at a reasonable price with the rest of Lucas thrown in for, say, £250m. TRW must have thought it through.

6 Relief and Recovery

The Shaftmoor Lane meeting caught Lucas at its point of lowest confidence, when the directors came to terms with the unpalatable fact that they had no choices, only alternatives, neither of which would be comfortable. The group could slog on or it could give up. The second never received more than fleeting attention. As it turned out, pursuit of the first ushered in a lengthy period of recovery and transformation, when all the numbers turned upwards and confidence returned. Choices became available.

From mid-1983 until the 1989–90 financial year, when the markets again became troublesome, economic conditions generally favoured Lucas and British groups like it. Exports became easier as sterling fell back in international value. Raw-material prices dropped, at least until 1987. Industrial relations shifted from confrontation to control and cooperation. With a lower number of people to pay, after the sharp contraction of 1979–82 and gradual contraction afterwards, the secret of success for Lucas would be to organise higher productivity.

Drawing attention to the calculation that the employment cost of a skilled production worker in Japan, Germany or the US in 1986 was more than twice as much as in the UK, David Shackley observed that, still, competitors, 'through higher productivity . . . have competitive unit labour costs'. With low employment costs, Shackley drew an obvious moral for Lucas: 'The opportunity presented by this situation is one which if seized and secured will create a highly cost competitive manufacturing base in our UK factories.' Coupled with expansion overseas, the attempt to grasp this opportunity made a major contribution to the 1980s transformation.

Inevitably the recovery of the different Lucas operations was uneven; Electrical remained a financial drag until the late 1980s. But the group results hid the disparities in a series of steady rises. In August 1984 Bob Brown reported to the board the unusual phenomenon that 1983–84 sales had actually been higher than forecast. Five months later, so the board minutes said, 'Mr Brown reported that February 1985 had been the best single month for the company since May 1979, with profits of £7m compared with £3.4m in February 1984.' Clearly wanting to dampen any excitement, he reminded the directors that 'reduction of borrowing continued as a top priority'.

At least, with higher sales and profits, the need for a dip into reserves or for use of bank facilities to run the group faded away. Pre-tax profits, which in the year to July 1983 had been a humble £2.1m (saved from a loss by compensation payments from GM), rose to £32.6m in 1984 as the group found its balance again and then to £57.8m in 1985. By 1986, at £95.2m, they had surpassed the record of 1977. A series of further climbs took the pre-tax profits to £187.1m in 1989 and then they flattened out to £191.2m in 1990. As a percentage of the capital the group used, the pre-tax profits constituted 0.5% in 1983 at the end of the recession but 25% at the end of the decade.

The figures measured the Lucas recovery. Underneath them, two crucial financial factors underpinned the process set off by the better trading. The first was a combination of the rights issues of 1985 and 1988 with a readiness to use relatively congenial market conditions to attract loan capital. The second was a halt, called a holiday, to the making of contributions to the group pension funds.

Coming out of the recession, the Lucas share price had been languishing under 170p, but during 1984, in fits and starts it began to rise enough for the group's finance specialists to start calculations on how much might be raised, and at what price, from the markets. In the autumn, directors received a paper setting out the range of figures and possibilities from share issues to raise sums between £36m and £183m. Only in 1985 though did the share price move to the levels where a share issue looked attractive. Starting the year moving around 260p, the share price rose to over 300p by the summer and over 400p by the autumn, helped by a management campaign to provide the brokers' analysts with more information. The analysts, in any case, held generally sympathetic to the group, although they expressed concern about the lack of profitability at Electrical. During this period, the Buy recommendations far outweighed those to Sell or Take Profits.

In May 1985, the opportunity to test market reaction to any capital-raising by Lucas came when Industrial Systems needed money to take over Duralith, a US corporation making control panels and assemblies. The technique chosen was a share placing. Brown told the board in May that Cazenove, the group's broker, 'had advised that a vendor placing in connection with the proposed acquisition . . . could proceed on the basis that the institutions were aware of the Lucas Electrical problems and that the City profit expectation of £50m would be achieved'. No problem emerged. During July, Lucas

Westland Agusta EH101 helicopter
fitted with Lucas electrical
generating, ice protection, switch
gear and actuation systems, 1988.

raised £17.8m, after it had met expenses, by selling over 6m shares at 295p each.

The waters tested, directors talked about a rights issue during the summer and then discussed it in more detail during their September meeting. By that time senior executives had seen Cazenove and agreed that the best time for a rights issue would be when the group published its 1984–85 results during November. But Electrical's problems hung over the feeling that, as Jean-Maxine Lévêque put it, 'In his experience when the market was favourable and all conditions were satisfied, an issue should take place as quickly as possible'. Hull warned 'Steps should be taken to avoid the accusation that money was being raised to assist the Lucas Electrical problem'.

Sure enough, when the issue prospectus came, the stress lay on investment in Aerospace and Industrial Systems, continued development on the automotive side but restructuring the UK business to match the expected demand, and financial flexibility in the light of all the reorganisation costs. The prospectus acknowledged but brushed away Electrical. 'In the automotive sector, although much further rationalisation is necessary in Lucas Electrical, and this is well in hand, our other companies . . . ' it went on as quickly as words could carry it.

The formula worked. Shareholders took up their entitlement: one share for every four they held at a price of 365p, which was 5p more than the most Lucas thought it could charge only three days before the announcement. The sale raised, after all the expenses, £89.4m. The market liked it, helped by the bullish tone of brokers. 'The shares still have some way to go,' Scrimgeour Vickers asserted. 'Lucas has the potential for both organic growth and business development,' considered Albert E. Sharp. 'The shares look outstandingly cheap,' concluded W. Greenwell. Contrary to the normal behaviour after a share issue, the price continued to rise throughout the winter.

The enthusiasm on the markets did not solely relate to the group's likely operational performance. It owed something to the effect of the pension fund holiday on the profit and loss account. Not for the first time, the pension fund played, for Lucas, a wider role than the mere collection of money for the dissemination of benefits. Pension funds had existed in Lucas since 1928 and the company had always contributed to them; indeed, setting up the funds in the first place had been a corporate initiative.

During the 1970s their existence, remembered Roy Middleton, 'gave the unions a lever. For a period there were pay controls but exempted were improvements to pension schemes. So that gave the unions something to talk about.' At that time Middleton was pensions adviser to the shop stewards of the Lucas Aerospace Combine Committee; now he runs the Lucas Pension Scheme. Then, 'When successive actuarial valuations had been done showing a surplus, the unions thought this was money to spend – that

Lucas Pension Scheme
personalities.

Percy Bristow, Scheme secretary,
1944–70.

Hugh Spottiswood, Scheme
secretary, 1970–83.

Nellie Parlett, first woman trustee,
appointed, 1963.

trades union aspirations could be met without costing anything, but that would have been stacking up problems, increasing the funding rate all the time.'

Negotiations between the company and the unions led both to increased benefits for employees and for the right of employees to become trustees. The attraction of worker trustees for the idealists of the Combine Committee was that it was, as the Committee's historians described it, 'the wedge that could open the door to workers' control over the investment institutions, of which pension funds make up over 50%'. Already trades unionists had 'amended the deeds of the staff pension fund to enable investment to be made which do not require an immediate return. And they have followed this up with discussions about investing in the West Midlands Enterprise Board to create jobs in an area where Lucas is fast destroying them'.

Pension payments to former employees increased regularly and, with the change in industrial relations caused by recession, the present running and future organisation of the two main pension funds, for staff and works, did not become an issue. Bryan Mason believed that one of the reasons why the mass redundancies of the early 1980s passed peacefully was the mobilisation of the pension funds. 'We tried to make it as painless as possible by enabling the pension to be pulled forward.'

Into the 1980s the company contribution was 10.25% of staff salaries and 8.25% of works wages. In the executive, concern remained about the weight of the shareholding held by the pension funds. When the board discussed the matter, in February 1983, without easing its discomfort, the staff fund held 8.68% of Lucas equity, the works fund 4.34% and the employees share fund 4.7%. By comparison, Prudential Assurance, the biggest outside shareholder, held 3.98%. Bill Shield feared what the Combine Committee hoped: 'The trade unions had a desire to influence the company.'

Neither had the expectation fulfilled. Lucas executives, of course, wanted to reduce corporate expenses by stopping contributions to the funds. They felt well able to do this, given that the assets of the funds were considerably greater than any liability they would face. Brown and Mason negotiated with the unions and won their approval for a payments holiday of two years. The matter was delicate but the agreement came without fuss. Trouble only came two years later, with token strikes, when the company calculated that it still did not need to make payments. In line with the rules of the funds, Lucas gave the unions six months' notice of its plan to revert, as the internal documents have it, 'to a balance of cost situation' starting in 1989 after a further two years of holiday. This simply meant that the company would pay into the funds if an actuarial need arose. So well-endowed had the funds become that it never did. In exchange for what became a freedom from payment, the company approved a range of increased benefits.

The City quickly grasped the effect of the payments holiday agreed in 1985. If it had any concern it was what would happen when the holiday came to an end; analysts had no notion that the holiday would become indefinite. Certainly the reduction in expenditure came immediately through to the profit and loss account. In the first half of 1985–86, pre-tax profits at £38m were £22.7m higher than the previous year, and of that difference £13.6m related to the pension contribution holiday.

The equity injection of £89m and the cash saving of around £20m a year gave Lucas a sounder financial base than at any time since before the recession. Gearing at less than 20% left plenty of space for more borrowing; the days fearing that banking covenants might be breached had passed.

The rights issue, Brown reminded the board in May 1986,

> was the first step to improve the group's capital structure. The second step, which has been an agreed objective with Schroders [the group's merchant banker] for some time, is the need to increase our long-term debt . . . over two thirds of the group's borrowing mature in under five years and are at floating, rather than fixed, rates of interest.

The way he chose to move from short-term borrowing to long-term debt and from fluctuating interest rates to fixed interest rates was to issue two convertible bonds on the Eurodollar market. Each of them matured 15 years later, and together they raised the equivalent of £92m.

Brown also acted to secure flexibility by instructing Schroders to arrange and manage a multi option facility of £116m, lasting for five years. This would allow the group quick access to a variety of sterling or dollar advances and, by having available options on different types of advance, Schroders would be able to provide funds when they were needed at the cheapest rate going.

Lucas Aerospace, Willesden, propulsion system for UK StingRay, lightweight air droppable torpedo.

Aerospace Luton, plastic based transparencies – cockpit and cabin windows.

With Lucas continuing to restructure its UK operations, build up its presence abroad, hold its position in its chosen automotive areas and expand the aerospace and industrial sides by acquisition, the call for funds remained heavy. Within two years of the rights issue, the board again turned to the advisability of more capital-raising. This time, the omens seemed less favourable.

In the summer of 1987 the price of Lucas shares rose strongly. But on Black Monday in October, London followed Wall Street in a giddy tumble. Lucas shares at 765p lost over a third of their value. Although brokers continued to look sympathetically at Lucas shares, generally seeing them as undervalued, stock market conditions remained uncertain when, in February 1988, the directors started to discuss a second rights issue.

Facing page, Lucas Industrial
Equipment and its associate
company Keelavite Hydraulics
were involved with off-shore oil
development from the Persian Gulf
to the North Sea. Applications
included hydraulic jacking
systems, high pressure couplings
and turbine fuel supply pumps and
starters.

Nor, with the domestic economy running strongly, could the directors anticipate which way the UK government might jump in its forthcoming budget. But for all that, they could see merit in being among the first companies to seek capital in a new round of rights issues as the market recovered its equilibrium after Black Monday.

So, in April, Lucas accompanied its announcement of a 32% increase in its half yearly 1987–88 pre-tax profits with a call for £162.7m. It asked the shareholders to buy one new share for every four they held at 500p each. The reasons it gave for wanting the money came down to reassurance that the programme to build up the business – strengthen the traditional and weld on the new, while finding a better balance between automotive, aerospace and industrial – had gone very well and therefore it should continue, for which new funds would be necessary.

After the issue, the market analysts, with few exceptions, maintained their Buy recommendations, but the share price, instead of rising as it had done in 1985, slipped under 600p and stayed there for the next nine months. Brown, however, continued to look at long-term fixed interest capital and seized the opportunity of feeding the London market's revived appetite for corporate bonds. For the first time since 1971, Lucas issued a long-term bond for £100m at an interest rate of 10 7/8% and due for repayment in 2020.

The visits to the capital markets marked the confidence which returned to Lucas during the 1980s. Executives knew they would not be turned away. This financial reorganisation was one facet of a wider pattern of change in the group. Another facet of this change involved people, and it started at the very top.

Jeffrey Wilkinson resigned in January 1984 'to pursue his other interests' as the board minutes recording the event gently stated. More accurately and crudely, he had been pushed out, having lost the struggle which had been taking place at the top of Lucas ever since he and Tony Gill had been made joint managing directors. Non-executive directors had told Godfrey Messervy a year before that he should decide on his successor but that they had no particular preference for either Gill or Wilkinson. Messervy was slow to make up his mind. Wilkinson knew perfectly well what was going on and he saw his departure coming when, he remembered, 'Messervy came into my office for the first time ever'.

At a personal level, Messervy made the obvious choice. Outside Lucas, he and Gill were friends and neighbours. Wilkinson, however, from the vantage point of his own sharp intelligence, ambition and massive self-confidence, tended to be dismissive of Messervy. On his own account he seems to have been barely polite with him: 'I didn't

Tony Gill appointed sole Managing
Director, 1984.

pander to Messervy and my lack of regard for what he did must have shown.' Yet, at a professional level, Wilkinson had run into difficulties with his portfolio of responsibilities. The recession bore most heavily on the UK companies and the most exposed of them in a financial sense were the commodity businesses in Electrical. In strategic terms, Lucas saw its future in the high-technology companies and they tended to be in Gill's portfolio. In other words the future did not seem to be with Electrical unless new ways of harnessing its business to the international rather than national motor industry could be found. Wilkinson's solution in the form of a significant European alliance, Lucas-Ducellier-Paris-Rhône (LDP), came near only to slide away. Messervy let Wilkinson pursue the European solution but viewed it with only limited enthusiasm. 'At the time Messervy decided on Gill, I was at my most disadvantaged,' Wilkinson said. 'The board was sick of listening to me, bringing bad news. Electrical was at the nadir of its fortunes.'

With Wilkinson gone, Gill became the sole managing director and Messervy's heir apparent. He took over as chairman and chief executive in 1987. Because of Messervy's keenness to push executive responsibility downwards, Gill ran Lucas from the point of Wilkinson's departure until he handed over to George (later Lord) Simpson ten years on. He found, not surprisingly, that working with Messervy alone was easier than working with Messervy and Wilkinson together.

> Becoming sole managing director simplified the relationship. We didn't have to have pre-arranged three-way discussions. What we had were informal sessions, much more user friendly. Personal tension went out of it. We played to our strengths. Messervy managed the board; he'd talk to other directors when we wanted to get something. I kept him informed, took directions from him. Muddles and tensions disappeared. With his approval I delegated some functions to the managing directors of individual businesses. Messervy took an interest, helped but didn't interfere.

Gill took control as Lucas moved into a new phase. The industrial conflicts of the 1970s had largely disappeared and if differences broke out into action then, by comparison, they were little more than scuffles. Survival of the group, after the desperate cutbacks of the early 1980s, had been secured, even though the shock of the first loss in Lucas history had not faded from corporate memory. With trading conditions improving, 'management started to manage', as Bob Dale put it. Gill, then, faced the long-term task of ensuring that management was fit to manage and it had the tools to do so. To succeed in that, new practices and techniques had to weld on to the best of the old style, for, in some respects and despite the hostile pressures from the outside, Lucas was introverted, conservative, stodgy even.

Starting his Lucas career in an operating company and only moving to the centre later, Gill understood this perfectly well. 'There was cultural arrogance in Lucas, the belief that Lucas could go on being Lucas and customers would go on buying. We needed to turn that round so that we provided what the customer needed.' To bring the more wayward Lucas managers close to the outside world and to set up the operating companies with plans and targets to compete internationally, Gill introduced Competitiveness Achievement Plans (CAPs). They became the group's basic management tool, an instrument devised locally but meeting central strategic criteria, gradually becoming more elaborate and sophisticated so that they would eventually be not just a guide to operations but also a financial planner. Anxious to make local managers both respon-sible and accountable, Gill saw the CAPs as 'a democratic way of planning the future'.

Each CAP, Alan Gaves noted in a strategic review for the board, is based on

> an understanding of the performance achieved by the best competitor; the detailed
> actions needed to achieve at least equivalent performance levels; understanding of the
> resources, i.e: people, skills, technology and money, needed to implement these actions.

In other words, Gill explained, 'people in a business were telling you what they had to do to be competitive. If they were saying it was beyond them, they were reasoning towards the obvious result – closure or sale.' Although the 85 business units were told that they had no local power to make decisions without a CAP approved by the centre and that no business plan meant management changes, some companies were slow to grasp the purport of the exercise. Gill related how, going to an Aerospace company to hear its CAP presentation, 'there was not a single Japanese name. Was there no Japanese competition? The reply was "Yes, but they're buying their way in" as if that made it invalid. Yet the most formidable competitor was Japanese. That was the size of the problem.'

It took 18 months for CAPs to spread across the group and in that time, according to Gaves, deficiencies emerged: inadequate information about competitors, targets set too short to match competition, not enough talented people in manufacturing systems development and insufficient management time devoted to innovation and change. On the plus side, the plans showed that customers commended both Lucas product tech-nology, which, however, could be applied more quickly and effectively, and manufac-turing process technology although it was 'thin and patchy in application.' Alongside the

Lucas supplied control systems for Sasol Jordan Formula One racing cars.

operational audit of the CAPs, Gill supported an audit of managers, starting with the top 75. Bryan Mason, by this time group personnel director, and Whitehead Mann, the group's recruitment and personnel consultancy, assessed these managers against a matrix of business skills and found broadly what they would have expected to find. Lucas had a leadership problem. The 1987 report of the group's appointments and salaries committee said,

> The following general characteristics have been identified: there was a very low level of entrepreneurial and/or marketing skill; a large proportion of the 75 were equipped to manage and maintain their current business but only a small number had the qualities to take the business forward; the group were very homogeneous – having the same values and being inclined to perpetuate these values; personal weaknesses had seldom been identified and discussed before.

The findings prompted a managerial reshuffle and reinforced Gill's determination to bring in new blood to revive the old. Indeed, the appointment of executives such as Jack Fryer and Ken Maciver, both of whom were to play significant roles in the group, dates back to this period. But the findings also prompted the development of a strategic leadership programme, aimed at turning managerial thoughts towards customer satisfaction.

'We asked three universities – business schools – to bid for the job of creating a marketing course. I put the top 100 in the organisation through it and then took it further down,' recollected Gill. Eventually about 1200 Lucas executives went through the course.

The best bid came from INSEAD: they came to Lucas and developed a course on what they thought were our problems. The INSEAD group was mainly Americans: eventually they formed a company and ran courses in the UK and US. The company went to the people; that was cheaper than sending our people to Fontainebleau. It was the nearest thing you can get to indoctrination, to turn towards customer orientation from continuing Lucas arrogance.

Gill explained that, after the start on marketing, the training approach extended to whatever the operating companies wanted, whatever had been thrown up in their CAPs. 'If a unit identified issues, we used training as a response to that.'

To what extent this approach improved the general Lucas business is difficult to say, Mason concluded: 'Lucas people thereafter could talk the right game, strut their stuff, demonstrate how knowledgeable they were about ways forward.' That was one thing. 'The confidence in giving freedom to executives to run their own businesses was greatly enhanced – they didn't need to be nudged and pushed.' But the downside for Mason was that Lucas 'became vulnerable to executives taking short cuts verging on the improper. So there are examples of assets misused, of poor contracts entered into.'

Managerial training, however, formed only one part of a much broader process of change. Throughout the 1980s Lucas continued to put more and more stress on training at every level of the organisation as different manufacturing and managerial skills came into play, rendering traditional job definitions obsolete and demanding a new mix of expertise. Part of this training was directed to production skills immediately needed; for example, at the Girling plant in Pontypool, Wales, making anti-lock braking systems, employees during the mid-1980s spent a day a month training off-the-job. Another part related to the training, according to the official standards of the Youth Training Scheme, of apprentice technicians and craftsmen. Lucas also promoted among the workforce individual programmes of study at Open Learning Centres throughout the group. The group sought to ensure the arrival of a steady stream of engineers, especially systems engineers, by sponsoring courses or paying for professorial chairs at a range of universities: Birmingham, Southampton, Warwick.

The ferment of change in manufacturing caused the increasingly urgent demand for training. Japanese industry reached the high point of its international influence over manufacturing processes during the 1980s. Western car manufacturers, steel makers and engineers of all sorts rushed to find out how the Japanese could produce more, at higher quality, for relatively less cost than they could. Lucas was among them. Indeed the group, with its history of interest in technical innovation, emerged as one of the UK leaders at some of its plants in fostering improvements in manufacturing technology based on the Japanese experience.

The conduit for, and the guide of, change in Lucas was John Parnaby. Headhunted to fill a specific post by Whitehead Mann, he joined Lucas in September 1983 as group director of manufacturing technology, with a place on the group executive. Then, and later, Parnaby attracted controversy. The very post he occupied caused disagreement between Gill and Wilkinson, the one believing such a director necessary, the other not. At a more personal level, Parnaby's critics charged him with being more of a boffin than a businessman, but that was harsh for someone who had started in the steel industry at 16. For Gill, what mattered was not so much that Parnaby was the first manufacturing systems professor in the UK but that he had been to Japan and seen that it worked; he understood the Japanese system. Parnaby had the responsibility to create change but he did not have battalions behind him to force change. He wanted to apply what he called 'the systems engineering approach'; this required changes in the pattern of thinking, innovation led by education and business reorganisation. It was a heady mixture. His ability to create change would be as good as his ability to convince managers that they needed it on the factory floor; there were many in Lucas who harboured suspicions about what Parnaby wanted to do and did not believe that he would be necessary anyway.

He found out about that even before he started work. When he was wondering whether to take the job, he related,

> I asked to see one of the big sites, Great King Street. I walked around it. It was awful. There were many floors. There was stock everywhere, mounds everywhere, you couldn't see people for it. I detected despair – there appeared to be no effective leadership, and modern practices dealing with high product variety weren't there. I asked to meet potential colleagues; there would be so much to do and it would be impossible if they didn't want to do it. At least three thought it would be a complete waste of time and I told Gill they could kill it – without his support to hold them back.

Gill and Parnaby needed each other. Most Lucas managers had no planning background. Parnaby, though, had an endless capacity to absorb facts and the unrelenting ability to organise them. He worked systematically on the deceptively simple premise of Think-Plan-Do with restless energy, ready to be theorist, playmaker and manager. But the all-encompassing approach deterred some managers from using his expertise.

Parnaby believed that manufacturing performance could not be seen in isolation; it depended on innovation in other areas such as training and the application of a variety of disciplines. So throwing investment at a factory, in the form of expensive machine tools or information technology, would not improve its performance unless, first, its manufacturing systems had been re-designed to be simple. Simplicity meant designing an integrated factory system around the products coming from it rather than around the processes used to make the products; cells not lines. Simplicity would be out of reach if the factory did not know what the market wanted and where its products fitted in to the market. All of this meshed neatly with the drawing up of CAPs.

Parnaby built up a team, he proselytised among the Lucas general managers, he ran workshops about how the Japanese acted, he gathered manufacturing managers together and took them to other companies which offered a good example. In effect, he set up an internal consultancy, Lucas Engineering & Systems (LE&S), and offered its services, for adequate payment, to companies in the group. Once at a company he persuaded the management to set up a taskforce or taskforces, embracing the different sections and strata, to be trained and then to apply that training in factory diagnosis and system design. The first major taskforce started work in Birmingham at Electrical's starters and alternators business, seven months after Parnaby arrived at the group.

John Parnaby, Group Director of Manufacturing Technology, was good at recruiting talent and motivating graduates.

This business, the group's annual engineering report noted in 1985,

> represents a classic mismatch between manufacturing technology and market place requirements. Production facilities have been conceived around a low variety/high volume demand pattern and the concurrent volume reduction and increase in variety have generated the need for massive stock support and consequential manufacturing inefficiency.

That the product ranges were obsolete did not help, so analysis of the factory, the initial appraisal, took into account new ranges. The new manufacturing plan called for a 35% reduction in the number of employees and consolidation of all the manufacturing on one site. It meant the introduction of the just-in-time system with all that involved: rigid control of stock, quick tool changes and a readiness among employees to turn their hand to a variety of tasks.

By the end of 1984, two manufacturing modules or cells had started to work, one handling a high variety of products, the second a low variety. These two modules provided both experience in the new system and a base for training. In four months, productivity rose, respectively by 25% and 7.5%, manufacturing lead times dropped in one module from 14 days to one day and in the other from 10 hours to 4.5 hours. 'The

Following the formation of a new joint-venture company in Hong Kong, Sir Godfrey Messervy led a visit to the Chinese Military Aircraft factory at Chengdu, China, April 1987.

results achieved to date,' said the engineering report, 'have far exceeded initial expectations . . . Many of the changes have in fact been welcomed by the workforce and the traditional communication channel to management has been fundamentally changed.' The quick results set off changes in the commercial and technical support activities of the plant and laid the basis for the development, during 1985, of a further 11 modules.

Parnaby's influence spread. At the new Pontypool factory, Derek Savage, the product general manager, reported in 1986 editions of the staff newspaper on how 'we took advantage of the new concepts in factory design and layout now available and introduced a Japanese-style system of workflow which is proving very successful'. By early 1986, Parnaby told the board, manufacturing cells had been installed or were being installed on 12 sites, he had training for task forces going at 19 sites and manufacturing systems training on two levels taking place at 32 sites for the first level and 48 for the second.

By the end of the decade Parnaby had built LE&S into a £20m a year business. In five years it had supported more than 300 task forces and other projects related to manu-

facturing systems across the group from Pontypool to Madras. It had developed a set of over 50 products setting out methods of coping with innovation and introducing new technologies. It is, Parnaby reported in 1989,

'Hilver', Moseley, Birmingham, Lucas Management Training Centre.

> a very significant element in the technology transfer and innovation process across Lucas
> . . . With over 170 young, well qualified engineers engaged on projects across Lucas
> ranging from machine systems engineering to total quality methodology implementation,
> there is good potential for continual technology transfer and the exploitation of synergies.

At the same time LE&S had started to work with other companies. 'Via its projects with major Lucas customers such as Rolls-Royce, Jaguar and Westland, [it] is able to develop its products to meet perceived customer expectation of Lucas divisions.'

7 Gill and the 1980s Expansion

Tony Gill at the wheel of the Lucas racing truck, first in Europe to be fitted with the advanced Lucas electronic diesel fuel-injection system.

Facing page, Lucas Aerospace Hot-air balloon used in the 1980s for charity and other public relations events.

For Tony Gill, the mid- and late 1980s were good years as Lucas reorganised, consolidated here and expanded there, and reached a state of better financial health.

> We weren't spending on group research where there was no likely return. We were shutting down businesses unlikely to make it. We were getting the manufacturing technology changed. We were getting plant investment to bring in flexible machinery. Profitability was going up; cashflow improved and gearing became easier. We went through a period of really making progress. And it fed on itself – until the recession hit us.

Underneath the progress a debate took place. At the time of the recession in the early 1980s all thought of lessening dependence on the automotive sector by creating new profit streams had been abandoned. But by 1984 the financial position at Lucas had improved enough to start discussing the future shape of the group. Industrial Systems became what Alan Gaves called in a 1984 strategy paper 'the principal vehicle for implementing the objective of broadening the base of earnings'.

This 'broadening the base' became the running debate, never completely resolved, on whether and by how much Lucas should diversify. Diversification in the 1980s attracted more sympathy than it did in the 1990s; corporate strategists thought the availability of different streams of income to be desirable, although there seemed little taste for buying companies just to do something different. Gill argued at a board meeting in October 1984 that

> the distinction should be made between diversification into entirely new areas, and diversification by development of existing products and technologies into related areas. He mentioned the expansion of Aerospace activities from aircraft to weapon systems and the Industrial Systems development of noise-measurement systems. These moves illustrated

his favoured approach of going into new businesses only if they were related to existing management skills in at least two of three key requirements: market knowledge, product technology and manufacturing technology.

Of course, as funds became available so did a rising temptation to spend them. The City liked to see something taking place with the funds raised on the market. Retrospectively, Gill hinted that not all the money had been wisely spent.

> There were lots of companies on the market, not all run very well, not all having the strength in the market they appeared to have. We came rather late to realise that the ambition of being less dependent on automotive and aerospace should not take too much investment.

Throughout the 1980s there was a gentle rumble of concern among some directors about the spending. Even towards the end of the decade some directors argued that the industrial side should be sold out. During 1989 James White, the chief executive of Bunzl who became a non-executive Lucas director in 1985, wrote to Gill: 'I would favour a strategy that saw Lucas concentrate on Automotive/Aerospace and exit everything else. I do not think we have the firepower to pursue all three to major scale.'

Without being too prescriptive about it, Lucas worked through the 1980s to achieve a balance of sales made up of 60% automotive, 20% aerospace and 20% industrial. This accounted for two of the four distinct factors which came into play during the period. The first of the four concerned the organisation. Although Gill clung to his belief in operational and financial autonomy, he sought to create a unity among what remained a federation of relatively small companies. Second, Lucas Electrical continued its struggle with the issues thrown up during the 1970s and during the recession; while it tidied up, other fiefdoms covering diesel, braking, wiring and services came into an automotive division. Third, Aerospace made a big push into the US market with a string of takeovers. Fourth, Industrial Systems, in the interests of 'broadening the base', itself made a string of takeovers.

Shortly after succeeding Godfrey Messervy, Gill put his own pattern on the group. He moved away from the design of a series of automotive companies, plus Aerospace, plus Industrial Systems underneath an executive committee and shoe-horned the operating companies into three divisions.

Lucas Aerospace Electric Actuator
Team, based at Bradford, won the
Queen's Award for Industry, 1986.

Bob Dale became managing director of the automotive companies – Electrical, CAV, Girling, Rists, World Service and the new Engine Management Systems – and had a seat on the board. For him this was the culmination of a steady movement through the management hierarchy; he had won a reputation as a clear-thinking troubleshooter as he handled operations which, at the time he took over, had serious problems needing urgent resolution. He had been through Batteries, World Service and Electrical, where, in spite of new responsibilities, he continued to exercise direct control.

At Aerospace, with Alan Watkins as managing director, also having a seat on the board, the operations were run on a geographical rather than a product base, so that there were three companies, one each for the UK, North America and France; this recognised the highly political nature of both civil and military business. Watkins brought to his new job extensive operational experience, honed in Aerospace since the mid-1970s, coupled with searching and free-speaking intelligence.

Gill kept under his own wing a third division – Industrial and Group Functions, made up of the congeries of Industrial Systems companies, managed by the ebullient Bunty Wootten, and the departments dealing with Finance, Personnel, Product and Manufacturing Technology and Public Affairs. He thus avoided the confusion caused by Messervy when, in the interests of creative tension, he gave his two managing directors, Gill and Wilkinson, a mixture of operational and functional responsibilities so that they could not avoid crossing into the territory of each other.

In short, he had taken the responsibility of seeing that activities potentially valuable to Lucas would not slip through the nets of the new organisation; the group functions acted as a centrifugal force on the autonomous operating companies. Gill looked too for other mechanisms which would ensure that expertise in one part of the group – electronics, for example – could become available to other parts by establishing later a Group Technology Council, the better to encourage technological flows. He understood Tony Jarrett's warning, in his 1984 engineering report, that 'the present decentralisation philosophy does not facilitate the essential systems engineering approach, both inside Lucas and at the customer interface'.

The executive still sat above the three divisions, bringing together Gill, the operational divisional chiefs and some of their senior subordinates – Jack Fryer, now running CAV, Ken Maciver, in charge of World Service, Derek Whitaker from Girling and Bunty Wootten – with Bob Brown, Bryan Mason and John Parnaby. The strategic running of the group, nestled above the executive but below the board, Gill placed in the chairman's committee where he gathered with Dale, Watkins and Brown.

When Gill made these arrangements, Lucas had around 62,500 employees, of whom more than 42,800 were in the UK. Automotive employed 45,800, Aerospace 10,700 and Industrial just over 6,000. Automotive provided 61% of sales, Aerospace 28% and Industrial 11%.

Bob Dale, Managing Director of Lucas Automotive.

The impetus to solve the problems of Electrical by alliance in continental Europe lost force after Wilkinson's departure in January 1984. The focus of discussion inside Lucas shifted sharply, away from the search for a combination to rival Bosch and towards finding a means of extricating the company. Nearly four years of negotiation and discussion to create Wilkinson's ambition of a new European grouping looked unlikely to come to fruition. What had seemed so desirable, so near to achievement in autumn 1983, looked tattered in spring 1984. Partly this disillusion came from growing concern about the plight of Ducellier; mounting losses and the demands of the French banks for a refinancing of the company as a condition of extending their credit lines pushed attention away from the formation of a new grouping to the immediate problem of money. Lucas wanted at all costs to keep Ducellier's financial problems off its balance sheet even though, as the company had run as a partnership with Valeo, it had no option under French law but to acknowledge its liability for its near half share. Keith Wills, who, the previous year, had been negotiating new partnership arrangements with Valeo, now had the task of organising Electrical's retreat from France. He entered a maze of discussion, not only with Valeo but with the banks, the French carmakers, French government agencies and teams of lawyers.

In a paper presented to a worried board in March, Wills put the position starkly:

Alan Watkins, Managing Director of Lucas Aerospace.

> The lack of support received by Lucas for its plans for Ducellier means that long-term viability is not assured. In order, therefore, to avoid the worst for Ducellier, and in order to allow Valeo to continue with its plans for rotating machines, Lucas is prepared to concede to Valeo full ownership and control of Ducellier.

When the directors met on 29 March, Gill reported that it had been made clear to Peugeot and Renault that 'we had come to the end of the road'. Practically this meant that either an agreement would be reached with Valeo on future control of Ducellier, or Lucas would lodge Ducellier's balance sheet in the appropriate French court, the first stage towards liquidating the company or putting it into administration. Going down the legal route would be a defeat for Lucas, the board felt, but it would be worse for Valeo.

Lucas had given Valeo a deadline of 5 April: a deal or the court. In Paris, on that day, Lucas severed the link of 22 years with Ducellier, a link which until the 1980s recession had been profitable. Valeo bought the Lucas share for one French franc. Lucas injected FFrs35m into Ducellier's equity, assumed its share of the 1983–84 losses and granted Valeo a FFrs50m convertible loan and gave up its right to licence payments.

The result of these transactions for the Lucas 1983–84 financial results was an extraordinary loss of £3.4m. The wider effect was more difficult to enumerate. Withdrawal from Ducellier, the biggest independent electrical equipment supplier to the French motor industry, reduced the direct Lucas exposure to a motor industry which, in contrast to the British experience, continued to grow, leaving only Freins Girling and RotoDiesel as its French automotive operating companies. But the Lucas position at Ducellier had always been difficult; it had never been able to assume sole and continuous control. It had been forced to subordinate its commercial considerations to French government policy. At the end, however, the French government quietly provided Lucas with tax relief as implicit recompense.

Yet the politics of using Valeo as a means to consolidate a fragmented local industry and as the nucleus for a group to compete with Bosch did not go away. IDICA floated the idea, even as the ink dried on the Ducellier agreement, for a holding company to take between 20% and 30% of Valeo's equity, so its management could be made more effective. Nippondenso, the Japanese components group, might also be persuaded to join. This looked like a weaker French version of Wilkinson's original plan. The discussions eventually lapsed, but in 1985 Lucas found itself with 4.8% of Valeo's equity anyway, as its loan converted into shares. A year later Lucas sold the shares at a profit of £5.9m, wiping out the extraordinary loss of 1983–84.

Wilkinson's intellectual ghost, though, did not disappear. Messervy and Gill on 27 June 1986 met Carlo De Benedetti, a Valeo non-executive director who, with 42% of the voting rights, had a major influence on Valeo's affairs. He had two propositions: the first, a narrow and cautious suggestion of exploration to see whether the electrical interests of the two groups could cooperate, and the second, a bolder and wider approach of automotive merger with the sale of the Lucas automotive businesses to a company controlled by De Benedetti for cash and shares. The Lucas board declared it would prefer the first but would agree to discussion of the second provided a meeting stuck to principles and did not involve outside advisers.

By September, De Benedetti had refined his ideas and, at another meeting, made clear to Gill that he would like a holding company into which each group would put 49% of their automotive interest with a bank holding the balance of 2%. Gill responded that he would prefer a teaming approach. Neither side seems to have focussed intently on the ideas; in any event, both had been talking with other groups about alliances and transfer of businesses, and this they continued to do. Gill and De Benedetti met again in June 1987 but Gill turned down the overtures. The Lucas board minutes recorded that De Benedetti 'had said that he remained interested in such a merger in order to establish a strong European group. He had been told that Lucas had difficulty in seeing the advantage of such a merger from its own point of view.'

Ducellier notwithstanding, Gill's main preoccupation at Electrical when he became sole managing director of the group was not alliances in Europe but losses in the UK. He saw Electrical as a low value-added commodity business making losses, when Lucas should be concentrating on higher technology, higher value-added activities. Electrical, then, was a financial problem to be resolved rather than an opportunity to be nurtured. His brief for Wills was simply to reduce the losses calculated on a management basis as £18.6m in 1979–80, £42.1m in 1980–81, £14.0m in 1981–82, £20.9m in 1982–83 and £19.5m in 1983–84. When Dale took over in 1985, Wills and Gill having come to a parting of the ways, he received the same message: 'My brief in '85 was to get this company sorted – "Don't buy, but get rid of, if you can't turn it round" – stem the losses, the haemorrhage.'

Wills worked up and then, helped by Parnaby's manufacturing processes, started to implement the plan to sort out the starters and alternators business which, scattered over different sites in Birmingham and manufacturing outdated products, lost £17.8m in 1980–81, £8m in 1981–82 and £7.6m in 1982–83. Of the accumulated problems of Electrical, starters and alternators was probably the worst, the least tractable.

Brian Henderson, General Manager of Rists, the Lucas wiring business.

Mike Higginson and George Reid
servicing the battery pack of an
Electric vehicle with power train,
motor and controller from Lucas
Batteries.

The investment plan came up to the board periodically through 1984 and finally won approval in early 1985. The caution of the directors arose from the cost involved at £21.9m, including capital expenditure of £12.1m. Whatever the decision, it would be costly. Internal analyses showed that to shut down the operations and walk away with the loss of 5,000 jobs would cost £10m more than the investment plan. Although Electrical hoped to sell its new range of products more widely, the initial firm contracts came from Ford and British Leyland, thus increasing dependence on the UK rather than decreasing it, as group strategy demanded. But a running business, and the forecast was for a pre-tax profit of £4.5m for 1987–88, opened up the possibility of merger or sale to another company later on. That seemed a reasonable prospect. 'By this time the industry was starting to consolidate and everybody was talking to everybody else,' Dale recalled.

But the starters and alternators business fitted into a wider picture: a smaller UK vehicle production base, Electrical's static export performance, the decline of the parts and services business as products became more reliable, the fall of prices in real terms.

When Dale looked at his rickety range of responsibilities and examined the CAPs of the individual businesses, he calculated, he told the board, that there could be a further drain of cash coming to £118m over the next three years. Looking at the businesses in the light of Lucas criteria about international competitivity, market position and cash generation, he devised a plan which, effectively, would bring Electrical's days to an end and acknowledge that the Lucas future lay apart from its traditional base.

The only product group in which Dale wanted to invest covered engine management systems, 'a major opportunity . . . even though we are rather late in exploiting it'. Based in the UK, the business had an electronic components factory in Malaysia. 'We have developed good software, including now a gasoline injector, but . . . we have limited manufacturing capacity (ignition modules only; all fuelling modules being purchased from competitors),' Dale told the board. 'Major investments are required and a joint venture arrangement might bring in complementary strengths and markets.'

For the rest of the Electrical businesses, Dale planned divestment or joint venturing. Either would be suitable for the starters and alternators and batteries, both of which had an international base. A range of other businesses, which Lucas did not think important strategically, became available for sale: lighting, switchgear, screenwash products, screen wipers, rubber and instrumentation. Six more plants would simply be shut down because they had no financial prospects and they included Great King Street, the complex where the Lucas business had started.

Instrumentation was the joint venture with Smiths Industries, called Lucas Electrical – Electronics and Systems. It had existed for only two years, long enough to destroy the hopes vested in it. Indeed, its performance had been precisely the opposite of what had been intended: far from being a profitable electronics base for the British motor industry, it had been a loss-making complication. It quickly emerged that Lucas had not made a very accurate assessment of what it had taken on when it absorbed the Smiths instrumentation business. Laying out his plans to dispose of it, Dale told directors, 'The introduction of Smiths products in the last two years has undoubtedly exacerbated our dependence on the UK and has brought additional problems with regard to product quality, poor supply reputation and complexity of components for the aftermarket.'

Preferably Dale wanted to sell a basket of companies all at once but if that would not work he would adopt a more fragmented approach and if that, in turn, would not work then he would have to consider, as a third step, either closing a particular business down or retaining it. The first choice did not work. Lucas had discussions running over several weeks exploring a sale to Hitachi or Mitsubishi or Delco or TRW but when they failed Dale had to fall back on piecemeal divestment.

Right, Aerospatiale Dolphin helicopter for the US Coastguard. Lucas Full Authority Digital Electronic Control (FADEC) on the Avco Lycoming engine, *below,* AC and DC Generating Systems for civil and military aircraft and helicopters.

The prospect of the Lucas disposals and the future course of its engine management company fell into a maelstrom of corporate discussions as major US groups sought to expand and European companies plotted effective rivalry to Bosch. Dale provided a flavour of that when he talked at a board meeting on 21 May 1987.

> Starters and alternators. Magneti Marelli, Valeo and Bosch continued to express interest . . . but Marelli were the front runners . . . Mr Gill mentioned that Mr De Benedetti, whose actions had triggered European discussions regarding the lighting and starters and alternators businesses, may in fact acquire nothing as a result of the current negotiations.

On engine management systems, Dale said,

> Magneti Marelli, Siemens and Allied-Signal were all in discussion with one another as well as with Lucas. There was a possibility that Siemens and Allied-Signal might link their engine-management systems businesses, which would make them a formidable second to Bosch. For its part, Lucas would continue to discuss possible options and permutations with all three.

Throughout 1987, Lucas struck deals and organised joint ventures so that by the end of the year the major rationalisation of Lucas Electrical had been completed. Starters and alternators went into a joint venture with Magneti Marelli, which would own 70%. Lighting went to Fausto Carello, the Italian company and longtime joint venturer with Lucas in Italy. Delanair, a subsidiary of Hanson, bought a screenwash and commercial instrumentation business. Batteries went into a 50-50 joint venture with Yuasa. Although not formally part of Electrical, Lucas left the electric vehicle project to Chloride. 'We turned the Lucas Electrical loss into break-even in two years through a combination of divestments, closures, productivity improvements and some price reviews,' Dale reminisced.

Apart from the interests in the joint ventures, the only elements remaining in Lucas Electrical at the end of 1987 were Engine Management Systems, a company in its own right, 60% of Lucas Kienzle Instruments, the consistently profitable tachograph business, the parts and services and switchgear businesses, and 11 profitable businesses overseas, including Lucas TVS, the leading auto-electrical equipment company in India and Martin Amato in Argentina. The historic bastion of the group finally crumbled; the future would be elsewhere.

To win its future, Lucas Aerospace understood perfectly that it needed a stronger presence in the US, home of the biggest aerospace industry, home of the biggest customer base. When Alan Watkins took over Aerospace from Blyth in 1982, he faced an industry in recession. Like others in the sector, he had to deal with reducing margins. 'During my first period we were making sure we'd done enough cutting of costs to get back to profit. Having got the organisation into tolerable shape, we could look at strategy,' he remembered. The possibilities of significant US expansion began to appear in 1983–84 and, in January 1984, Watkins reported to the board, 'The organic growth of the business [in the US] is beginning and this may result in some cash usage. However, a growth-by-acquisition strategy is under review . . . This would require funds.' At the time total sales to the US ran at about $20m a year and the group had two onshore facilities at Fairfield and Englewood, New Jersey, which provided engineering and servicing for running contracts such as equipment on the Harrier jump-jet and the RB211 engine. 'We didn't measure on the Richter scale.'

As Watkins explained later, growth at Aerospace would not take place unless it moved into the US. As the company examined its position, coming out of recession, it noted that although the existing order prospects for the next five years would secure moderate sales growth, there could be a decline in volume afterwards; major programmes such as the Tornado European fighter aircraft would wind down and nothing new seemed to be starting. Aerospace was already as strong in the UK as it was likely to be and Europe was industrially and politically fragmented. Further, Aerospace needed to break out of its heavy dependence on Rolls-Royce, which at one point in the early 1980s absorbed nearly one-half of Aerospace sales. Acquisitions would help to enlarge the Lucas product range, which looked mature and needed anyway a stronger electronic element.

During summer 1985 Aerospace moved out of the studying and planning phase into the marketplace with a request to the Lucas board for authority to buy AUL Instruments, a private company in the defence electronics sector, for up to $10m. Watkins broke new ground: 'I had never made acquisitions before. We started modestly and set down some criteria – size, technical field and so on – and then went through the listings. We didn't want to buy basket cases. Then we contacted companies on the shortlist.' Buying AUL meant obtaining special US security clearances. After AUL, Watkins went for Weinschel Engineering, a publicly quoted company, at a cost of $11m and $3m for plant improvements; he wanted Weinschel to be the first of three acquisitions in the defence microwave sector. 'We couldn't buy a systems house because of the cost and security problems. So we tried to buy a company making components. If we bought separate companies we could get a sub-systems capability.'

For Lucas, the third acquisition would prove, a decade later, to be the most important and testing of all the 1980s purchases. Watkins did not know that when he sought the authority to buy Western Gear Corporation in September 1986. But even for him, it turned out to be the biggest item of his American shopping basket. The opportunity came suddenly. 'A call came out of the blue: Western Gear was available. It had been for sale for a while – in the hands of a dragline manufacturer who wanted it to be sold but didn't want a US competitor to buy it.' Watkins told the board that 'the acquisition of Western Gear would represent a significant expansion in actuation systems in the USA. Lucas Aerospace is particularly strong in Europe in actuation systems with products in hydraulic, pneumatic and electric actuation. These products are manufactured in the UK divisions, in the Aerospace associated companies in France and with work share partners in Germany.' The cost was $128.5m.

A year later, Aerospace in the US looked very different, according to the internal annual report on North American activities.

> AUL and Weinschel and Western Gear (which was too good a fit to miss) have transformed the business and Lucas Aerospace Inc now has a mainly self-sufficient activity under a director of Lucas Aerospace based in a new Washington HQ with total sales, including imports, of $311m, compared to $62m in 1985–86.

But Watkins did not stop there. In November 1987 he moved for Lear Siegler Power Equipment Corporation and won board approval to spend up to $50m on the company, a well-established generating and actuation equipment manufacturer of Cleveland, Ohio. It was quickly renamed Lucas Aerospace Power Equipment Corporation. The proposal for the Lucas directors contained information which, had they but known it, proved an unfortunate augury. 'During 1985–86, Erie [the Lucas codename for the company] came under heavy government scrutiny following alleged irregularities in quality procedures, and on progress billing. The subsequent investigations and stipulated corrective actions placed severe burdens on the overhead structure whilst depressing sales, with the result that the company was in losses in both 1986 and 1987.' Good enough reason there to change the name.

During 1988 Aerospace pursued its microwave ambition. After screening about 200 companies over the previous four years, Watkins sought permission from his fellow directors to start negotiations on buying two more microwave companies. This time the board resisted a quick decision. In April and May 1988, reservations came out: the future level of US defence expenditure looked uncertain; perhaps defence electronics might not be a profitable area in the future; the companies looked expensive; the underlying strategy looked unclear; Aerospace management might be overloaded; perhaps the time had come to consolidate (at this time Aerospace was busy with its successful attempt to wind up Thomson-Lucas, the French joint venture, and acquire Bronzavia and Air Equipement, the flight controls business). In June, though, Watkins won his case and the following month Lucas bought EPSCO, a microwave communications equipment company for $23m.

By this time growth in the US aerospace industry had slowed down, bringing with it consolidation of companies at considerably easier prices than in 1986–87. Taking advantage of these conditions, Aerospace bought another microwave company, this time one specialising in communications transmission, reception and interception, called Zeta Laboratories. Based in San Jose, California, Zeta had been the victim of an accounting fraud, subsequently rectified by Whittaker Corporation, the owner. The cost to Aerospace was $15.8m against $39m which Whittaker had paid to buy it in early 1986 before it knew about the fraud.

The final manufacturing company bought by Aerospace during Watkins's time was Utica Power Systems, a power transmissions company which went into Allied-Signal from the Bendix group but which Allied-Signal now thought peripheral to its main interests, and, indeed, seemed to have allowed to run down. For Lucas though there would be advantages in that its driveshafts connected directly with the gearboxes made by Lucas Western, as Western Gear had been named, and by Lucas Air Equipement in France. Purchase, Watkins recommended, would give the opportunity 'to consolidate

Lucas Girling Manufacturing Systems Symposium, 1986. Senior engineers from all operating companies and licencees around the world attended.

system expertise on engine and airframe mounted gearboxes and adds to Aerospace's hydraulic capability with servo pumps for future actuation systems'. It would take Lucas closer to the engine and airframe makers.

Watkins left Lucas in May 1989 to become managing director of Hawker Siddeley. By the end of the 1988–89 Aerospace sales in America had swollen to $428m, producing operating profits of $38m. Total Aerospace sales that year were £602m, making an operating profit of £55.8m. In three years $282m had been spent on acquisitions. The City was sorry he was leaving; still, some analysts liked the acquisitions: 'growing recognition of its strategic positioning' said Sheppards; 'great strides in building up its US business' said Warburg.

The heyday of the Lucas industrial arm, under its different names, came between the recessions of the 1980s and the 1990s. Plans for growth existed as long before as 1974 when fluid power and electronic measurements and controls seemed favourable sectors for expansion; they had international spread and the fragmented nature of the sectors provided chances of consolidation. They could form a muscular third leg, alongside the automotive and aerospace businesses. But the plans did not run far. The cash shortage of the 1970s stopped expansion in its tracks. Only after the 1980s

recession did strategic thinking shift back again to the third leg. Only then did cash become available.

The 1985 rights-issue prospectus described how the group intended to end dependence on the declining UK automotive industry and, in listing five policies, it included 'add, by development and acquisition, to the range of industrial systems and components supplied by our industrial division to provide a range of quality products for growing industries'.

Coming out of recession, industrial sales were under £100m a year, but growing after the disposal of some small and unprofitable companies. In January 1985 Bunty Wootten reminded the board that, in 1983–84, Industrial Systems contributed 15% of group profits on 5% of group sales. At the end of the year, Lucas bought Duralith, 'marking our first significant step in growth by acquisition since our acquisition of shares in Siliconix in 1978,' Wootten said. (Lucas later sold Siliconix and spent the takings on Ledex, which made solenoids and switches.) It also marked the commitment to growth. By early 1987 Wootten could make the cheery prediction of £500m sales by 1990 – not reached, in fact, as he was £200m over-optimistic.

Schaevitz, making electronic measuring equipment, followed Duralith into the group at a cost of £22.8m. These additions meant that measurement and control electronic

Presentation of the grant on behalf of Girling (Cwmbran) Trust to build a youth centre in Cwmbran. Torfaen's Mayor receiving a cheque from Ken Strangward and colleagues. Far right, Bryn Richards, senior shop steward and previous Mayor of Torfaen.

The 1984 Chairman's Top Award went to David Middleton of Lucas Aerospace. From the many suggestions selected by local committees a few of special merit received an additional award from the Chairman.

components and systems had reached sales of around £80m a year. A succession of fluid power distribution operations, generally small, in the US, Canada and continental Europe also came into the group lifting annual fluid power sales to about £35m.

In spite of Wootten's efforts to fit the different companies into categories, there was little unity. Wootten noted in his 1987 report to the board that the constituent parts of Industrial Systems – 27 different profit centres – 'are not essential or complementary parts of a whole with a clear market/product driven mission.' The businesses, he went on, 'are all small or very small separate independently viable enterprises, any one of which can be lost or sold without any effect on the whole, other than financial.'

The board nodded through the fluid power acquisitions of 1989 but sat up sharply when Bob Brown, who had succeeded Wootten as managing director of Industrial Systems, proposed to spend £130m on two US instrumentation companies. Spending on that scale, combined with an Aerospace acquisition proposal, would take group gearing to over 40%. But the objections centred on the old question of how the group should be spending its money and on concerns that even after the re-financing of the 1980s there would not be enough funds to support expansion in three sectors. This gave rise to the concept that expansion in Industrial Systems should be seen not just as a means of creating new business but of supporting the existing mainstream businesses of Automotive and Aerospace.

Colin (later Sir Colin) Southgate, who had joined the board in 1987 when he was managing director of Thorn EMI, told his colleagues in November 1989 when they discussed Brown's proposal that acquisition of the two instrumentation companies would be 'strategically the wrong move. Benefits of synergy, between the two businesses and with the Lucas group, had been taken into account, but in view of Lucas's record in achieving such benefits, it was dangerous to justify the price on these grounds.' Gill was unenthusiastic: 'it was difficult to understand how these two businesses would support the other two sectors, even though instrumentation may be a growth area . . . it might prove to be a diversion which was risky and unaffordable.' With other directors stacking up against him, Brown failed to win the backing he wanted.

But the acquisitions went on. Nova Sensor, with its silicon-based sensing technology, Metier, the software company, and DeeCo, with touchscreen and display control capabilities all came into the group during spring and early summer 1990. When Brown and Parnaby, due to be the next managing director of the industrial wing, presented a strategy to build up the group's sensing capabilities to a critical mass which could serve both the group and outside customers, the board concerns came out again. The non-executive directors generally took the view that the third leg of the group should be

RAC Dewar Trophy presented to Lucas Girling for the development of its anti-lock braking system. Centre, Lucas Chairman, Sir Godfrey Messervy; far right, Derek Whitaker, Girling Managing Director and his team.

converted into what was called 'a technology plinth' for the other two sectors. Gill did not take such a rigid position believing 'it was possible to adopt a middle course of buying technology for in-house development which could result in sales to outside customers.' On that day the the argument was not finally resolved – but smaller acquisitions went ahead in the following months.

With some years of rising sales and profits behind them, Lucas directors at the end of November 1989 thought increasingly about the future shape of the group. Goldman Sachs, the merchant bankers, had prepared a report looking at the strength, or otherwise, of the group in the face of any bid. Group strategists had been looking for a year at the three-sector strategy. But the latest internal financial projections had not been encouraging when set against the ambition of the group; they reflected inadequate operating profit and earnings per share, low organic growth, poor productivity increases, excessive working capital and inadequate cash generation. They looked like a softer variant of the harsh diagnosis of the early 1980s.

When the board reviewed strategy, Jean-Maxine Lévêque observed that the group 'had advanced towards the goal of becoming a world-class player in its selected fields, but the problem was the lack of sufficient strength in each of the chosen fields. It was necessary to identify the means of gaining sufficient strength in each chosen field.'

Southgate by now had come out firmly against maintaining three sectors. Brown commented that 'it was much less expensive to become a world player in the industrial sector than in either the automotive or aerospace sectors'. Gill made the enigmatic point that 'while some acquisitions had been disappointing, the group had never regretted any of its divestments'. The weight of opinion was moving towards the subordination of the interests of Industrial Systems to those of Lucas Automotive and Lucas Aerospace.

This certainly reflected the report commissioned from Goldman Sachs, circulated internally during June 1989. Goldman Sachs had noted the slow progress towards achieving a balanced three sector strategy and suggested it should be reconsidered, bearing in mind the perceptions of investors. It saw Industrial as an ill-defined agglomeration of diverse activities, not as a coherent business grouping. Goldman Sachs recalled that financing acquisitions had come from the funds raised by the rights issues, rather than debt, therefore depressing earnings per share. It considered businesses in Industrial Systems might need to be divested to release funds for the other sectors.

Bob Dale at Automotive had concluded that there would not be funds to allow the expansion of all the companies in the division and he favoured 'concentrating upon two core businesses – Chassis Systems (including car and truck braking) and Powertrain

Dealers and their families outside the Lucas-TVS factory. Over 100 authorised dealers attended the Lucas Indian Service Golden Jubilee Celebrations at Madras, December 1981.

Systems (including diesel and gasoline systems), supported by an infrastructure of electronics, sensors and aftermarket operations. Tony Edwards, the new managing director at Aerospace, who had come from Canadair Aerospace after posts at Motorola, General Electric (US) and Rolls-Royce, stressed the importance of maintaining a critical mass; he considered there could be some synergies with Automotive and accepted that some businesses could be divested. Brown described the refocussing of Industrial and put the case for acquisitions in growth areas, including the two £130m instrumentation companies; he warned 'if the proposed acquisitions did not proceed, the more able employees of Lucas Industrial would leave and he believed that the sector should then be divested'.

By this time Lucas had a new group financial director, David Hankinson, who had held similar posts at Chloride and Rover group. He advised his new colleagues of the City view that Lucas gearing should not increase and that 40% should be the maximum. Nothing, he argued, should be done to dilute earnings per share, a view with which Goldman Sachs would have been sympathetic. In fact, Lucas ended its 1989–90 financial year with static earnings per share of 20.2p and gearing of 15.9%. But change was in the air again and the breezy expansion of the 1980s looked blown out.

8 Recession Again

The 1990's recession hit harder and lasted longer than Lucas expected. 'We did not expect the turmoil in world markets to be quite as it has been,' Tony Gill confided to shareholders. Like the first, of the late 1970s and early 1980s, the recession of the 1990s came in waves, first to the automotive sector before spreading to aerospace. Expansion turned into retrenchment, or as the gloss of an internal document had it, 'post-acquisition rationalisation'.

In 1990–91 pre-tax profits ended at less than half the level of the previous year, down to £82.8m. The slide continued, to £22.5m for 1991–92, but then profits briefly recovered to £49.5m in 1992–93. In the following two years special provisions and exceptional items in the accounts hid the increase of operating profits. Only in 1995–96, the last full year of Lucas Industries, did pre-tax profits approach the level reached in 1989–90. Between 1989–90 and 1991–92 the return on the capital Lucas employed slumped from 25% to 2.9%. But dividends right through the recession stayed at the same level of 7p a share, even though in 1991–92 the group did not earn enough from its operations to cover the payment.

A mixture of factors in the outside market hit Lucas, as they did companies in its peer group. Earnings from the group's automotive companies fell as their customers put more and more pressure on prices; component and systems prices fell faster than the ability of Lucas to cut its own costs. On the aerospace side, demand fell away in 1991–92, as the group had expected when, the previous year, it could not work hard enough to keep up with the flow of orders. Defence spending cuts – these were the years when governments talked of the peace dividend after the collapse of the Soviet Union – combined with a reduction of demand from civil users.

Inside Lucas, other reasons for financial pain came into play, two of them long-standing. The group continued to invest in the future at a rate which compared favourably with other UK engineering companies. In the last year before the recession struck hard, spending on research and development came to £98.8m; in 1990–91 it increased slightly to £104m; even when earnings fell badly in 1991–92, research and development expenditure held at £98m before jumping to £133m in 1992–93.

At the same time, Lucas continued to deal with historic problems; the sharp cutbacks of the early 1980s had been followed by continued trimming throughout the decade, as it tried to reduce the costs of excess capacity, especially in the UK. With another recession, restructuring resumed with greater intensity, meaning, for the company, payments now for greater economy later. The annual report for the year to July 1993 told shareholders that 'employee numbers fell by 4860 to show a cumulative 20% reduction since July 1990'. Redundancy and reorganisation costs reached £24.4m in 1990–91 and £23.7m the following year, when the accounts also carried a provision of £88.4m for restructuring. Redundancies cost another £9.7m in 1992–93.

Ever since the early 1980s, the accounts had received some bolstering from the flow of property sales as the group disposed of old factory sites and a variety of accumulated buildings and land, like sports grounds, no longer thought necessary for corporate health in a less paternalistic age. But by the time the 1990s recession arrived, when the financial lubrication would have been helpful, the flow of funds had dried up. They could have been used to offset a series of stock write-offs and exceptional warranty costs which cropped up during this period.

Financial pressures inevitably caused borrowing to rise. In the five years before July 1993, net borrowing rose from £246m to £329m, proportionately less than the increase during the 1980s recession. Gearing, which had touched a low 7.2% after the 1988 rights issue, climbed steadily to 44.2% in July 1992, or 4.2 percentage points above the level David Hankinson and the board thought should be the limit. The group had its credit rating at Moody's, Standard & Poors and IBCA reduced in 1992–93, meaning that it would have to borrow at a higher rate of interest than hitherto. But its overall financial strength did not deteriorate in the same way as the early 1980s when there were worries that the value of shareholders' funds were declining to a point where loan covenants would be breached. Shareholders' funds, which had hovered over £800m until July 1991, fell back to £725m. John Grant, who succeeded Hankinson as finance director, told the directors that the most onerous loan covenant specified a minimum tangible net worth of £650m: 'Any major action to establish further provisions could reduce the margin of safety to an unacceptable level,' he warned.

Yet funds became available to hold back the rise in borrowing. In the first place, retrenchment meant the sale of companies which either did not perform or failed to meet any wider strategic aim. As shareholders learned in 1993, 'The remodelling of core businesses is on schedule. The divestment programme realised £56m in the year and over £75m to date. Further divestments will be made of businesses which do not contribute significantly to the company's core strengths.'

Second, the Lucas Pension Fund came to help, just as it had in the mid-1980s. This time it made a distribution from its surplus. In its 1989 report on drawing up a plan to repel predators, Goldman Sachs placed the Pension Fund surplus as an attraction to any company contemplating a bid for Lucas. It observed that a successful predator might be able to use the surplus, either by merging the Lucas Fund with its own and then, under the rules of its own fund, repay the surplus to itself, or by using the Lucas Fund to lift the benefits to its own employees. Goldman Sachs recommended that Lucas use the surplus for the benefit of the group, although it conceded the legal complexities would be considerable.

After two years of talks with the trustees of the Pension Fund, who engaged their own lawyers independently of the company, and the regulators, Lucas became in 1991 the first company, using new laws of 1988, to use the surplus of a corporate pension fund. It managed to ride over a legal challenge from Simon O'Leary, a former employee and, indeed, a former trustee, who charged the company with breach of trust. It won

Above, Wing Rotation Actuator. designed for, *below,* Bell Boeing V22 Osprey, USA.

the approval of trades unions by raising pension benefits, increasing annual spending by £220m, as a *quid pro quo*. To allow the company to use the surplus funds, it had been necessary to change the trust deeds of the Pension Fund and to win the support of the Occupational Pensions Board, the government regulator. After all that had been done, the immediate cost to the Pension Fund was £150m; of that, the government received £60m in tax and the company £90m.

The Pension Fund contribution effectively offset the provision for restructuring in the 1991–92 accounts; it underpinned the balance sheet as, without it, it is doubtful whether the shareholders would have received a dividend. But expressions of hope, in November 1991 at the time of the first announcement of the boost to Lucas finances, that gearing would be reduced, proved too optimistic. By the end of the 1991–92 financial year, it had become clear that the group found it difficult simultaneously to carry on with capital investment, keep up research and development spending, restructure and keep shareholders quiescent with dividends. The Pension Fund, though, had allowed it to try.

Hankinson believed the Pension Fund could be used again. In December 1991, in his annual financial report for the directors, when he looked at opportunities for lifting performance, he asserted that

> much of the pension fund surplus of £225m remaining after the recent refund can be accessed and, in addition, some part of the further surplus of more than £500m (representing the difference between 'full service' and 'past service only' actuarial liabilities) can be realised by transferring UK employees into separate schemes or selling the businesses which employ them.

In fact, the notion would be no more than a finance director's daydream, especially after Robert Maxwell pillaged the pension fund at Mirror Group Newspapers.

Still, the Pension Fund release of £90m provided Lucas with a financial stopgap at a time when, together, external pressures and internal performance forced the redesign of the group. By the start of the recession the three sector approach had been abandoned to two sectors and another to support them. Hankinson's analysis of what had been happening within the group appeared less than encouraging financially. At the end of 1991, surveying the previous five years, he worked out that what he called incremental investment, or acquisitions and organic growth together, had not provided a return; rather there was a negative rate of return of 3.2%. He also calculated the rate of return on the Aerospace acquisitions to be higher than that on those of Applied

Lucas CAV Unit Injector simulated on a Computer Assisted Engineering screen.

Technology (the old Industrial arm). But, he reported, 'The overall return on acquisitions of 8.8% compares unfavourably with a geographically weighted average interest cost of 11–12%', or, put more crudely, Lucas would have been better off financially with the money in a savings account.

Responding to the financial problems, Bob Dale, by this time director for business development, had another attempt at what had first been tried in the early 1980s: more stringent selection of where the group should place its funds. In 1992 he broke the group into categories: winners, potential winners and support businesses, and those destined for divestment. As they had been through the 1980s, the automotive winners were car and heavy-duty braking, car and van diesels including the new electronic unit injector (EUI) and aftermarket operations. Aerospace included flight control systems, electromechanical actuation, electronic systems, electric power for small aircraft, flight structures and customer support. Dale identified 22 businesses for divestment; they included Rists, Kienzle, the remaining shareholding in the batteries business and overseas operations in areas as diverse as Argentina and South Africa.

The recession brought with it another embargo on any but essential expenditure, so that the operating companies had both to combat hostile market conditions and secure their position in the marketplace in onerous conditions of restraint. They had to find a means of paying for the long term with the short term pulling at all the pursestrings. On the automotive side, the braking operations faced the problem of what policy to follow on ABS (the common abbreviation for anti-lock braking systems) while the diesel business tried at a time of rapid and competing technological changes to secure the future of EUI, where Lucas claimed a technological lead. Aerospace, meanwhile, found that winning secure relationships with engine suppliers demanded more front-end money.

The Lucas braking business, by the end of the 1980s, had worked itself into the anomalous position where its basic business for cars and light vans continued success-fully – Girling had for long been a mainstay of the group – but its potential capability of winning new business had started to slip away because it had not exploited technology it devised. In 1992, the year when the number of Colette calipers, the Lucas disc brake, coming off the production line reached 200m, about 30% of the world market for foundation brakes was filled with products of Lucas design origin; further, Lucas had 16% of the actuation market, but a lowly 5% of the ABS market. The totality kept Lucas among the top four world producers, with Teves, Bendix of Allied-Signal and Bosch, but overlooked the fact that the share of ABS in the car braking market had risen to 43% and looked like moving higher.

Lucas truck, fitted with a CAV Injector, leads the field at Nürburgring.

There had been serious doubts within Lucas during the 1980s that ABS would ever be more than an optional extra on expensive cars. Having made that calculation, it did not press forward with developing its own electronic ABS system, based on flow valve technology. This it left to Sumitomo, its Japanese joint venturer. Lucas instead devised an electro-mechanical system which did 80% of what ABS did but at a much lower price and, although this was sold for a Ford model, it never attracted customers on a large scale. Demand for electronic ABS proved stronger than Lucas expected and Bosch, the world leader, managed to keep pressing down prices, which left Lucas without a price advantage and a technologically inferior product. It was, Dale said retrospectively, 'a commercial mistake'.

In 1990 Lucas decided that it wanted to make up for lost time, to base a world ABS strategy on partnership with Sumitomo, using the Lucas technology. But the costs of the enterprise changed rapidly as the recession pushed prices down. Where it had been assumed that 2.5m sets a year would be viable output, by 1991 that had changed to

Lucas Sumitomo, Ohio. Left to right, Keishi Koba, Bob Burnica, Allan Gilmour and Derek Savage.

3.5m. With the group financial position deteriorating, the strategists jibbed at the investment involved.

In Dale's review of automotive strategy presented to the board in 1991, the technology won acknowledgement as state-of-the-art with a lower cost potential than other systems. But, and here were the problems,

> The disadvantage of our low initial market share on the one hand, and the very high risk of the volume-price profile on the other, have combined to persuade us that we should not persist with the 1990 plan for car ABS. The plan required Lucas to invest about £8m p.a. in product engineering and £10m p.a. in manufacturing capacities for each year between 1991–92 and 1995–96. Given the changed ABS prospects and the need for Lucas to restrict and prioritise investment, an alternative strategy is called for.

Ken Maciver, who ran the braking business from 1992, looked back on that decision with great bitterness as 'one of the worst mistakes in the history of the company. Lucas should have sold something to do it. It threw away its birthright on ABS; there was no excuse for the decision.' The uncertainties of the Lucas approach to ABS led it now into internal discussions about whether it should stay in the brakes business at all and into external discussions with Bosch about an alliance. These talks, based on bringing together Bosch ABS with Lucas foundation brakes, achieved little but still unsettled Sumitomo. They ran their course and broke down with Lucas always fearful that a brakes alliance would be the first step to a Bosch takeover. Even had the companies ever managed to agree, it is doubtful if the competition authorities would have allowed it.

That left Lucas pretty well where it was when it started. It decided to retain car braking in the portfolio and to develop the foundation range while trying to enlarge and deepen the relationship with Sumitomo. But it never quite gave up on the idea of finding a partner with which it could make a quantitative leap in the market. When, in 1989, Fruehauf put up for sale Kelsey-Hayes, the US manufacturer with ABS in its product range and an expanding presence in the US and Europe, Lucas had bid tentatively, offering first about $350m and then later $450m. The offers had been brushed aside. Later Lucas had talks with Varity, the new owner of Kelsey-Hayes, about some form of collaboration. It also explored alliance with Bendix and had discussions with Delphi, the GM component maker, about licensing. In 1996, the situation resolved itself.

The problems of the brakes business, with a small market position for respected high technology, found a mirror in the diesels business with the EUI, the next generation, or so it appeared in 1988, of fuel-injection equipment. That year, Powertrain Systems, the successor to CAV, set up a special division to exploit the EUI, taking Lucas back into the large truck market.

Partly the EUI was a response to emissions legislation, but it went further than that, seeking to be a product which would as easily cope with stricter and stricter legislation. Jack Fryer in a 1992 report for the board, wrote:

> The unit injector is very much a product for the future . . . It cannot easily be applied to existing engines as the cylinder head requires modification to take the injector. Thus development programmes with OEMs [original equipment manufacturers] must be timed to coincide with new engine range plans. The planned emissions legislation is providing a major opportunity for EUIs as engine manufacturers are forced to revise their existing engine ranges to meet the new limits.

Where an engine manufacturer had been prepared to change engine design then the EUI had worked well. That had been proved by Caterpillar, the first EUI customer, with its 3176 engine. Volvo also had given Lucas a development

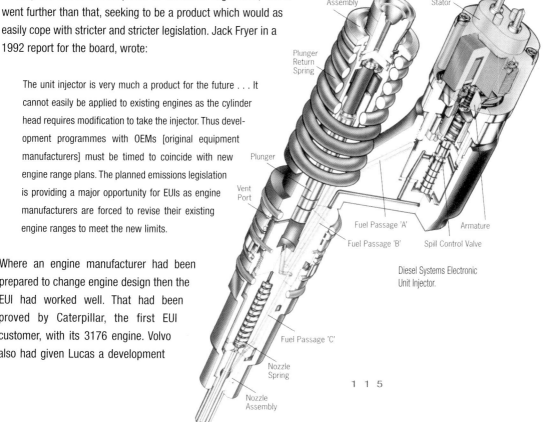

Diesel Systems Electronic Unit Injector.

1 1 5

and production contract. But the danger always existed, and Lucas executives understood it well, of an arrival on the market of a different product which did not demand changes to engine design. Indeed, other manufacturers were in the field: Bosch in the early 1990s worked on its own injector, Nippondenso sought to develop another system called common rail.

Lucas established a sound base of work from the major truck manufacturers. That was fine as far as it went, but recession caused a sharp decline in the truck market and the truck manufacturers made deep cuts in their schedules for 1992–93. 'These changes in the heavy-duty truck market have coincided with a major increase in interest in the use of EUI for cars and vans,' Fryer reported in November 1992. The carmakers turned their attention to high-speed direct-injection engines, as opposed to the hitherto conventional indirect-injection engines. For these the EUI represented appropriate technology. BMW, Rover and Volkswagen wanted development programmes for engines coming into production from 1997 onwards.

The car and van plans looked promising, but the fact remained that EUI continued to drain resources away from the group, even though its sales, rising to over £33m in 1993–94 had been much according to forecasts. In the four years to 1993–94, its sales had reached £60m and its trading losses nearly £34m. By comparison, sales of rotary pumps, the staple of diesel business, over the same period were over £1.4bn giving trading profits of nearly £156m. The group thus far had been consistent in its belief that the EUI was a technological and commercial asset with a bountiful future and that therefore the costs, notwithstanding recession, should be absorbed. It had not lost its nerve in the way that it had with ABS.

However, the lurking threat of a different product to achieve the same technical end had started to emerge in early 1994. Fryer told the board,

> The European situation has been thrown into turmoil by the Mercedes Benz announcement that they will be moving to a common rail system for their car/van range. Mercedes Benz hope that this will give them a technological leap over the competition but the industry considers their plan to be extremely high-risk.
>
> A number of common rail systems have been proposed (notably the Nippondenso version) but Mercedes Benz appear to be developing their own based upon a Fiat system. They are working with Bosch on this system but there appear to be considerable doubts regarding the Bosch motivation.
>
> The Lucas approach to common rail is to monitor the situation closely and recognise that we need an insurance policy in case the system becomes widely accepted.

New factory at Burnley combining local metal forming expertise with modern manufacturing systems. Lucas Engineering and Systems beat international competition for the production of rocket motor cases.

And there was the first crack in the consistent confidence. But, said Gill many years later, 'If we were to develop common rail as well, it would have been very expensive. If we were convinced that pump injectors were the answer and the customers agreed, it was better to concentrate the resources there.'

The third – and less contentious – area where long term meant a short-term outlay was at Aerospace, which now found itself engaged in vendor financing. It concerned the price of an entry ticket to the status of preferred supplier at an aircraft engine manufacturer, in this case Allison Gas Turbine, a division of General Motors. Lucas would pay $35m in engineering and certification costs and it would guarantee a $70m loan, which would enable Allison to arrange more off-balance sheet financing. But in return Lucas would be, in effect, the exclusive supplier of fuel control systems, guide vane actuators, gearboxes and generators to a new series of Allison engines for small aircraft.

Negotiations on this deal took place in 1991 as Aerospace sales started to slide and as a new round of cuts started at group factories. So the Allison agreement had some stabilising effect at a difficult time. It promised, after the development period, probably $1.2bn of sales over 20 years as the products went in to about 7500 engines. The agreement fortified the Lucas position as the leading European aircraft components supplier and it made it a serious player in the gigantic US market. The agreement also went some way to reducing the dominance of Rolls-Royce in the Lucas customer list.

Left to right, David Hankinson, Finance Director; Bob Dale, Managing Director Automotive; Tony Gill, Chairman and Chief Executive; Antony Edwards, Managing Director Aerospace; Bob Brown, Managing Director Industrial, 1989.

But Rolls-Royce remained too important to be ignored, the love-hate relationship too deep to be brushed aside. Indeed, from the end of 1990 to the middle of 1992, amiable talks went on between the two on the pooling of some of their resources in the very area which had been at the centre of the relationship. They explored setting up a joint venture pulling together the Rolls-Royce controls and accessories division with Aerospace's electronic systems division to design and manufacture electronic engine control systems. As an interim measure, they signed a memorandum of understanding for a risk- and revenue-sharing joint venture for the Rolls-Royce Trent engine.

The exploration on a joint-venture company went a long way. The equity division would have been 60% Lucas and 40% Rolls-Royce. The two sides settled the lines of responsibility. They worked on harmonising conditions of employment. They tried to adapt differing management practices. But they could not settle issues of control and funding within the joint venture and they tangled over the future of the Lucas hydromechanical controls business with Rolls-Royce. So the scheme collapsed, leaving the relationship to develop, or not, on a project-by-project basis.

Six months later the two reached a risk-sharing agreement for a full authority digital electronic control (FADEC) for the Trent engine. The central element was a payment by Lucas to Rolls-Royce of £12m for 3.5% of Rolls-Royce's income stream from the engine. Lucas became the preferred supplier of large FADECs and accepted a promise that it would have a level playing field for small and medium-sized FADECs. Rolls-Royce would pay 96.5% of the Lucas costs on future development work.

Rolls Royce Trent 800 engine, which entered service on Boeing 777s in 1996 with a Lucas Full Authority Digital Engine Control (FADEC).

In September 1992, Gill set off a reorganisation in the top echelons of the group. In the briefing notes for members of the group executive to explain what would be going on, there appears the sentence, 'Under current circumstances, we must close ranks'. The sentence gave the impression of a management under siege. Certainly, events inside and outside the group conspired to make 1992 and early 1993 a period of extreme diffi- culty; unwelcome at any time, but particularly so for Gill at the end of his career.

In the depths of recession, Gill needed a stable team around him. But this was not to be. The year started promisingly enough in terms of providing for the succession. It had been agreed, in line with prevailing outside opinion, that the roles of chairman and chief executive should be split. The board moved to put a new chief executive into place by appointing, in February 1992, Tony Edwards as group managing director. This was a polite way of saying he was on trial. In terms of running Lucas, the idea was that, in addition to his operational duties, Edwards would review the organisation and then, when confirmed as chief executive, he would take whatever steps he thought necessary. Gill meanwhile would be able to retreat from executive responsibilities as the first step towards becoming a non-executive chairman, which he would remain, the board said, until the end of 1994.

Retreat did not last long. Two weeks after the Edwards appointment, Hankinson left, leaving Gill to be the acting finance director until a replacement arrived. Hankinson and his colleagues on the group executive had an uneasy relationship and that broke down on questions of style and manners. Nobody questioned his competence. He had been in the job just short of three years. The group at the time dismissed the matter as the sort of thing which could happen in any family or team, which it probably could, but the timing at best seemed unfortunate: the City, worried about the forthcoming interims, knew that Lucas finances suffered in the recession and speculated about maintenance of the dividend.

In the summer it began to become clear that the Edwards appointment had not been a happy one. Colleagues went to Gill and said, as Gill recalled,

> It was not going well; Edwards was risk averse, there were no decisions, there were rumblings of discontent. This had to go to the board. There would be no confidence if he was given the leadership. The board agreed. They asked me to carry on.

So he did. Edwards left in October 1992 to run Dowty, TI's new subsidiary. Old Lucas executives doubt whether he ever had the mixture of qualities to run a group as large and diverse as Lucas. Edwards was a man of easy charm and keen technical enquiry. Rather like Messervy, he could forge the most agreeable of relationships with customers. Sales were his strength, not operational management. At the time, the departure of Edwards sparked speculation about troubles in the Lucas boardroom. That the group denied, with the comment about Edwards, 'He has proved unsuitable for the appointment'.

In the City, the loss of a second main board executive director in a year did nothing for the reputation of either Lucas or Gill. One loss might be understandable, two looked careless. It gave rise to the charge that Gill could not bear to lose control. He resented that, especially as he had planned to spread his wings on the offer of two outside chair-manships. But the losses threw up the question of why they had happened anyway. Gill won much respect for his integrity but rather less for his choice of people. Edwards had been a relative newcomer to the group; his appointment indicated that Gill had run out of internal candidates for the top job. In the past Lucas had always promoted from within and the succession – Waring to Corley to Scott to Messervy to Gill himself – had been a seamless and well-signposted process.

During the late 1980s, the obvious internal candidates were Watkins and Dale. But Alan Watkins left to be a chief executive elsewhere. Dale did not guess then, and Gill did not tell him later, that he might be in line as the next chief executive. Gill, a discreet man known for great loyalty to those he trusted, found it hard to confide; this frustrated Dale, who decided he had had enough of the executive life and retired early.

While all of this was going on, John Grant arrived in September, carrying with him extensive treasury, financial services and corporate strategy experience from Ford

John Smith, left, leader of the
Labour Party, visiting Aerospace's
Fordhouses factory, with Mike
Francis, centre, and Frank Turner.

where his most recent post had been executive director of international financing at the company's US financial services group. Frank Turner arrived in November to be the new managing director of Aerospace; he had previously been at Rolls-Royce where, after a succession of line appointments, he became director, civil engines. With these appointments, following the departures of Hankinson and Edwards, Gill had fashioned a new executive.

His reorganisation in September 1992 stripped out the divisional structure which had been in place since 1987. The group executive took control of all the Lucas businesses, which were grouped into five portfolios: three automotive, Aerospace and Applied Technology. The portfolio managing directors were Dale, who also handled business development, Fryer and Maciver on the automotive side, Parnaby and Turner; the functional directors on the executive were Grant and Bryan Mason. 'The leader of each business became responsible to a designated member of the group executive. The new team undertook a commitment to speed up the application of best practice while reducing all forms of corporate overhead by at least 25%,' said the annual personnel report of January 1993.

These executive and organisational movements took place against a background of frustration with, and speculation about, Lucas in the City. The sagging share price did not help. It lost half its value between May and September 1992 when it touched its

HRH the Princess Royal visiting Lucas Automotive, Birmingham. Left, Bill Betts, right, Mike Johnson.

lowest level for seven years at 78p. (A share split in 1990 had multiplied the number of shares four times.) In this year of poor results, the pension fund surplus contribution and executive difficulties, there was also what Grant called 'a low point in Lucas credibility'. Towards the end of the year, MORI carried out a poll of investors and analysts which threw up the disheartening findings that favourable views of Lucas had hit an all-time low and that unfavourable views had spread to 39% of investors and 66% of analysts. Between the poll of 1991 and the poll of 1992, the percentage of analysts listing management as a perceived weakness rose from 26 to 69 and the percentage of investors thinking likewise rose from 12 to 37. But Grant's meetings in the City and information he received from Cazenove led him to report to the board in June 1993 that the strategic course of Lucas – core businesses, divestment, cost control, productivity improvement – had been accepted as right, but scepticism existed about the ability of Lucas to produce acceptable financial results.

Combination of the uncertainty about Lucas and the low stock price made the group, especially in the second half of 1992, look vulnerable. Bid gossip helped the share price to rise. In January 1993, when the share price had climbed back to 141p, Société Générale Strauss Turnbull Securities told clients 'a hostile bid remains a real possibility . . . an appropriate exit price would seem to be in the region of 200p . . . a ceiling exit price would be around 260p.' It listed four possible bidders: Siebe, BTR, Siemens and Rockwell. Yet bid chatter and Lucas had clung together for much longer than a few months in 1992 and 1993: the market loved to ponder the future of the group.

For all that, in the last months of 1992, Lucas dusted off the defence strategy documents and put a defence team on alert; it even carried out dry runs of the defensive tactics with Schroders. It also looked at alternative strategies to deter a hostile bid, including putting major businesses into joint ventures and an agreed merger with a company of similar size and compatible objectives. At the time, Lucas anyway had a string of discussions either planned or taking place with a wide variety of companies on alliances of one kind or another: Allied-Signal, Deutsche Airbus, Echlin, Fiat, Snecma, Sundstrand and Varity. It had been talking with Bosch, Siemens and TI. Its survey of companies which might be interested in an agreed merger canvassed the usual range of British companies with which it had had talks at some stage in the past such as GKN, Smiths and TI and eliminated others where there was no or little complementary activity such as Delta, Laird, Siebe, BBA and T&N.

While executives prepared to repel hostile bids from the outside, the frustration with the group experienced by the City spilled over to the inside. No written record is in the company documents, but the recollections of Lucas directors, while at odds on the

Sir Antony Gill, Chairman, centre, at the Lucas Suggestion Scheme Awards.

detail, are clear that, in March 1993, two non-executive directors, claiming the support of the group's City advisers, made an attempt to unseat Gill. Out of the blue, Gill was told in a private meeting that he should resign.

Tenacious and determined, Gill did not lie down. He made certain he had the support of James White. He told the other executive directors on the board they would have to make a choice: him or the unknown. Grant and Turner at this stage seemed to have tried to play some sort of mediating role, but then threw their lot in with Gill; Dale and Mason did not waver in support of Gill. With a majority of directors now in his favour, the attempted coup was foiled.

The only clue to boardroom difficulties in the company documents is the sudden flurry of directors' movements and a single letter. Southgate and Philippe Souviron, a French banker who had joined the board in 1991, resigned. Gill moved quickly to recruit new non-executive directors, men whom he knew personally and who had high commercial reputations: Richard Giordano, Sir Alastair Morton and Paul Bossonet. A letter came from Souviron confirming his resignation, regretting he 'cannot share any longer the minimum level of solidarity and community of views with other members of the board'.

The episode gave the search for a new chief executive a fresh stimulus. Giordano agreed to become chairman of the nominations committee of the board; 'With the story going about that I didn't want to be succeeded, I had to distance myself from the nomi-nations,' Gill remembered. With Giordano in charge, the search for a successor led six months later to George Simpson, the first Lucas chief executive who had not made his career in the group. Gill had reached calmer waters.

9 The Simpson Interregnum

Simpson's appointment won acclaim. One of the better known British industrialists, he came fresh from negotiating the sale of Rover to BMW, credited with putting the carmaker back into the league where it might be taken seriously again. That Simpson would go to Lucas helped restore good feeling about the group in the City. He would arrive with the group in recovery. 'Post the final results and the appointment of George Simpson as chief executive, the stock's performance has continued unabated,' Panmure Gordon told clients. As the share price passed 200p in early 1994, Albert E. Sharp commented that 'with George Simpson at the operating helm and the continuing influence of John Grant on the financial base, the hope surrounding the rating should eventually be translated into reality'.

There was satisfaction too at the appointment of Sir Brian Pearse as the new chairman. True to the undertakings of 1992, Tony Gill stepped back to non-executive chairman when Simpson arrived and then handed over to Pearse after receiving a standing ovation from shareholders at his valedictory annual general meeting of November 1994. Pearse came with a lifetime's financial experience, first at Barclays Bank, latterly running Midland Bank. He would provide financial and City expertise to balance Simpson's industrial background.

But Lucas had to wait several months for Simpson's arrival. British Aerospace, where he had been deputy chief executive since 1992 as well as running Rover, did not wish to see him go. But that was hardly surprising given his background and reputation; Sir Graham Day, one of Simpson's predecessors at Rover, called him 'the best manager I've ever known'. He came steeped in the motor industry, but he had always been with the manufacturers, never with the component makers. So Simpson came with a personal challenge, which other courses open to him did not have. BMW had suggested that he should stay at Rover, but that had not seemed a good idea to him. He could not see a future role at British Aerospace.

Simpson came across as the practical man, poised and streetwise. As a manager he had a very different style from Gill. Where Gill would marshal facts and present them methodically as a means of winning consensus around a course he wanted to follow, Simpson was more rhetorical in his approach. 'He thought people should do things for themselves. He got results by clearly articulating what he wanted and getting rid of people if they didn't meet that,' Frank Turner said.

Lucas disputed Government pollution figures that suggested diesel emissions were more harmful than petrol.

At any rate, he brought to Lucas an aura of success after the experience with Rover. But his influence did not move in the direction anyone outside expected nor did his presence in the group last as long as either he or Lucas expected. His period of control proved to be an interregnum which became final. Simpson saw running Lucas as the swansong of his career. Before he took the job he told Bob Dale that and repeated it later: 'When I went I intended it to be my last job, to spend five to ten years there. And the board there, especially Gill, expected me to be there a long time.'

He actually arrived in April 1994 and left when the merger with Varity Corporation of the US came into effect on 6 September 1996. His short tenure, seen against the background of the original intention, gave rise to bitterness and accusations that he had negotiated the merger to facilitate his departure to greener pastures at GEC.

In September and November 1993 there were two letters, the second a confirmation of the first which had been handwritten and hand delivered, from Gill to Simpson, dealing with the terms and conditions of the appointment, setting down what had been discussed and settled. The first paragraph ended, 'We both agreed that your appointment as executive leader at Lucas is in the context of our joint hope and belief that it will be in your own, as well as the company's interests, for your employment by Lucas to be for at least five years.' The contract of employment had a fixed term of three years; there would be a review at the end of the second year to usher in one year rolling contracts. So Simpson served 29 months of the fixed term of the 36 months contract, but did not meet 'our joint hope'.

The charge of using the Lucas merger to organise an exit is harsh. There are too many economic interests involved to suggest that corporate mergers involving groups of Lucas's size knit together on the whim of an individual. GEC, the most powerful UK industrial group, started to look seriously for a successor to Lord Weinstock, the managing director for more than 30 years, at about the same time as Simpson took over at Lucas. On offer – what many regarded as the top job in British industry. 'A year and a quarter in [to his contract], Arnold Weinstock had a conversation with me. At that time I was very committed. I told them to go away,' Simpson remembered. That would have been in or around June 1995. But dates vary, according to recollection.

Rumours linking Simpson to GEC certainly circulated by the end of 1994. GEC appears to have been in touch with Simpson in early 1995. In the middle of the year, Pearse sought from Simpson a firm indication of his intentions and established from him that he wished to throw his hat into the GEC ring. Shortly afterwards, Pearse went to see Lord Prior, the GEC chairman: 'I said it was important to announce it by September. There was urgency in sorting out Lucas – to appoint a new chief executive – or to merge.' In fact, GEC did not announce Simpson's appointment until March 1996, and then put no date on his arrival.

Bombardier long-range executive
jet. Lucas supplied the complete
electrical system.

The significance of this sequence, imprecise though it may be, for the controversy which later surrounded Simpson and the merger, is that Simpson's future was known to him, and to Lucas, by the summer of 1995; the announcement itself is irrelevant. At that stage, talks swirled around with a host of groups but no firm plan to merge or buy or sell existed. The decision to explore a merger or an alliance which would change the face of Lucas did not come until December 1995, at least five months after it had become clear Simpson would leave.

On that basis, there is no question of Simpson merging Lucas in order to advance his own career. Knowledge of his departure, however, may have made merger talks easier by removing one of the points of tension frequent in negotiations: settling who will have the top job, who will be in control afterwards. It may also have given merger negotiations an urgency for him which otherwise they might not have had.

Simpson arrived at Lucas after making some enquiries: 'I did a bit of due diligence, talking around: what I found was that Lucas had some good technologies, processes and people but a poor reputation.' After six weeks in the job he drew up a list of first impressions which followed the same theme. On one hand, he found CAPs a sound process although they needed to be sharper; he had been encouraged by the talent, commitment and knowledge of Lucas people; he had been encouraged too by the strong range of positions Lucas had in technology, in the market and in its programmes; finally he had been encouraged by the 'change management capability' and 'advanced management thinking'. On the other hand, he expressed concern about the apparent absence of 'well communicated strategic vision, performance management culture, strong quality/customer focus'; he found a short-term need to organise for performance and deal with balance-sheet issues.

By July, Simpson had crystallised his impressions and thinking into a strategy review. His conclusions followed the lines which Gill and his colleagues had laid down as they moved away from the concept of Lucas based on three sectors.

For Lucas to succeed, it needs to focus its efforts on building strong core businesses that can compete aggressively in the increasingly global markets . . . To support this aim it needs to increase dramatically its operating performance and underpin this with more robust mechanisms to sustain high levels of performance.

This led him to five objectives. First, to create a balance sheet from which Lucas could quickly and safely move forward; second, to organise for high levels of financial and operational performance; third, to focus more on the core businesses and cleanse the portfolio of niche, under-performing businesses; fourth, to develop the industry position by exploiting Lucas technology, developing systems integration, expanding influence in Far Eastern markets and taking part in industry restructuring; fifth, to create a range of strategic portfolio options by the end of the 1995–96 financial year.

Following Dale's splitting of Lucas companies into three sections, Simpson designated core businesses, financial contributors and candidates for divestment. The companies chosen for each category broadly matched Dale's choices. Where Simpson broke with past practice was in his organisation. He made the managing directors of the six businesses report directly to him rather than to a group executive. Indeed, he disbanded the executive and replaced it with an executive director forum and an enlarged operating committee. At the same time he restored the group's strategic planning capability by setting up a unit under Jack Fryer who reported directly to him.

Within six months of his arrival, the reversion to the core businesses had started. If Lucas needed services it could buy them in; it did not require a series of companies to provide consultancies within the group. That seemed the reasoning behind the decision to sell Management Systems, a software company, and Engineering & Systems, the company which John Parnaby had established to spread the best manufacturing practices throughout the group and which also had been in demand from other companies, not least Rolls-Royce. When the group, in October 1994, announced its 1993–94 annual results, it became clear that the cull and restructuring of companies would be extensive. US companies, such as Aul, Epsco and Weinschel, bought when, in the 1980s, Aerospace tried to build a defence electronics arm, became available; consideration of their disposal was not new but, under Gill, the group had jibbed at the loss it would have to carry.

The provisions made to cope with change came to £110m; goodwill written off came to £94.3m; losses on the sale of businesses added up to £18.4m. So many exceptional charges pushed the group into a pre-tax loss of £129.7m. It looked as if Simpson and Grant had thrown into the figures every conceivable piece of bad news they could imagine and put a cost on it. Certainly the size of the loss exceeded the most pessimistic City estimates. But instead of calls for the dismissal of the chief executive, the share price rose strongly. That owed something to the reputation Simpson then had in the City.

But it also reflected the understanding that the exceptional numbers disguised the strong movement of the group out of recession. To that extent Simpson had been lucky with the timing of his arrival. The demand for diesel equipment had reached levels where the group could not satisfy the demand and had in place £90m of investment programmes to expand capacity. The prospects for EUI looked firmer as production volumes for trucks increased and Volkswagen joined Rover in signing up to a development programme. Seeing the VW programme through would cost Lucas £81m of capital expenditure. Almost immediately, though, technical problems started to emerge so that by early 1996 it looked as if there could be a delay of 21 months. Hedging the bets, Simpson launched a programme to develop common rail technology and in mid-1995 talks started with Siemens about cooperation, in effect trying to match up the diesel expertise of Lucas with the electronics strength of Siemens.

In the braking operations, Ken Maciver managed to build up profits by, he explained later, redesigning manufacturing processes, starting the strategic sourcing of materials and more aggressive product marketing. He used the US factory, owned by the joint venture with Sumitomo and praised by Ford, as his benchmark. Still troubled by the tiny position of the group in the ABS market, Lucas used its alliance with Sumitomo as its main means of staking its presence, selling to Japanese carmakers active in the US.

The main trouble for Simpson in immediate operational terms lay in Aerospace, where the markets remained stagnant. Turner carried on the restructuring which had started before his arrival at the end of 1992 with the object of bringing costs into line with likely sales. He recalled:

> There was a headquarters staff of 125; we got it down to 29. We brought the division back to four businesses: engine controls, flight controls, power systems, and cargo handling in the US and customer support. Seven factories were closed, seven businesses were sold: one of them was aircraft repair in Santa Barbara, California – you can only make money with that sort of business in a cheap labour place, but Santa Barbara has about the most expensive labour in the world.

Simpson's reorganisation cut across some of the work which Gill had been doing. In his last two years Gill had become increasingly preoccupied with trying to ensure that the expertise in Lucas became available to all in the group who needed it; the group should

Left to right, Sir Anthony Gill,
George Simpson and Sir Brian
Pearce.

not be a collection of petty fiefdoms. To that end he put members of the group executive in charge of different aspects of best practice with a brief for spreading expertise through the group and getting people to approach problems in the same way. Thus Grant produced a finance manual and Maciver worked on techniques of production innovation management. Gill and his colleagues called the whole process The Lucas Way. Simpson appeared uninterested and the initiatives tended to wither. One, however, could not be ignored: Electronics had been classified by Simpson in his July 1994 review as a core business.

Gill, conscious that the use of electronics had spread and would continue to spread quickly, becoming increasingly an integral part of Lucas products, had pulled together pockets of electronics expertise, numerous independent and small businesses which he put together in two companies under Parnaby in Applied Technology. Called Lucas Electronics and Lucas Control Systems Products, the companies crossed the auto-motive-aerospace divide. 'Aerospace people were good at product and technology inno-vation, but not as good as Automotive engineers at achieving very low-cost, high-productivity systems and low engineering costs with high product quality,' Parnaby recollected. For his part Gill believed that

if we could get the electronics people in Automotive and Aerospace to work together, we could reduce Aerospace costs and get into Automotive more sophisticated technology. If we had one organisation we could replicate the success of others, like Siemens. We could form an electronics business with Aerospace and Automotive as customers.

But the business did not last long. Simpson, as with Engineering & Systems, appeared little interested in internal businesses selling services and expertise to the operating companies. So Simpson put the bulk of electronics into what had become Vehicle Body Systems, which took in both the rump of the old Lucas Electrical businesses and more recent and sophisticated ventures like electric power-assisted steering (EPAS). Simpson said, sitting in judgment on his time at Lucas:

> There was about a year of operational management. I kicked on pretty hard. Profits went up. We made a lot of progress. The share price went up. As we were driving the opera-
> tional performance, we really struggled with the question of how the company sat in the
> motor industry, how it could compete or consolidate. What occupied Fryer and me was –
> could we make it on our own?

But Lucas nearly reached the position where it was not going to make it anywhere.

When Gill made preparations for his handover to Simpson, he prepared a list of the topics he wanted to discuss. The first item was 'Settlement of US Government investigation into Lucas Aerospace businesses'. Neither knew at the time that the investigation would threaten the very existence of the group, that it would be one of the most testing experiences in the group's history.

The whole business turned into a legal labyrinth where another twist would appear as soon as the path looked straight. Lucas found itself dealing with at least six branches of the US authorities; it had three firms of lawyers and teams of consultants – quality auditors, gear experts, Pentagon liaison, Congressional relations, public relations. The longer the affair went on the more damaging it became, both commercially and financially; provisions in the accounts which looked enough one month proved inadequate the next; customers, by turns, became worried, tetchy and litigious.

The government investigations centred on two Lucas companies, AUL and the geared systems division of Western, once known as Western Gear, both of which had been acquired in the expansion of the 1980s. The two investigations were not related. That at Western lasted longer, had wide ramifications and finished with prohibitive cost. That at AUL started first, ended first and finished less expensively.

In May 1992 the US Attorney started investigating the way in which AUL manufac-
tured and tested launch electronic units for Maverick missiles, made under a contract with the US Air Force, at Garden City, New York. 'This could have been very sensitive because it was Mavericks which killed Brits in the Gulf War – the friendly fire case,'

Facing page, Rescue hoist, Lucas Western, USA.

1 3 0

Aerospace Burnley won a Multi-launch Rocket Motor Case order against international competion.

remembered Turner, who inherited the responsibility when he became chief of Aerospace.

Lucas called in its own lawyers to arrange its own investigation. Both the official and internal investigations uncovered testing irregularities. A year after the US Attorney's first move, the government proposed that the matter could be settled by the payment of a fine and costs for inspection and repairs along with the adoption of a programme which would prevent irregularities appearing again. A year after that, the local court accepted a settlement which cost Lucas a $4m fine, $7.5m of restitution for the repairs and $0.5m to cover the cost of the investigation – $12m in all.

That settlement also covered other testing irregularities alleged at AUL's plant in Hazleton, Pennsylvania, making radios for the US Army. There the matter might have rested but for two further issues. First, three weeks before the court approved the Maverick settlement, a US government quality control review at Garden City found deficiencies. Second, the Hazleton investigation opened up another front. 'It is alleged,' a Lucas internal document explained, 'that certain components of the radio were knowingly gold-plated to a thickness of only five millionths of an inch when the contract called for plating to 50 millionths.'

US criminal and civil investigators indicated that the matter could be settled by Lucas paying a small criminal fine and meeting US Army contractual claims which amounted to more than half of the $18.5m contract value. Lucas quibbled, prompting the US criminal authorities to threaten that, if the matter dragged on, they would apply for a criminal indictment against AUL. By autumn 1995, Lucas had settled at a cost of $14m. This turned out to be a fraction of the cost incurred in the Western saga.

Not long after Lucas had started its haggle with the US Army, Turner had a shock. The FBI had visited the Los Angeles factory, in the City of Industry, where Western made airframe mounted accessory drives, better known as gearboxes, for the US Navy's F/A-18 fighter aircraft, and azimuth drive units which controlled how the US Army's multiple launch rocket systems swivelled and moved up and down.

> The first thing I knew about it was a phone call from the local manager saying he couldn't run the factory – the FBI had arrived with 50 U-Haul trailers and taken away all the inspection records. They served us with a Method C. I said 'What the hell is that?' I was told you can't trade while it is in place.

The first communication to the Lucas board came with Gill's operations report in September 1993, which recorded the arrival of the FBI and the Department of Defense

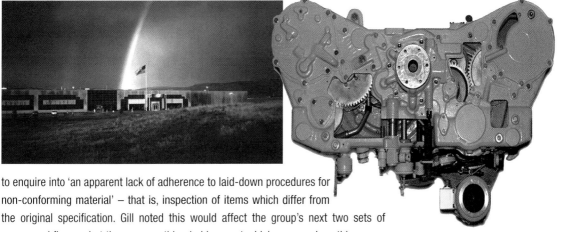

to enquire into 'an apparent lack of adherence to laid-down procedures for non-conforming material' – that is, inspection of items which differ from the original specification. Gill noted this would affect the group's next two sets of announced figures, but there was nothing in his report which conveyed anything more alarming than the unusual. 'We are cooperating fully with the investigations and have instituted an across-the-board audit of non-conforming material control procedures in all our US Department of Defense contracting facilities.'

Above, Military engine gearbox made by Lucas Western for F18 fighter aircraft became the subject of a major US Federal investigation, *left*, Western's factory, Park City, Utah.

For Lucas, the investigation came at a difficult operational time: Western had started to relocate its factory from expensive Los Angeles to cheaper – and subsidised – Park City, Utah. Inspections dragged on; the Department of Defense watched the gearboxes and drive units being stripped down and it looked at procedures in other plants. The tone of the Lucas reports at the time suggested that the whole matter concerned technical questions capable of resolution with a little goodwill and patience: 'The recovery plan and corrective actions in relation to the federal investigation at Utah and Los Angeles are progressing satisfactorily,' the board heard in November 1993.

Extensive meetings took place between Lucas and its representatives, from the chairman downwards, and the various branches of the US authorities. But on 25 March 1994, the question escalated from the technical to the general and political. Counsel for the US Navy wrote to Gill – and this would have been a week before Simpson arrived as chief executive – asking the company to demonstrate by 4 May that it was responsible to do business with the US government.

The following month, the officials dealing with questions relating to the debarment of companies from doing business with the government said they had no current intention of cutting Lucas off from government contracts. This reassured Lucas but a new threat emerged. It appeared that some Navy officials had started to use press leaks as a means of exerting pressure on Lucas: the *Wall Street Journal* on 20 May 1994 carried

Final assembly station for the Honda 'Synchro' rear Colette disc brake. Lucas produced its 200 millionth Colette disc brake – the world's most popular – in 1992.

an article which tried to link F/A18 forced landings to alleged failures in Western's gear-boxes – which was the first Lucas had heard about it.

The *Wall Street Journal's* article served to make public Lucas's difficulties with the Department of Defense. This fed through to customers. In June, Simpson reported to the board that Rolls-Royce had been asking about it. Airbus Industries and Boeing had worried to the point of asking whether a fundamental quality problem existed with gear-boxes and actuators, prompting Lucas to make special presentations as a means of quietening concern.

By this time the situation had become more fluid. Inside Lucas, talks and calculations took place on how much it might cost to settle with the Department of Defense. The company had agreed to hand over to the US prosecutor all the evidence gathered from its own investigations into reporting and testing procedures; this improved the atmos-phere. Work started with the US Navy – which, of course, needed the gearboxes to keep its aircraft flying – to release the accumulated gearboxes which had been piling up since mid-1993. During September negotiations started with the Justice Department on the level of fines and damages to settle the whole affair.

Inevitably the negotiations immediately exposed a wide gap between what each side thought reasonable. But Lucas believed the prosecutors based their claim on a false premise, as Simpson told the board in his operations report at the end of September:

> It is based on their view that the AMAD gearbox is achieving only 1285 hours between failures as compared with our guarantee of 3,000 hours and the Northrop and McDonnell Douglas view, and testament, that the gearbox comfortably exceeds guarantee. This gives us a real opportunity, if we can gain access to the data, to undermine the basis of the prosecutors' claims.

For Lucas, hopes that the issues might steadily be resolved looked misplaced by the autumn as the US Navy served another Method C notice on the Park City plant. This seemed to go back over ground already covered and arranged. But talks with US Navy admirals, and a visit by one of them to the Western plant, seemed constructively directed towards long-term plans to raise production and towards the necessary steps to have the Method C restrictions lifted.

Negotiations with the prosecutors led to Lucas's acceptance of an $18.5m fine to settle the criminal investigation. 'This would remove the involvement of the US government agents,' Turner told the board. But the civil issues remained to be settled. The technical issue about the mean time between failures faded away as reviews, using

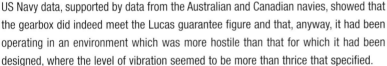

Major investment in modernisation programmes at Pontypool, which manufactured brakes, *above*, for the Rover 400, *left*, led to a growth in productivity.

US Navy data, supported by data from the Australian and Canadian navies, showed that the gearbox did indeed meet the Lucas guarantee figure and that, anyway, it had been operating in an environment which was more hostile than that for which it had been designed, where the level of vibration seemed to be more than thrice that specified.

Lucas appeared to be moving out of the shade and in February 1995 made an offer to the US authorities to settle the civil aspects of the case. The timing, and the amount offered, was an attempt to prevent another case bursting out, brought this time not by the US authorities but by a whistleblower contesting dismissal from Western at Park City for falsifying records – this, when, as Turner described, 'The place was crawling with Department of Defense inspectors and the FBI.' But the offer was to no avail; the whistleblower case lodged in court and the US attorney rejected the settlement plan.

If anything, Lucas was now in a worse position with the authorities, who gave notice that the company would be debarred from doing business with the US government because it failed to meet the quality control issues of the Method C Notice, because it failed to meet gearbox delivery schedules and because the government was concerned that Park City employees engaged in wrongdoing had not been disciplined.

Simpson sent Parnaby into the Park City factory to improve its operations and thus, he hoped, satisfy the US Navy. Parnaby had not been dealt a strong hand. Clearly the relocation from Los Angeles had not been a success. It looked by this time, though based on the best motives, to have been wholly misconceived: it had been carried out in the expectation of finding an educated workforce willing to work conscientiously according to the Mormon ethic. Instead, according to internal documents, 'We are finding great difficulty in attracting competent people to the area, where housing is extremely expensive and there is no local industry infrastructure.'

But Parnaby went into what he called 'direct diagnosis' and set out about putting the factory operations on an even keel: 'Facts-projects-plans-training courses from the day I took over.' On top of that, however, the factory had to cope with a loss on stock valuations which meant that, on an annual turnover of $52m, it would lose $47m. It took Parnaby and his team, burdened by the presence of government inspectors on the site, up to 18 months to bring the business back on course.

Talks on a settlement, which Lucas was anxious to disclose before the announcement in mid-October of its 1994–95 results, led to an expensive resolution. The agreement with the US authorities specified that Lucas would pay $88m (£55.6m) civil damages. On top of the $18.5m paid as a criminal fine and the $12m and $14m paid as the AUL settlements, this lifted the obvious cost of the tussle with the US government to $132.5m. Legal and other costs added on a further $17m. The 1994–95 accounts took exceptional charges of £95m to cover the damages and the costs of restructuring the manufacturing processes, or more than three times what the group had expected in October 1994 and, indeed, as late as March 1995.

Simpson's summary of these events led to the conclusion that the settlement prevented worse pain.

> Nobody in the group had experience of dealing with this. The FBI was in the plants and US lawyers were warning that if we were not careful there would be huge costs. It was damaging the share price. It was making it difficult to get on with restructuring. It was taking up management time. So against our convictions, we took the pain. It was an important point in Lucas development; it allowed other things to happen. But we couldn't afford $88m. The issue was dragging the company down. It was a misdemeanour, not following proper processes, it wasn't that the gearboxes didn't work.

Lucas may not have been able to afford $88m, but it could find it. The looming and much greater danger had been that if Lucas could not have the factory back to rights, making deliveries, it would open itself to civil suits from customers whose own delivery schedules failed because the Lucas products had not arrived. With the US system of triple damages, whereby the cost of harm done to the suing company is multiplied by three, claims on Lucas could have reached levels which would have wiped out its funds and broken the group. As the affair dragged on through 1994 and into 1995, significant companies such as Boeing, General Electric, Grumman, Loral, Allison, Pratt & Whitney

HRH Diana, Princess of Wales at Lucas CAV's Sudbury injector factory, July 1993.

and the BMW-Rolls-Royce joint venture expressed their worries. The settlement with the US government enabled Lucas to head off their potential claims.

The tangles with the authorities did not quite end with the October settlement. An audit of quality procedures allowed the lifting of the Method C notice during early December but the notice of proposed debarment from future government business remained in place – much to Parnaby's aggravation. He and his team requested a meeting in Washington with the US Navy. They rehearsed how everything that needed to be done had been done, the plant was world class but, Parnaby said, as he related later, '"I can't get anybody to sign us off. I've come to tell you that I will announce the closing of the factory on Friday – all the contracts run out at the end of the year." "Gee, John," they said, "you've really got our attention."' Within a week, in July 1996, the debarment was lifted, closing the chapter. The postscript came later when Lucas sold the business to Allison, by then a subsidiary of Rolls-Royce.

10 Pressure for Merger

George Simpson wanted Lucas to take part in the general restructuring of the motor components industry as it adapted to the changing demands of its customers and the shift in procurement trends from components to systems. And he wanted to produce by July 1996 a range of 'strategic portfolio options' for the board's decision. These two aims he set out in his first review of July 1994. During 1995, the pressures of the first, as Lucas courted and was courted, lent a sense of urgency to consideration of the second.

Put in charge of strategic planning by Simpson, Jack Fryer began to produce an analysis of Lucas in relation to its industry along lines which Alan Gaves and Bob Dale before him would have recognised. After 2000 there would be a few core suppliers – super integrators – serving motor manufacturers worldwide. 'Lucas would need to become part of an SI, or aligned to one, in order to protect its core business.' As he refined his proposition, Fryer found two types of Tier 1 suppliers – the broad integrator capable of multi systems and the super-niche player providing individual sub-systems. The first would be companies such as Delphi, Bosch and Nippondenso, the second companies such as Lucas, Valeo and Allied Signal. To be a super-niche player Lucas would have to fill the gaps in its product range and the geographical gaps in its market coverage. Although this thinking applied to the automotive industry, it remained valid for the aerospace sector.

Against this background, the Lucas board met on 20 December 1995 to listen to Fryer and then to discuss the future. 'Sufficient data had been collected in order to plan the future direction of the Lucas group,' the board minutes recorded Simpson as saying, 'and, in the light of the several opportunities currently available, it was essential to form a view on a number of issues by the end of the meeting.' If any one meeting set off the process leading to the merger with Varity nine months later, it was this one.

Lucas in 1995 was the world's nineteenth largest automotive component supplier

Left to right from top, Lucas directors, 1995: Sir Brian Pearse, Non-executive Chairman; George Simpson, CEO; John Grant, Finance Director; Bryan Mason, Personnel Director; Non-executive Directors, Paul Bosonnet, Professor Alec Broers, Sir John Fairclough, Sir Alastair Morton and Ed Wallis.

with revenues of £2.3bn. The assumption was that it needed to build revenues to more than £3bn a year to remain viable in the long term, and to be one of the top ten component makers. But there were the gaps to be filled. Fryer listed these as 'Car Braking Systems (weak in ABS, friction and global capabilities), Diesel Systems (common rail, electronics and global coverage), Body Systems (scale, market position and capability to develop modules) and Electrical Systems (scale and silicon integration).'

Given general expansion, it seemed doubtful that Lucas could improve its position relative to other makers simply by organic growth. Nor would small acquisitions and alliances achieve the growth. Fryer did have some options available though. In the UK, TI and T&N expressed interest in working with Lucas and GKN had done in the past, but they would offer largely unrelated growth. Bosch proposed Lucas as a partner in braking. There was the option in braking of working with Kelsey-Hayes, owned by Varity. The possibility of merger with Valeo had arisen because De Benedetti proposed to sell his 28% shareholding. Siemens might be prepared to part with its automotive business, although Lucas was not prepared to sell its business to Siemens. For Aerospace, Allied Signal and Lockheed Martin were potential buyers.

So the board's response to Simpson's injunction came down to agreement for Simpson and his colleague to pursue the Kelsey-Hayes, Bosch, Siemens and Valeo options. By February the choices had started to whittle down. Bosch was only interested if it could buy the whole of the Lucas braking business, not a joint venture with Lucas as junior partner; it was, in any case, close to forging a braking alliance with Bendix. The Lucas strategists thought this alliance made discussions with Varity more urgent; acquisition of Varity looked the most attractive choice in terms of shareholder value analysis, according to John Grant at a board meeting in February. Valeo looked less attractive given the demand that an offer for the De Benedetti shares had to be unconditional. Siemens did not wish to sell its automotive business and, although Simpson had suggested an automotive alliance, it seemed unlikely Siemens would be enthusiastic. There was some thought at the February meeting that Siemens might be cultivated as a potential white knight if Lucas became subject to a hostile bid. The board decided that this cultivation and the possible acquisition of Varity should be the immediate focus.

By this time, personal interventions had begun to play a part. At Davos, Switzerland, where the good and the great mingle in the networking opportunity of the World Economic Forum, Simpson ran into Victor Rice, chief executive of Varity. Rice had already approached Sir Brian Pearse about having talks. The two chief executives arranged to have breakfast together – which they did, shortly afterwards, at the discreet Halkin Hotel in Mayfair, London, one Saturday morning during February 1996. Simpson recalled that 'he [Rice] raised the possibility of putting the two companies together. What we decided was to set up two teams and have a look at it.' Rice then had started to move towards Lucas as Lucas had started to move towards him. Talks started.

With Siemens hovering in the background and the Valeo prospects pushed aside, events now gathered pace so that by the time the board met on 24 April, the broad plans for bringing about a merger had been arranged by the two teams. 'The status of the main issues was that the valuation method, structure outline and management outline had been agreed, but not the valuation timing, structure detail and management detail. The board structure and name of the company had also not been agreed.'

Although Varity had not won much more than passing reference in Dale's alliance analyses of 1991–92, except for its ownership of Kelsey-Hayes, the reasons for a merger appealed to the board more in 1995.

Lucas Varity CEO, Victor Rice, 1996.

> Mr Fryer described Varity as a £1.6bn automotive company with 52% of its turnover in car
> and light truck braking systems, 5% in heavy-duty braking and 43% in diesel, with small
> interests in electronics. It had strong market positions, being the US market leader in ABS,
> third in foundation brakes and European off-highway leader in diesel systems.

A merger then would meet the interests of the Lucas car braking business and partially meet its diesel interests because of Varity's common rail developments and ownership of Perkins, but the combined business would still need an alliance in electronics. Geographical gaps in Lucas's market coverage would close somewhat as US sales went from 24% to 34% and European sales dropped from 67% to 58%. The combined group would be in the top ten of the world's component suppliers.

Rice constructed Varity out of the Massey Ferguson tractor business. He became president in 1978, helped by a good word from Pearse, who had met him and been impressed, during Massey Ferguson's interminable rescue negotiations with the banks. He nursed Massey Ferguson away from bankruptcy and used that as a basis to create Varity. He built the group around Perkins and bought Kelsey-Hayes and Dayton Walther, thus creating a position in wheels and braking. Rice had a keen eye for commercial opportunities combined with a fine appreciation of financial engineering. 'His style was in keeping with that of the chief executive of a North American company,' noted Tony Gilroy, a close associate who brought determination, long experience and straight-forward thinking to Varity's operational concerns. Because his approach and practice

1 4 1

Facing page, Lucas Varity Diesel
Systems Electronic Unit Injectors.

were fundamentally American, Rice had a live sense of values and remuneration and he expected those to translate into any combined group. Actually, he was British and had started work on cost analysis at Ford before joining Perkins in Peterborough. Now he engaged in negotiations with basically the same motive as Lucas: combination would give greater strength in a hostile world.

When the Lucas board met with its advisers in May, the general tone of discussion came out strongly in favour of the principle of merger with Varity. The directors instructed Pearse and Simpson to continue negotiations.

> The executives were not very keen – that was the Lucas independent feeling. The board recognised the theoretical sense of what was being proposed. Where they had some reservations – Morton knew Rice – it was that they did not trust how Rice might behave. There was general support for the value, for the transaction, but some concern for some of the people, Simpson said later.

Pearse remembered how 'I had enormous battles with Victor Rice – one of the key issues was that Rice was afraid he would not have enough power. He was hedged around with protection.' Pulling the deal together to mutual satisfaction proved 'long, protracted and difficult' in Simpson's words. 'It was a long difficult process to the last day,' remembered Pearse who, on that last day, started the board meeting at 10 o'clock one morning and reconvened it again the following morning at four.

The board minutes carry staid and guarded references to the tensions which Pearse and Simpson reflected. 'Mr Grant . . . confirmed that the merged company would be resident in the UK.' 'Sir Alastair Morton emphasised the board's responsibility to ensure that the chief executive of LucasVarity plc would be subject to the control of the board.' 'Sir Alastair Morton concluded by expressing his opposition to the appointment of Mr Rice to be chief executive of the merged company on the terms of employment and with the level of authority so far described.'

On 31 May 1996 Lucas and Varity announced their merger. It came into effect on 6 September. In an arrangement without premium for either side, Lucas and Varity placed their shares into the new company, LucasVarity. This gave Lucas shareholders 62% of the new group. Pearse and Simpson believed they had negotiated Lucas interests into the stronger position. 'The structure of the board gave Lucas people a majority, six to five. The chairman had the casting vote,' explained Pearse. He stayed on as chairman. With Simpson leaving anyway, Rice naturally became the chief executive – and that enabled Lucas to have the finance directorship, so Grant carried on into the merged company.

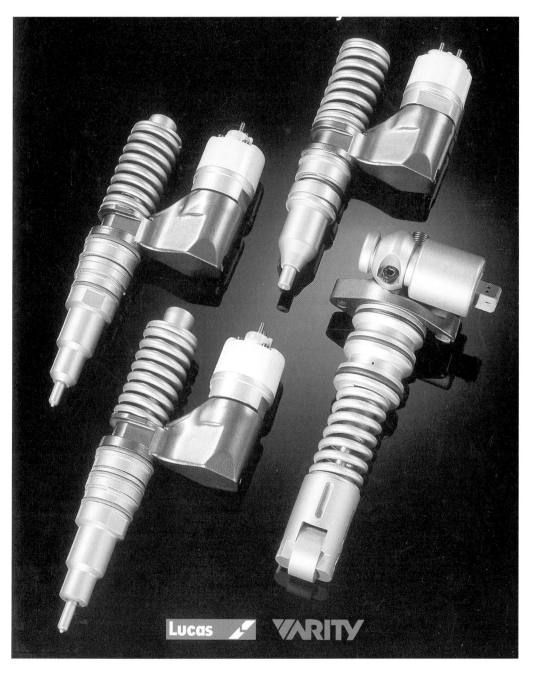

Three determined walkers, Chris Hillocks, Mark Ramsey and Barry Jackson, occupational firefighters at Lucas Diesel Systems, Gillingham, Kent, step out for charity, 1996.

LucasVarity's public life of two and a half years formed at once a coda to Lucas Industries, old Lucas, and an overture to TRW.

In truth, the influence of old Lucas lasted for a very short time; at the time of the merger, of the Lucas directors, Simpson, Bryan Mason and Professor Alec Broers, who had become a director the year before, all resigned. At the end of 1996, both Sir John Fairclough, on the board since 1993, and Grant resigned, the latter to all intents and purposes fired by Rice, without discouragement from Pearse, who believed him 'not clinical enough with numbers'. In April, Paul Bossonet went. By then, the only LucasVarity directors who had been on the Lucas board before the merger were Pearse, Ed Wallis, the chairman of PowerGen who had joined in 1995, and Sydney Gillibrand, who had been vice-chairman of British Aerospace and had also joined in 1995. At the highest level, then, the links with old Lucas had been severed. The post-World War II historical chain, running from Waring through Corley, Scott, Messervy and Gill, snapped in 1994 and was finally discarded when those linked to it, like Mason, went a separate way. With the arrival on the board of Tony Gilroy in January 1997 and Neil Arnold in October 1997, Rice had recreated the triumvirate which had run Varity. Gilroy became chief operating officer and Arnold succeeded Grant.

Pearse carried on as chairman until May 1998, when Wallis succeeded him, but felt isolated and uncomfortable as, in effect, Varity took control of the highest reaches of the new corporation. He recalled:

> John Grant went quickly, I sought to ensure that Arnold would live in London. But he didn't and I couldn't do a thing about it. It was the worst year of my life. From two months before the takeover until I left there was nobody to talk to, nobody to trust, nobody who knew enough. The possible exception was Wallis. Suddenly the number of board meetings reduced to five with two telephonic. They didn't go through budgets and numbers. They went through strategy.

Certainly Rice and his immediate colleagues had corralled the power, but they had also created a new company.

This creation came through a skillful and energetic management of the transition. Ken Maciver, who continued to run Aerospace, a job he had been given by Simpson when Frank Turner left in 1995, called the transition 'a model of its kind'. Pearse thought it reflected 'the highest credit'. Before the merger came into effect, a transition team had been established, headed by Gilroy for Varity and Fryer for Lucas. The Varity team arrived well-prepared, clear what it wanted to achieve – better prepared, it turned out, than the Lucas side. From May to September 1996, the transition team worked on the future structure of the group, the synergies between the different operating units, the costs which could be cut – £162.5m, more than double the amount mentioned in the merger negotiations – the companies worth keeping and the companies destined for disposal. One aim was to leave the past behind.

'In picking teams for the business we wanted to pick young people. We picked teams for the seven businesses: our ambition was to have an average age under 40, a balance of Lucas and Varity people, without the baggage of history,' Gilroy said. He and Rice, by contrast, were veterans, respectively, of 59 and 55. Calling the selection 'a culture shock', Rice said it made the transition a success.

> We took the top 160 people [from both Lucas and Varity] and went through four pieces of information on each: their own self-assessment on a specially designed form, an assessment by their existing boss, a psychometric analysis and a personal interview with an outside company, Egon Zehnder. We were able to rate everybody against predetermined criteria and we said, irrespective of where they came from, we would only choose people in the upper quartile.

The top 160 had to be reduced to 88 to fit the number of positions available. The systematic approach to filling the jobs showed that the new company would be interested only in the best, according to its own criteria and that it would be, Rice believed, 'extraordinarily fair – no Lucas, no Varity, only LucasVarity people.' The majority of those selected were British.

Varity brought with it the business measurement system of Economic Value Added, devised by Stern Stewart, the US consultancy, and spread it across the group. 'EVA measures a company's net operating profit after tax, less the cost of all capital employed, including the cost of equity,' wrote Martin Dickson in the *Financial Times*. 'It is calculated after making adjustments to a company's conventional earnings to get rid of accounting anomalies, such as the treatment of research and development costs. The aim to is to get managers to focus on more efficient resource allocation.' Within three months, the LucasVarity businesses had settled EVA targets three years ahead, written business plans five years ahead and had top management in place.

LucasVarity split its business into seven divisions which followed naturally from where the former groups had left off. Light Vehicle Braking Systems embraced the Lucas car braking business and Kelsey-Hayes, concluding their sporadic courtship. Heavy Vehicle Braking Systems took in the former Lucas operation and VarityDaytonWalther, consum-

mating a plan of the 1980s. Diesel Systems was the old Lucas business. Diesel Engines was Perkins. Electrical and Electronic Systems came from the companies which had emerged from the old Lucas Electrical and VarityZecal. Aftermarket Operations brought together the respective sectors of Lucas and Varity. Aerospace was old Lucas Aerospace.

Lucas Body Systems Switch Controls factory.

Rice and Gilroy had more closely defined ideas about autonomy and centralisation than old Lucas. Certain practices – EVA and Total Quality for example – they imposed across the group. EVA targets and business plans had to be agreed by the centre. Gilroy said:

> Once the parameters were set, it was up to the individual and team. It was a no-excuse environment. We wanted people to over-achieve, so we had an uncapped bonus system. But a bonus was only earned if a business added real economic value – so people were motivated to get the whole business right.

To bring the different businesses together, the group established six functional councils – marketing technology, information technology, purchasing, human resources and finance – each with a senior officer or divisional managing director in the chair. This took further an approach to cross-fertilisation that Gill had begun.

But the group soon began to change shape. Rice, Gilroy and Arnold had privately planned to sell Perkins before merger with Lucas became a possibility. In fact, Caterpillar made an offer even while the negotiations with Lucas were taking place. At that stage, had Lucas also made a bid for Kelsey-Hayes and abandoned thoughts of merger, it might have been able to maintain independence. Caterpillar met a cold shoulder then but talks resumed in 1997 and eventually Caterpillar paid £803m for the business in December. The following year talks started to sell the heavy-duty braking businesses and the sale to Meritor for £235m was announced in December. Meanwhile, LucasVarity bought the 66% of Freios Varga, the Brazilian brakes manufacturer, it did not already own for £71m, and acquired a Mexican brakes maker serving especially Chrysler and GM.

Operationally, LucasVarity could ride on the improvement of the markets, but at the same time it developed and tied up loose ends of old Lucas. The first order for diesel-injection equipment using common rail came in summer 1997; by the end of the year it had £650m worth of commitments from Ford, Kia and Renault. By March 1998, the group had started to consider a £200m investment programme for diesel. But the new group backed away from EUI for cars, cancelling the VW contract, after accumulated losses going back to old Lucas of more than £100m. Continued restructuring of Aerospace and the infusion of new personnel brought improvements in performance to the extent that Rolls-Royce stopped complaining and started calling LucasVarity its best supplier. Aerospace had £2bn worth of work coming through on the Trent engine. It bought the Smiths Industries controls business but finally disposed of the ill-fated gearbox business at Park City, Utah, which had threatened the existence of Lucas.

The ownership of LucasVarity did not turn out in the way that old Lucas had expected. Cazenove, its broker, had thought that, after merger, there would be a flow back to the UK of 25 to 30% of the equity held in the US. It worked in the opposite direction so that, Rice explained, after nine months, US investors held 60% of the equity and UK investors 40%: 'Basically US shareholders were liking the management and the company and in the UK they had the opposite attitude.'

The disparity of attitudes would now settle the fate of the group. 'It was obvious to me and the senior managers that, if LucasVarity was going to be a success, it would be unable to do it from a UK base,' Rice said. In early 1998, prompted by Morgan Stanley, the investment bank, the LucasVarity directors started to explore how to change domicile. The Morgan Stanley arguments, with which Rice agreed, were that LucasVarity had been strategically limited since the merger because it was domiciled in the UK, that the US accepted leverage more readily than the UK, that LucasVarity had disadvantages in making investments and that it had an inherently unstable shareholder base; a shift to the US would solve those problems.

Preparations had reached the point of discussions in the board, with Morgan Stanley and now Merrill Lynch and Cazenove present, on the likely movements of the share price. Arnold planned an extensive share buyback campaign – 20% of the share capital in 18 months – to run with the change of domicile. Although behaviour on the stock markets became erratic in late August, the background work continued and the announcement of a change of domicile came on 9 September, with the American advisers confident of a rise in the share price. UK institutional investors, approached before the announcement, had been at best cautious, at worst disappointed.

LucasVarity had not had an easy run with UK investors. Longstanding shareholders accused the old management of selling without a premium, giving Varity a low-cost reverse takeover. British investment habits did not embrace share buybacks too readily; dividends remained the traditional preference. EVA seemed alien; it had not spread into the UK and seemed, if anything, a trifle gimmicky. Although Rice and his managers had met the operational promises of the merger, the share price had not responded. Rice himself had done little to endear himself to the City, which found him offhand; nor had he given nearly as much attention to British investors as to those from the US. Criticism of him became sharp and personal which he attributed as much as anything else to the fact that he had left the UK and become successful in the US. Now, as LucasVarity took what was mildly described as an unusual step, it found its arguments for change contested and dismissed.

The Lex column of comment in the *Financial Times* was typical but at the same time politely hostile.

> True, US investors are more accustomed to higher leverage, lower dividend yields and share repurchases as a means to lower companies' cost of capital. But with net cash, LucasVarity has hardly been stretching UK tolerance of gearing. There is plenty of room for a more efficient capital structure without crossing the Atlantic.

It found equally flawed the notion that just by being close to peers made it easier to compete more effectively for investment. 'For old Lucas shareholders who sold out cheaply in the merger, watched the new shares underperform by 30% and are now effectively being asked to sell out completely, this is a sorry end indeed.'

But not, as it turned out, the end expected in September 1998. Rice and his colleagues had two months to woo the shareholders before an extraordinary general meeting to vote on the proposal. In spite of the wall of opposition, bricks of which were the two former chairmen, they nearly did it. They would have done it had one big institutional shareholder, Schroders, swung their way. For two hours shareholders argued and then cast their votes, influenced probably by the fact that the share price had not been rising as LucasVarity advisers had assumed it would.

The official announcement blandly set out the percentages.

> At the court meeting, a 57.2% majority in number representing 74.42% in value of the shareholders present and voting in person or by proxy voted in favour of the proposal, which required a 50% majority in number representing 75% in value of the shareholders present and voting in person or by proxy to be approved. At the extraordinary general meeting, 73.9% voted in favour of the proposal, which required 75% approval. Approximately 80% of the share capital of the company was voted at each meeting.

Rice believed the proposal went down because, as the board minutes after the vote recorded him saying,

> We were defeated by financial market conditions, as reflected in the severe weakness of our stock price. Also we, and our advisors, underestimated the reluctance of US institutions to buy without the certainty of a positive vote and of UK institutions to sell at such depressed price levels. Cazenove misread the voting intentions of UK institutional shareholders and the basis upon which they would make their decision. They were also unable to persuade the UK shareholders to change their decision.

So that was that, at a cost of about £25m.

The Path to Cleveland

'It is business as usual', Ed Wallis declared, when he made the formal announcement of the board's failure to win approval for the change of domicile. But the normality implied in his statement was more hope than reality.

Certainly, at the operational level, there was little to complain about. The latest figures had shown profits increasing in each of the three main divisions of the business and, if a strike at General Motors in the US could be ignored, margins improving across the board. The sale of Perkins to Caterpillar had given the group a cushion of cash plump enough to make the managers of the 1980s and early 1990s green with envy. It was widely assumed in the markets, and Victor Rice said nothing to disabuse the impression, that LucasVarity had £1bn to spend on acquisitions.

Yet the fact remained that Rice and his colleagues had backed a course and lost. The *Financial Times* acknowledged that on most counts Rice had delivered the cost reductions and financial improvements he had promised, but it reflected on the setback at the extraordinary general meeting under the headline 'The Day The Brakes Locked'.

The effect of that seizure left Rice and the board in a dilemma. 'Do we run the company,' he asked the directors when they met at the Waldorf Towers in New York on 2 December, 'for the benefit of the 60% who supported the transaction or the 20% who blocked it?' There could be no definitive response but it was clear to all the directors that fences would have to be mended with dissident UK shareholders and especially with Schroders, the fund manager most antagonistic to the proposed change of domicile. It was also clear that, if LucasVarity clung to its desire for a move to the US, it would be unlikely to realise it with a simple re-run of the vote, in the hope of a marginal shift of opinion. It might win the backing of all the shareholders if change in domicile could be linked to a major acquisition, or, indeed, to a break-up of the group.

But, to continue the *FT* analogy, this was really cleaning the grease off the brake mountings. To unlock the brakes, Rice would have to be seen to be doing something decisive, to be defining a way of expansion different from that linked to the change of domicile. The group strategists told the directors that the stock was illiquid and the price becalmed, that the ability to conduct business transactions had been damaged. Time, the board agreed, was of the essence. 'The company must make a bold move to execute its strategy and deliver shareholder value in the near term if it is to retain its shareholders and its key employees,' recorded the minutes of the December board meeting. Rice believed that the company had until March 1999, when it would announce its 1998 results, to declare its intentions.

In the meantime, Rice could stir the pot of market speculation with a trickle of information. Less than a week after the board's meeting in the Waldorf Towers, LucasVarity produced a comfortable set of third quarter figures and teased the market with an announcement of a review of its operations to be completed by March. In the early days of the New Year, it went a stage further and admitted preliminary talks with a number of companies. The statements were suitably vague; companies are always reviewing their operations and, in the automotive sector at least, they are always talking to each other. But the statements gave an impression of corporate energy, of a group gathering speed after the halt of the previous November; they put some life into the share price.

The impression was misleading, not because of a lack of energy in the upper reaches of LucasVarity, but because the momentum for change was far more vigorous than the statements suggested; a quest for alliance with another group, in some form or another, had gone further than mere reviews and preliminary talks implied.

Talks with Tenneco resumed in early December and reached the point of joint teams discussing how to establish synergy between the two groups. There had been detailed discussions with Delphi, the General Motors components subsidiary, which broke down on price. The option of merger with TI, the British group, discussed spasmodically for the previous 15 years, had been rejected. Consideration had been given to trying to work out a deal with Nippondenso of Japan and, in Europe, with Valeo or Magnetti Marelli. But the favoured potential partner was TRW, whose automotive expertise was complementary but knitted perfectly with that of LucasVarity at a time when electronics had started to link together the different component systems; TRW's steering technology and manufacturing, for example, linked naturally with LucasVarity's braking technology and manufacturing.

Within days of the November meeting of LucasVarity shareholders, Rice and Joe Gorman, the TRW chairman and chief executive, had started talking about the possibilities of bringing the two groups closer together. Who took the initiative is unclear; both sides claim to have started the exploration. At any rate, by December the talks had become more specific: Gorman and Rice had dinner together and at a meeting in Detroit considered a combination. That, in turn, led to a more formal management meeting in New York on 5 January when both sides set out their aspirations. There was a lengthy adjournment while TRW considered its position. Then the meeting resumed. This, Rice recalled later, was the watershed meeting. 'All of this was about a merger. Gorman and I sat down. He said, "We've changed our minds, we'd like to buy you." Then after talking to the board, it was just an issue of price.'

The two groups knew each other quite well. Their paths criss-crossed from time to time. Indeed, only the year before they had signed a joint-venture agreement to design, develop and manufacture steering systems for the international car and light commercial vehicle markets. The two groups wanted to harness the experience of Lucas Electrical & Electronic Systems in electronic actuation systems with TRW's strength as a maker of steering systems.

Over the previous 20 years, TRW and Lucas had been different enough to reduce commercial rivalry but close enough to think of cooperation. In 1980 they treated each other with cautious camaraderie when TRW, wanting to clean up its British interests by folding Cam Gears into Clifford Motor Components, found it needed to buy a Lucas shareholding. The Lucas board raised no objection: 'Lucas were continuing to develop useful links with TRW who were good people and a suitable disposal to them of the Cam Gears holding was to be commended.' Charles Ohly, then TRW's executive vice-president automotive, wrote to Godfrey Messervy about how pleased he was with past business relations. 'I . . . eagerly look forward to an expanded business association with Lucas in connection with the development and manufacture of electronic control modules for fuel-injection equipment sold by Lucas CAV.' And, he declared roundly, he hoped for 'a long and mutually profitable association based on compatible and sound business relationships.'

That 'expanded business association', designed by the groups to steal a march on rivals at a high point of interest in diesel systems, was a high point for CAV, its North American representatives reported back to Birmingham: 'The business relationship with TRW has been excellent so far with TRW performing well.' As it turned out, American enthusiasm for car diesel engines proved short-lived and when, in 1983, Lucas consequently had spare capacity at its Greenville, South Carolina plant, it undertook for TRW sub-contract manufacturing.

During the 1980s, the name of TRW tended to come forward when Lucas wanted to re-organise or when it became sensitive to the possibility of takeover. No surprise then that TRW emerged during 1986 in Lucas calculations as, if not a buyer, at least a partner for a portfolio of companies in the troublesome Electrical business. TRW cooperated to the extent of sending a six-man team to visit the UK operations, and there were, reported the Lucas executives involved, 'Several weeks of unproductive discussions with four potential collaborators'. The other groups to which Lucas was talking at the time were Hitachi, Mitsubishi Electric and Delco.

The same year, as Lucas executives in North America wrestled with the problem of how, or if, to make the group a more significant player in the market, Bunty Wootten argued that 'Lucas is basically a Tier 1 Supplier – but major investment would be required to realise our potential in the USA . . . Teaming would seem the solution in several product areas.' As he looked at the field, he made TRW one of 12 companies which offer complementary skills in one or more fields and 'who could welcome our association'. Lucas Electrical and CAV had been discussing petrol injection and engine management with TRW.

Lucas Engine Management Systems wanted a partner to obtain access to a wider base of customers, to bring in fresh capital and, ideally, to offer complementary products and facilities. Relatively, it was technology rich but cash and manufacturing capacity poor. So, again, TRW sprang into the executive calculations: a short-list of companies who could be what the internal reports called 'potential collaborators'. TRW was one of seven, picked out because it had 'US-based electronics facility; declared strategy for growth in Europe; limited technology; has expressed acquisition interest in Lucas EMS'. Then, in 1990, talks between Lucas and TRW took place about chassis systems.

Although in 1989 Goldman Sachs, the investment banker, then advising Lucas on corporate defence against a predator, identified TRW as a possible bidder for the whole, or parts of, the group, it was only one of 126 companies mentioned. Certainly Lucas did not see TRW as a threat. Indeed, the history of contact gave the Gorman – Rice talks an immediate and more solid foundation than would have been the case with a hostile bid from a company less well known to Lucas and LucasVarity. TRW could obtain control through coalescence rather than conquest.

Gorman's first offer was $42.00 cash for each LucasVarity ADR (American Depositary Receipt, a certificate used in the US for trading in foreign stocks), which worked out at 255p a share. Then a higher offer came: $46.50, or 282p a share. When Gorman made the offer more formal in a letter, dated 18 January, to Wallis and Rice, the price had risen to $47.50, or 288p a share. And there the numbers rested when the LucasVarity board met for the discussions which would decide the future of the group. They had six defined choices.

The first, of course, was to do nothing, but given the group's reasoning about expansion, its concern about the share price and the raucous divisions among the shareholders, this did not seem realistic.

The second was to break up the group and sell its constituent parts. LucasVarity corporate planners valued the group at between £4.13bn and £4.8bn and that took account of the surplus in the pension fund, tax liabilities and cash in the bank. This range of value led to the estimate that each share would be worth between 275p and 320p. Here, then, was a benchmark against which offers for the group could be measured. LucasVarity operations could fit in, or be added on, to the activities of numerous other international groups, but the process of selling could be uncertain in timing and there would always be a risk about the price.

A third choice for the board would be to arrange a demerger. The idea would be to split the group into an automotive company, registered in the US, and an aerospace company registered in the UK. Before the redistribution of assets, planners thought, LucasVarity would have to use its shares to buy an aerospace company in order to make the demerger tax free. LucasVarity shareholders would be given shares in the new auto-motive company as a non-taxable dividend. If all this took place, the result would be that the automotive company would be highly geared while the aerospace company would have cash for acquisitions, share repurchases or a special dividend.

Together the two companies would have a value of between 220p and 240p a share. But the series of transactions could look like a re-run of the domicile argument, not likely to enhance LucasVarity in the eyes of the City of London, although Wall Street would be relaxed. Still, the whole matter could be settled by a resolution which would need to be passed by 50% of the shareholder vote, and the expected opposition of some UK shareholders could be chipped away with a dividend or a share buyback.

Merger and takeovers made up the fourth, fifth and sixth choices: the different approaches of Tenneco, TRW and a latecomer, Federal-Mogul.

Executives from LucasVarity and Tenneco had worked together and produced a scheme for a merger which would give LucasVarity between 42 and 47% of a new group. Immediately after the merger, the packaging interests of Tenneco, businesses with annual sales of over £2.6bn, would be spun off. That would leave an automotive and aerospace group with over £6bn of sales, of which the Tenneco contribution would be nearly £2bn.

LucasVarity would manage the combined business, a plus for the executive team.

A sad end to headquarters, Great King Street – it had become redundant by the early 1990s .

But, given that the merger would take place at current market prices, there would be no premium for the LucasVarity shareholders and 75% of them needed to approve a scheme of arrangement for the merger to take place. Alternatively the merger could be set up with a share exchange offer and that would need 90% acceptance. Knowing the sensitivity of the shareholders following the bitterness churned up by the change of domicile affair, the Tenneco package provided for a special LucasVarity dividend of £600m.

Starting from the share price of 214p on 14 January, the LucasVarity strategists worked out that the Tenneco merger, taking into account the packaging sale and the special dividend, would make every LucasVarity share worth 230p. So that was less than their value in the event of a break-up of the group, but roughly in line with what they might be worth if the automotive and aerospace business separated.

The possibility of merger with Tenneco may have been interesting but it was unattractive compared with the TRW offer of 288p a share. When the LucasVarity board met on 19 January to weigh up the choices and examined the Gorman letter to Wallis and Rice, two points about TRW's position stood out.

The first related to price: to think of negotiating the offer upwards would be futile. 'Our offer of $47.50 (for each ADR) represents a premium of more than 40% over the share trading price of LucasVarity prior to the commencement of discussions. We have stretched to put the best possible proposal on the table,' Gorman wrote.

The second related to timing. TRW wanted to hurry and had started to put in place the necessary financing. Gorman's letter continued:

> We are prepared to move forward rapidly to consummate a transaction . . . We will proceed immediately to negotiate definitive agreements, which would include an appropriate break-up fee (that is, a penalty which would be paid to TRW if the takeover plan broke down) and other customary provisions.

'We believe that an announcement within two weeks is feasible,' Gorman declared. There was a sting in the tail. TRW would not allow the offer to hang in the wind. 'In the absence of a positive and timely response', TRW would look at other options. In any case, if LucasVarity discussed the matter publicly, then TRW would revoke the offer. As it happened, financial newspapers ten days before had speculated that the two groups had started to talk as part of LucasVarity's publicly acknowledged review of its activities, but they had not seized on the likelihood of full merger or takeover.

Nor had the newspapers considered Federal-Mogul of Southfield, Michigan, as a potential ally of LucasVarity. In early 1996 Dick Snell became chairman and chief executive of Federal-Mogul. The following year he started a series of bold corporate shopping raids. In 18 months, Federal-Mogul made three significant acquisitions and trebled sales to £4.3bn. Snell raised debt for the purchases and then sold equity to pay off the debt. LucasVarity, he thought, might be the fourth buy.

The same day that Gorman put the TRW offer in writing, Snell wrote to Wallis and Rice. He only had public information at his disposal, so, in his letter, he went no further than 'contemplating an indicative offer of 270p per LucasVarity ordinary share.' He wanted to look at the books – conduct due diligence – then negotiate a definitive offer which the LucasVarity board could recommend to the shareholders. Snell believed this could be done in three weeks. His letter did not explain how the two groups might fit together but he asserted that the combination 'would create a formidable world-class company'. In any event, he sought from Wallis and Rice a response in five days.

When the LucasVarity board met the following day to plot the future, it rapidly dispensed with the possibility of demerger: there was little in the proposal for the shareholders. It did not pursue the possibility of a break-up. Nor, according to the minutes, did it spend much time on Tenneco.

The group strategists told the board that while a merger with Tenneco would be 'strategically compelling', it would be a complex and lengthy process to bring it about. Rice believed that, at that time, Tenneco was over-valued. Tony Gilroy, judging from the minutes, saw TRW as a better industrial partner for LucasVarity than Tenneco:

> In comparing TRW's offer with a possible transaction with Tenneco, Mr Gilroy observed that, whilst Tenneco was market leader in suspension, TRW had a significant presence in suspension and was one of only two steering companies (along with Delphi), the third building block (along with braking) for Vehicle Dynamics. In addition TRW had a systems capability, which Tenneco did not have.

Thus, with Tenneco pushed to the side, the board's discussion concentrated on the merits of the TRW and Federal-Mogul offers. At the industrial level, the LucasVarity strategists had made business evaluations of 33 different possible deals in the automotive sector and had concluded that a combination with TRW made the best sense. They thought 'excellent' the strategic fit with TRW. That with Federal-Mogul they deemed 'limited'. There is no record of the LucasVarity board even considering the industrial merits of an arrangement with Federal-Mogul.

Without knowing it, TRW had already stacked the financial cards against Federal-Mogul. It had made a bigger offer. It had made the offer in cash. There could be no very good reason for LucasVarity to dally with an offer worth 18p a share less than that of TRW, made up of 50% cash and 50% Federal-Mogul paper, especially when the view of UK investors towards US stocks was known to be suspicious. Lazards, the financial advisers of TRW, thought the TRW offer was full and fair. Probably, the TRW offer would be the best LucasVarity was likely to get.

The die had been cast. The LucasVarity board approved unanimously the pursuit of discussions with TRW. 'The chairman concluded by stating that the company should reply to TRW's letter emphasising that the company agreed to proceed based on the proposed price of 288p per share.' Federal-Mogul, on the other hand, should be told that LucasVarity did not want to proceed: the response would be 'Thank you, but no thank you'.

Federal-Mogul responded by raising its offer, although it remained in cash and shares and did not reach TRW's level. There was a deal of huffing and puffing in the financial press, but, in reality, Federal-Mogul had been played out of the game. It eventually made a dignified statement and faded away. Meanwhile, the TRW-LucasVarity discussions went ahead with great speed.

Ten days after Gorman's letter to Wallis and Rice, comfortably within the TRW target, Gorman and Rice in New York and Wallis in London combined telephonically to announce the plan for TRW to take over LucasVarity at a price of £4bn ($6.6bn), the largest cash acquisition in the history of the automotive supply industry. Together the two would be creating, said Gorman in the post-negotiation euphoria, 'A premier global supplier – the simple fact is we will be the second largest independent supplier.' Together, said Rice, 'TRW and LucasVarity become the leader in occupant safety and vehicle dynamics, together we will have the global scale and technological leadership to provide automobile manufacturers with advance module solutions in brakes, steering and suspension.'

At first the plan was for Rice to head the group's combined automotive operations, but Gorman withdrew the offer, leaving John Anthony, Ken Maciver and John Plant as the senior LucasVarity executives to move into the larger group. Gorman, on second thoughts, apparently had drawn the historical lesson that division of control at the top of a group can create disharmony. Such had been the case with the divided responsibilities of Gill and Wilkinson during the early 1980s at Lucas; it would be the case, only a few months after Gorman made his decision, between Jürgen Schrempp and Robert Eaton at DaimlerChrysler.

In early February TRW sent its formal offer to the LucasVarity shareholders and on 26 March, the offer was declared unconditional. Two days before, LucasVarity published its valedictory report and accounts, covering the year to 31 January 1999, disclosing a respectable 6.3% increase in turnover to £4.27bn and a modest increase in pre-tax profits to £345m, before exceptional gains of £188m.

There was little interest. The excitement of takeover gone, LucasVarity slid from public view and finally disappeared on 11 May when it re-registered as a private company. It was nearly 102 years since Joseph Lucas Ltd had first gone to the London market with a share issue to which 144 people wanted to subscribe.

With barely a murmur, the group which Joseph Lucas had started slid gently into American hands. It had been a long road, far longer, far wider than anything Joseph

Lucas could have dreamed when he sent his first cycle lamps to the US market in 1881 and, in an early display of international technological ambition, registered his first US patent in 1889.

For those engaged in the polemic of industrial chauvinism, the takeover was just another example of a chunk of British industry folding up before the Americans, the loss of a name sometimes regarded with despair, sometimes with affection, but a name of significance nevertheless in the British economy since World War I. For those close to the industry, the takeover was a natural, indeed a welcome, example of consolidation on the global markets. For those who followed Lucas and LucasVarity, the takeover was the ultimate answer to the search for new capital, sustained technological growth and wider markets, the arrival home of a group whose ambitions had frequently run ahead of its ability to achieve them.

For all that, there is a postscript of two teasing thoughts. The first, carrying a suggestion that the American embrace was inevitable, comes in the form of an anecdote. The story may be apocryphal; if true, it shows remarkable prescience. In the mid-1970s, Bernard Scott was the chairman at a management committee meeting of the Lucas Research Centre. One of his executives told him that Lucas had no independent future, it would end up as part of TRW. Scott's reaction is not recorded. At the very least his eyes would have hardened.

The second is conjecture, the indulgence of executive nostalgia. It runs along the line of supposing that another voting percentage point had swung towards Rice at the fateful extraordinary general meeting of November 1998. Then, runs the line of thinking, LucasVarity could have leveraged its finances, already strengthened by the sale of Caterpillar, to make the big acquisition which would have secured its future in the league of international systems suppliers. The acquisition would have been TRW.

Aftermath

TRW had scarcely absorbed LucasVarity when, in the febrile financial atmosphere of the late 1990s and early 2000s, it too came under pressure either to break itself up or allow itself to be taken over. In fact, both happened so that the old Lucas businesses found themselves again responding to different masters.

Some of the old Lucas businesses TRW had never wanted and had planned to sell. Overseas interests were sold off – in India, for example. But the most striking sale, agreed in December 1999, was that of the diesel business which went to Delphi Automotive Systems, the component group springing from General Motors, for $871m cash. This was a move of historic resonance; Oliver Lucas used to visit and consult with Delco-Remy, Delphi's predecessor during the 1930s.

Northrop Grumman, the US defence contractor, sought control of TRW's high-technology defence business. To obtain it, Northrop had to buy the whole group or find buyers for the parts it did not require. This set off a spasm of corporate activity. So, once TRW had agreed to the Northrop bid, it sold TRW Aeronautical Systems, what had been Lucas Aerospace, to Goodrich, another US aerospace company.

The old Lucas brakes and engine management and component business had meanwhile settled down in the TRW Chassis Systems and Automotive Electronics divisions. Now, as the Northrop bid for TRW moved to consummation, they moved into the ownership of Blackstone, a private US investment group, in a deal which valued the whole TRW automotive business at $4.7bn. Blackstone established TRW Automotive as an independent company. The link to old Lucas remained: the chief executive of TRW Automotive is John Plant and he started his career at Lucas in 1978.

John Plant, Chief Executive of TRW Automotive.

Index

Lucas divisions are entered under Lucas

Illustrations are in italic numerals

Subscribers

Norman Abbott	Girling Tyseley	1976	1981
Tony Abbott	Gt King St, Gt Hampton St	1970	1988
R G Acton	Lucas Aerospace	1964	1984
L G Adams	Aerospace Liverpool	1956	1990
Daniel Gerard Ahem			
	Girling Cwmbran	1964	1996
B Akhtar	Lucas Shirley	1997	2004
Brian Aldridge	Fradley	1958	1997
Benjamin and Nancy			
Alger (Carrier)	Gt King St	1930	1974
Antony Kieron Allan	CAV Acton	1949	1983
W J Allarton	Gt King St, CAV Acton	1952	1980
D H Allord-Brown	CAV Acton	1963	1995
Ahmed T Almulad	Formans Rd	1969	1988
Cecil Alway	CAV Acton	1949	1969
Donald Anderson			
Peter Angell	Automotive Electronics		
	Cirencester	1987	1998
G W Anstee	Aerospace Willesden	1955	1988
P J Arnott	Aerospace Hemel		
	Hempstead	1966	1988
George Arroll	Aerospace Wood Top	1948	1985
Steve Ascott	CAV Gillingham	1963	1999
S T Ascott			
Neil V Atkins	Fradley	1967	2001
Bill Baker	Aerospace Coventry	1972	1995
Peter Bacon	Aerospace Fordhouses	1987	
Thomas Badger	Girling Service		
	West Bromwich		
Charles Badger	Aerospace Hemel		
	Hempstead	1939	1981
Roy Alan Bailey	Aerospace Hemel		
	Hempstead	1967	1993
Adam Bailey	Fradley	1990	2002
H C L Baker-Duly	CAV Acton, CAV Overseas	1964	1970
Derek Ball			
Stephen Bamford	Aerospace Burnley	1990	1998
John W Banks	Lucas Corporate	1970	1981
S F Barber	CAV Acton	1948	1978
David Barlow	CAV Acton	1963	1987
Roy Barlow	Lucas Electrical	1942	1986
G Barnett	Electrical Shaftmoor Lane	1971	1980
Edward Barrett			
Albert G Barrett	CAV Acton, Aerospace		
	Hemel Hempstead	1974	1992
L A Barrett	CAV Acton	1939	1979
Roger Bater	Gt King St	1960	1993
J P Baverstock	Haddenham	1974	1994
A T Baxter	Aerospace Hemel		
	Hempstead	1964	2000
Harry Beeching	CAV Rochester,		
	CAV Gillingham	1955	1988
Derek Beeley	Aerospace Hemel		
	Hempstead	1963	1989
Martyn Bell	Gt Hampton St	1975	1988
Pauline Berry (Abbott)			
	CAV Rochester	1979	1997
W R Betts			
Roland Beveridge	Rists Accrington	1966	1991
G A Bills	CAV Acton	1969	2000
B N Binns			
David Birtwistle			
Eric Black	Lucas Litsa Switzerland	1948	1979
Robert Blassberg	Lucas Girling		
Kathleen Bolton	Rists Accrington	1974	1999
Fred Bolton	Gt King St, Aerospace		
	Shaftmoor Lane	1948	1986
Reginald Bonehill	Gt King St,		
	Mere Green, Holford	1977	2000
R W Bonsey	CAV Acton	1961	1980
J V G Bough	Lucas Export	1948	1993
John Bowes	Electrical Shaftmoor Lane,		
	CAV Acton,		
	Electrical Australia	1936	1974
Wiley and Penny			
Bowkett (Jones)	Gt King St, Electrical		
	Shaftmoor Lane	1955	2005
Olive May Boxall	CAV Acton	1963	1978
Geoffrey Boyle	Aerospace Hargherclough	1968	1997
E Bradford			
Hazel Braithwaite			
(Bennett)	CAV Acton	1978	1984
Louise Perryman			
(James)	CAV Acton	1978	1984
R J Brazier	Gloucester	1962	1990
Brian Brearley	Lucas Keighey NSF	1961	1981
Adrian and			
June Brennan	Aerospace Fordhouses,		
	Lucas Group Research		
	Centre	1965	2003
Keith Bromwich	Gt King St	1972	1999
David I Brown	TRW Corporate	1997	2001
Lavinia Mary Brown			
(Evitts)	Gt King St	1964	1990
Martyn Brown	Girling Tyseley,		
	Girling Cwmbran	1978	1999
Robert M Bruce	Gt Hampton St, Gt King St	1969	1979
Barry Bruce	Aerospace Hemel		
	Hempstead	1959	1997
R M Brydges			
P J Buckell	Gt King St, College Rd	1978	1989
Graham Bell	Lucas Group Research		
	Centre	1991	1997
M K Burdett	Aerospace Hemel		
	Hempstead	1964	1997
A S Burgess			
Doris May Burgess	Lucas Corporate	1934	1974
F A Burrell	CAV Acton	1940	1983
Ted Burston	Lucas Park St, CAV Acton	1982	2002
Michael Butterfield	Aerospace Bradford	1975	1985
P J Byfield	Plume Street	1971	1981
George Caen	Lucas Girling	1946	1983
John Edward Caley	CAV Sudbury	1967	1999
Derek Capstick	Aerospace Hargherclough	1968	1982
G Carbutt			
R W H Cardwell	Aerospace Hemel		
	Hempstead	1953	1986
Bernard T Carey	Lucas Corporate	1988	1994
John Carey	Gt King St	1961	1982
Shirley M Carlile	Gt King St, Lucas Shirley	1973	1996
David Carlton	CAV Rochester,		
	CAV Gillingham	1967	1998
Gerry Carty	Gt King St, Mere Green	1969	1989
Paul J Catlow	Gt King St	1958	1989
John Chard	Aerospace Hemel		
	Hempstead	1955	1998
Hilda Elizabeth			
Charlton	CAV Rochester,		
	CAV Gillingham	1964	1992
Carol Ann Charlton	College Rd, Gt King St	1976	1998
D N Charlwood			
Dick and Catherine			
Chase (Welch)	Gt King St, Electrical		
	Shaftmoor Lane, Lucas		
	Group Research Centre	1969	1995
R Chase	Aerospace Honiley	1958	1988
J G Cheasman	Aerospace Willesden	1952	1988
Peter Checketts	Aerospace Shaftmoor		
	Lane	1976	2001
Roy Chedzey	CAV Acton	1950	1981
Dawn Clark (Morrell)			
	Mere Green	1978	2000
Peter Clarke	Aerospace Hemel		
	Hempstead	1962	1988
John Clarke	Girling Tyseley, Girling		
	Service West Bromwich	1968	1983
William Clough	Aerospace Hargherclough	1948	1964
Maurice Coles			
E Colyer	Stonehouse	1989	1994
Les Cook	Lucas USA	1983	1995

Name	Location	From	To
David Hart	Lucas Service UK	1971	1998
S M Hartley	Electrical Eastern Avenue Burnley	1968	2002
Norman Harvey	Lucas Group Research Centre	1965	1987
Frederick Hassall	Rists Newcastle	1968	1997
D J Hathaway	CAV Acton	1930	1970
James Hattle	CAV Gillingham	1977	1998
Stan Hauptman	CAV Acton		
B S Hawkins	CAV Acton	1966	1982
Alice Hawkins	Gt King St	1969	1987
George Henry Hawksworth	Aerospace Victor Works	1952	1982
John Haworth	Aerospace Burnley	1954	1995
Wendy Haden	Aerospace Shirley	1992	2002
Margaret Haynes	Rists Newcastle	1967	1984
Ron Hayward	Electrical Shaftmoor Lane	1958	1987
Don Haywood	Aerospace Hemel Hempstead	1981	1991
J Healy		1969	1980
Peter Hearn	Aerospace Hemel Hempstead	1955	1988
Brian and Brenda Heath	Mere Green	1962	1999
Kenneth Heaton	Aerospace Wood Top	1948	1983
M J Hedderick		1961	1995
Colin Helsby	Aerospace Victor Works, Aerospace Huyton	1958	1993
Raymond Hemming	Electrical Shaftmoor Lane	1955	1987
Edward C Hemmings	Chester St, Mere Green	1948	1981
A J Heneberry			
Eric Henson	Lucas Girling	1959	1991
Donald B Hepworth	Aerospace Bradford	1947	1988
Frank Heron	Aerospace Huyton	1955	1988
Jim Hewitt	CAV Rochester	1956	1987
Margaret Hewitt-Edwards	Gt King St	1954	1988
Norman Hewlett	Lucas Service UK	1960	1999
Mike Heynes	Marshall Lake Rd, Gt King St	1969	1985
P G Hibberd	Girling Tyseley	1947	1988
Peter John High	CAV Gillingham	1987	1997
Edward Hill		1957	1990
Herbert Hill	Girling Service West Bromwich	1973	1992
Len Hill	Gt King St, Aerospace Shaftmoor Lane	1935	1976
David Hill	Gt Hampton St	1963	1996
Raymond H Hill	CAV Acton	1969	1989
Brian T Hill	Aerospace Liverpool, Gt King St	1945	1987
V Hill		1941	1980
P T Hillyard	Aerospace Marston Green, Gt King St	1954	1990
Pamela Hindle (Annison)	Aerospace York Rd	1977	2001
Tony Hine	Gt Hampton St	1960	1993
George Hinsley	Aerospace Shaftmoor Lane	1956	1993
W Hird	London	1933	1970
Ernest Hitchman	Gt King St, Lucas Electrical	1952	1984
Bob Hoare	Lucas Gt King St	1969	1997
M D Hobson	Rotax	1947	1987
Peter Hockley	Aerospace Shaftmoor Lane, Aerospace York Rd	1970	2001
Jenny Hodges	Mere Green	1969	1985
Edwyn Lambert Hodgson	Lucas Keighey NSF	1955	1983
John A Holland	CAV Acton	1954	1994
L B Holland	BW8 Spring Road	1955	1988
Edward William Holland	Chester St, Gt Hampton St	1937	1980
H Holland	CAV Rochester	1965	1986
Peter Holmes	Aerospace Shirley	2000	2003
Russell Holmes	Girling South Wales	1960	1999
Keith W Holmes	Aerospace Bradford	1969	1990
H B Homer	Gt King St, Marshall Lake Rd	1937	1981
Gary Hook	Girling Cwmbran	1963	1992
Colin Hook	Girling Cwmbran	1964	1987
Kenneth Hopes	Aerospace Hemel Hempstead	1954	1996
G J Hopkins	Aerospace Fordhouses	1971	1976
W J Hopkins	Gt King St	1943	1983
Christine Horne	Girling Service West Bromwich	1972	1995
Raymond Horsley	CAV Sudbury	1963	1978
Leonard John Horton	Rists Newcastle	1955	1990
Frederick T Houchin	CAV Acton	1948	1986
A J Howard	CAV Acton	1935	1981
Greta Howard (Turner)	Gt King St	1963	1987
Geoffrey S Howard	Lucas Aerospace	1945	1988
Alan Howarth	Electrical Burnley, Electrical Australia	1954	1986
G B Howarth	Burnley		
Graham Howarth	Lucas Service UK	1969	1999
George Emile Howarth	CAV Acton	1961	1991
William James Howell	CAV Acton	1954	1989
Bruce Howells	Girling Overseas Ops	1957	1997
Brian F Hubball	Gt King St	1968	1988
F G Hudman	Gt King St	1939	1982
Kenneth G Hudson	Aerospace Burnley	1966	1998
Eugene Hudson	Aerospace Shaftmoor Lane	1954	1988
W H (Harry) Hughes	Girling Pontypool	1972	1986
Roger Hughes	Lucas Service UK	1968	1999
William Henry Hughes	Formans Rd	1974	1988
Sidney Ralph Hughes	Aerospace Fordhouses	1950	1990
F Hulatt	CAV Acton	1947	1983
James R Humphries	Aerospace Fordhouses	1962	1988
John Hunt	Lucas Electrical, Lucas Corporate Shirley	1946	1991
Mrs J D Hunt (Seward)	Aerospace Willesden	1962	1977
Bill Hunt	Aerospace Hemel Hempstead	1955	1984
Angela Huntley (Roberts)	Lucas Shirley	1983	1997
Alan Hurford	Gt King St	1962	1987
Beryl Ann Hurl	Chester St, Gt King St	1968	1999
R J Hurley	Lucas Electrical	1951	1989
Bert Hurring	Lucas CAV, Lucas Service UK	1967	1996
David Hymas	Lucas CAV, Lucas USA	1957	1993
John and Sheila Idell	Gt Hampton St, Mere Green	1951	1991
T Illes	CAV Acton	1959	1994
Ron Ince	CAV Sudbury	1954	1992
Derick Ingall	Aerospace Hemel Hempstead	1939	1979
Robert David Ingram	CAV Acton	1974	1980
Brian Ingram	Lucas Girling	1960	1990
Stanley Richard Ingram	CAV Rochester, CAV Gillingham	1950	1981
S R Ingram			
John H Ingram	Gt King St	1958	1996
Dennis L R Ireland	Lucas Girling	1975	1988
Karen A Irvine (Lamb)	College Rd	1985	2001
R Irwin	Arle Court	1979	1995
Betty Isherwood (Cayless)	CAV Acton	1942	1978
Gary Ives	Aerospace Shaftmoor Lane, Aerospace Brueton House	1979	1992
J D Ivings	Witney	1992	1998
Douglas E Izon	Aerospace Shaftmoor Lane	1938	1984
John Jackman	CAV Acton	1973	1998
Norman Jackson	Gt King St	1940	1967
B A Jackson			
Charles Jackson	Gt King St	1953	1985
Peter Barrie Jackson	Aerospace Fordhouses	1986	2000
Ronald David Jackson	CAV Gillingham	1978	2000
Squire Ronald Jackson	Burnley	1945	1973
Frank Jacobs	Aerospace York Rd	1977	1992
William Jacques	Gt Hampton St	1953	1988
A F Jager	Shaftmoor Lane	1959	1990
David James	Gt Hampton St	1966	1991
Santokh Singh Jandu	CAV Acton	1984	1998

169

Name	Location		
James H Jarrett	CAV Rochester	1954	1992
Paul Jarvis	Gravelly Park	1966	2000
Aggie Jaschok	CAV Sudbury	1969	1972
David F Jebbitt	Gt Hampton St	1990	1999
George Jelf	Gt King St, Electrical Shaftmoor Lane, Chester St	1945	1975
R T Jenkins	Girling Pontypool	1973	2003
John Jenkinson	Fradley	1967	2000
Michael Jenner	Gt King St, CAV Acton, Aerospace Shirley	1957	1994
Guy Jennings	Aerospace Shaftmoor Lane	1987	1996
F Jennings	CAV Acton	1933	1979
K C R Jephson	Lucas CAV	1966	1993
Walter W H Jevons	Girling Tyseley	1973	1983
Albert E Jeynes	Aerospace Brueton House	1960	1987
Anthony Jirkhu	Girling Bromborough	1970	1980
I S Johnson	CAV Acton, CAV Overseas	1962	1998
Stan Johnson	Aerospace Burnley	1974	1999
Harry Johnson	Aerospace Burnley	1946	1982
Len Johnson	Electrical Shaftmoor Lane	1947	1986
Donald Stanley Johnson	Aerospace Shaftmoor Lane	1958	1994
D G Johnson	Lucas Engineering & Systems	1989	1995
G E Johnson	Cambridge	1950	1996
David William Johnston	Lucas CAV	1955	1980
Trevor Jones	Ystradgynlais	1984	1990
David W H Jones	Aerospace Hemel Hempstead	1981	1991
Bernard R Jones	Gt King St, CAV Acton	1953	1988
Ivor Jones	Gt Hampton St, Formans Rd	1959	1983
H Jones		1963	1995
T T Jones	Girling Cwmbran	1956	1991
Winifred M Jones (Bridges)	Gt Hampton St	1966	1987
Don Jones	Aerospace Bradford	1948	1976
Francis Victor Jones	CAV Acton	1943	1991
Phyllis Dorothy Jones	CAV Rochester, CAV Gillingham	1970	1990
Geoff Jones	Gt Hampton St	1966	2001
E Jones	Northbridge		
Colin M Joy	Frimley	1953	1991
Mykola Jurkewycz	CAV Acton	1957	1987
S D Kapur	Lucas Park St	1970	1987
John George Kaye	Aerospace Liverpool	1952	1982
Andrew Keating	CAV Rochester, CAV Gillingham	1957	1983
Geoffrey Keeble	Aerospace Fordhouses	1963	1989
William Keegin	Lucas Service UK	1949	1987
Gordon Keeley Lawrence Keen	Girling Service West Bromwich	1984	2003
Joyce Kell	CAV Acton, Aerospace Rotax	1947	1971
Stan Kelland	Gt Hampton St	1948	1991
John A Kellett	Girling Tyseley	1966	1980
Norman T Kelly	Aerospace Victor Works, Aerospace Huyton	1954	1988
Ralph Keme	Girling Cwmbran	1986	1994
Robert Kemish	Formans Rd, Gt King St	1960	1988
David Alan Kemp	Gt King St	1962	1993
Paul A Kendall	Aerospace Bradford	1966	2001
M A Kendall			
Edward John Kennedy	CAV Acton	1967	1988
John Kenning	Gt King St	1958	1992
J M Kent, MBE	Aerospace Hemel Hempstead	1962	1992
Charles Edward Kent	CAV Rochester, CAV Gillingham	1956	1986
Roger Kerrison	Aerospace Huyton	1961	2001
Keith Kershaw	Electrical Eastern Avenue Burnley	1954	1998
Roland Kershaw	Electrical Eastern Avenue Burnley	1965	1988
Kaz Kicinski	CAV Acton	1973	1979
Vincent Kielpinski	Aerospace Willesden	1955	1988
I P Killin	Northbridge	1959	1998
Dawn King (Kitchen)	Aerospace Shaftmoor Lane, Aerospace York Rd	1979	2000
M E King	Woodford Green	1960	1981
Mike King	Holford	1962	2002
John King	Aerospace Hemel Hempstead	1953	1988
Joe King	CAV Rochester, CAV Gillingham	1962	1999
Brian J Kingett	Gt King St	1952	1991
David Kings	Aerospace Fordhouses	1967	2002
George Kinman	Girling South Wales	1945	1986
Frank H Kirby	Aerospace Shaftmoor Lane	1956	1984
Jean Kirk	Cannock	1964	1987
Iris Knight (Johns)	Gt King St	1960	1987
P Edna Knowles	Lucas GKS	1944	1966
Graham Knowles	Aerospace Burnley	1984	2000
Gordon Knowles	Aerospace Shaftmoor Lane	1953	1984
David Knox	Lucas GKS	1962	1970
Paul Kocher	Aerospace Hemel Hempstead	1971	1997
W Kolebuk	CAV Acton	1956	1977
Stan Lambert	CAV Sudbury		1986
Mary Lamerton	Haddenham	1958	1978
John Lancaster	Lucas Burnley	1947	1980
K D W Lancaster	Gt King St	1948	1963
Anthony R Lane	Lucas USA	1955	1996
John W Lane	Aerospace Shaftmoor Lane	1956	1988
M E Langridge	CAV Rochester, CAV Gillingham	1954	1993
Anthony Langston	Girling Pontypool	1972	1998
Stephen Lapworth	Gt King St	1948	1981
Susan Law (Donaghy)		1969	1998
S T Law			
Malcolm Lawrence	Aerospace Hemel Hempstead, Aerospace Coventry	1973	1988
Peter Lawrence	Lucas Service UK	1972	1999
Richard Lawrence	Aerospace Shaftmoor Lane	1948	1983
D G Lawrence	Lucas Service UK	1940	1983
Martin Laycock	Lucas CAV	1972	2001
Ronnie Laycock	Lucas Burnley	1961	2000
P J Laycock	Gt King St, Gt Hampton St	1937	1981
Jack H J Leader	Aerospace Victor Works	1945	1990
Richard Leahy	CAV Acton	1975	1983
Allan E Leason	Girling Tyseley, Girling South Wales	1962	1994
David Lee	Electrical Burnley	1966	1982
Donald Lee	Lucas Gt King St, Lucas Service UK	1941	1982
Ernie Lee	CAV Hartridge	1971	1977
Andy Lees	CAV Overseas	1959	1999
Timothy and Jean Legg		1968	1988
Jack Lenham	Aerospace Fordhouses	1970	1982
Alfons Les	CAV Acton	1950	1990
Veronica Letters	Antrim	1972	1995
Colin Levi	CAV Acton	1955	1998
Frank Lewis	Lucas Gt King St	1941	1981
Renne Lewis (Cryer)	Lucas Burnley	1959	1988
J V Lewis	Electrical Burnley	1961	1980
Howard C Lilly	Gt Hampton St	1954	1989
L H Lincoln	CAV Acton	1967	1993
David Lindsay	CAV Acton, CAV Gillingham	1954	1994
Bernard Lister	Aerospace Fordhouses	1960	1988
Jane Littlejohns			
Les Lloyd	Aerospace Fordhouses	1970	1991
Steve Lockwood	Lucas Gt King St, Lucas Shirley	1968	1999
Bernard Loftus	Aerospace Shaftmoor Lane, Marston Green	1952	1983
Dennis Long	Lucas Birmingham	1962	1991
Edward L Longcroft	Aerospace Hemel Hempstead	1952	1979
R F Longmore	Gt Hampton St	1964	1991
Brenda Lonsdale (Furnival)	Electrical Eastern Avenue Burnley	1960	1987
Gordon Joseph Lonsdale	Lucas Park St, CAV Acton	1958	1998
Allan Lougher	CAV Acton	1963	1999
Alex Low	Gt King St, Electrical Shaftmoor Lane	1960	1990
Kenneth Low	Lucas GKS, Girling Cwmbran, Lucas France	1967	1999
Paul W Lucas	Lucas Aerospace	1978	1995

Name	Location	From	To
Vic Lucas	Lucas Birmingham	1964	2002
R E Lucas			
Kenneth Luce	Aerospace Fordhouses	1963	1987
G R Luckett	Gt King St, Telford	1960	1989
John Lucy	CAV Acton	1959	1991
W R Luff	Aerospace Willesden, Aerospace Hemel Hempstead	1936	1982
Ross Lumsden	Formans Rd, Gt Hampton St	1954	1986
D E Lyndsay	Gt King St, Formans Rd	1966	1980
John J Lyons	Aerospace Victor Works	1953	1988
Paul Lyons	Aerospace Burnley	1977	1988
Pauline J MacCauley (Smart)	Gt Hampton St	1951	1984
Stewart MacGill	CAV Acton, CAV Gillingham	1962	1989
G R Machin	Gt King St, Electrical Shaftmoor Lane	1946	1983
Don Mack	CAV Hartridge, CAV Bryce	1961	1989
Andrea Mackenzie	Girling Service West Bromwich, Gt Hampton St	1970	1999
Reg Mackie	Aerospace Luton	1967	1987
David MacLeod	Lucas Shirley, Rists Newcastle	1961	2000
Arnold MacPherson	Lucas Service UK	1960	1998
Kenneth L Maddox	Girling Cwmbran	1965	1997
Donald H Madeley	Aerospace Marston Green, Aerospace Shaftmoor Lane	1956	1988
Peter Magin	CAV Acton	1961	1993
Thomas Maiden	Gt King St, Holford	1975	1993
G Mustifa Malik	CAV Gillingham, CAV Rochester	1976	1992
Amna N Malik	CAV Rochester, CAV Gillingham	1976	1994
Brian Malin	Aerospace Shaftmoor Lane	1964	2000
Pat Mallett	Mono-Cam	1960	1982
C Mallouppa	CAV Acton	1953	1987
Arnold Mander	Lucas Gt King St	1937	1981
Malcom Norman Manley	Girling Cwmbran, Girling Pontypool	1959	1999
Frederick John Mant		1932	1975
E K Mantell			
Blanca and Marco Marandola	CAV Acton	1976	2001
Paul Marian	CAV Acton	1955	1999
William Marlow	Gt King St, Electrical Shaftmoor Lane	1954	1987
Mrs S M Marshall (Pearce)	Gt Hampton St, Fradley	1947	1986
David Marshall	Aerospace Fordhouses	1956	1989
Anthony Martin	Rists Newcastle	1969	1994
P Martin			
A Martins	CAV Acton	1975	2000
Granville A Marwood	Girling Cwmbran	1948	1985
Derek Mashford	Plymouth	1959	2000
C M Maslin	CAV Service UK	1965	1987
Arthur C Mason	Aerospace Hemel Hempstead	1968	1992
Betty Mason	Gt King St	1948	1980
Bryan Mason	Lucas Corporate	1957	1996
John A Massey	CAV Acton	1928	1976
Julie Matthews		1980	2000
E Matusiak	Aerospace Shaftmoor Lane	1964	1991
Derek May	CAV Acton, CAV Overseas	1962	2001
Harry May	CAV Bryce	1959	1981
Rex A May	Lucas GKS	1946	1984
A May	Lucas Birmingham	1945	1983
Philip Maybury	Holford	1982	1999
Anthony R Mays	CAV Acton	1943	1986
John McCarthy	CAV Acton	1964	1997
C D McCoy	Gt King St, Cannock, Chester St	1940	1984
Warren McDivitt	Gt Hampton St	1970	1987
Dr Keith McKewan	Gt King St, Formans Rd	1962	1997
Liz McGill	Lucas France	1997	2000
John J McGiveron	Aerospace Victor Works, Aerospace Huyton	1960	1992
John McGowan	Chester St, Gt King St	1952	1988
Raymond McKenna	CAV Sudbury	1960	2000
M J McKiernan	Lucas GKS		
Eileen McClean (Fitzgerald)	CAV Rochester, CAV Gillingham	1969	2002
Margaret McClean	Lucas Service UK	1973	1989
James McLeish	Aerospace Hemel Hempstead, Girling Cwmbran, Girling Overseas Ops	1963	1982
David J R McMullen	Lucas Gt King St, Girling Overseas Ops	1964	1996
G F McNally	Lucas Service UK	1949	1981
R N McRae	CAV Acton	1955	1987
Harold V Means	CAV Acton	1948	1981
Barrie Mears	Gt King St	1960	1988
Tony Measham	Lucas Gt King St	1952	1988
Richard Medhurst		1962	2000
Norman Meehan	Lucas Birmingham	1963	1989
Keith Meek	Girling Cwmbran, Girling Pontypool	1962	1999
John N Melbourne	Lucas Service UK	1973	2001
Kenneth Melleney	CAV Finchley	1966	1991
Frank Melling	Lucas Burnley		
Karl Menzies	Lucas Service UK	1967	1994
Alec J Mercer	Aerospace Hemel Hempstead	1951	1992
John Mercer	Girling Tyseley	1967	1982
Tom Meredith	Girling Pontypool, Girling Cwmbran	1967	1991
J R Meredith			
Fred Merrien	Fradley	1964	1987
John Patrick			
Merriman	Lucas GKS, Lucas Group Research Centre	1959	1993
Brian J Metcalf	Aerospace Burnley	1972	1982
P H Michell	CAV Acton	1962	2004
John Middlebrook	Aerospace Fordhouses	1960	1995
Brian Middlemass	Gt King St, College Rd	1971	1989
Derek Miller	Girling Cwmbran	1972	1999
D E Millington	Lucas Shirley, College Rd	1958	1991
Dave Mills	Aerospace Shaftmoor Lane	1979	1997
David J Mills	Mere Green, Gt King St, Formans Rd	1972	2000
Graham F Mills	CAV Acton	1959	1998
Mary Minchin	Aerospace Shaftmoor Lane, Aerospace Brueton House	1952	1986
M Minton			
Stuart Mitchell	Lucas Gt King St	1978	1984
Kit Mockett	Gt King St	1972	1987
Cahal C Moen	Formans Rd	1955	1987
Alex Moffat	Butlers, Gt King St	1961	1988
Ian Alistair Moffat	Gt Hampton St	1957	1994
John Moodie	Gt King St	1967	1988
John Moody	Gt King St, Chester St	1956	1981
James Moore		1977	1998
John Moore	Lucas Group Research Centre, Lucas CAV	1965	2001
Len Moore	CAV Acton, CAV Gillingham	1956	1996
Pat Moore	Gt King St, College Rd	1973	1999
Robert Moore	Lucas Shirley, Lucas Brueton House	1963	1997
H K Moorhouse	Aerospace Burnley	1965	1988
Delwyn Morgan	Girling Pontypool, Girling Cwmbran	1986	1993
Derek Morgan	Girling Cwmbran	1966	1999
Eric William Morgan	Aerospace Fordhouses, Aerospace Luton	1941	1989
Geoff Morgan	Lucas Electrical, Lucas CAV		
John Morgan	Lucas Service UK	1985	2000
J G Morley	Girling Bromborough	1967	1990
Mike Morrall	Lucas USA	1950	1976
Keith L Morrell	Gt King St, Lucas Shirley	1975	1997
Bill Morris	Aerospace Victor Works, Aerospace Huyton	1967	1993
Dennis William Morris	Gt King St, College Rd	1940	1984
Norman Morris	Gt King St	1944	1987
Raymond (Chris) Morris	Rists Newcastle	1953	1992
Leonard A Morrison	Lucas Service UK, Gt Hampton St	1941	1987
Alan Mortimer	Girling Cwmbran, Girling Pontypool	1961	1997
Bernard Powell Morton	Girling Cwmbran	1958	1990
C W Morton	Aerospace Hemel Hempstead	1955	1994

Name	Location	From	To
Roy Morton	Girling Tyseley, Girling Pontypool	1967	1991
D T Moseley	Girling Pontypool	1948	1989
Ivor H Moss	Hucclecote Gloucester	1969	1990
Ken Mothersole	CAV Acton, Lucas TVS	1951	1989
Anthony Mottram	Aerospace Huyton	1975	1991
Jean Mountford (Doody)	Lower Milehouse Lane	1949	1990
Donna Powell (Clark)	Aerospace Brueton House, Aerospace Shirley	1979	1998
R E Moxon	Lucas Birmingham	1960	1986
R F Mudge	Lucas Aerospace	1981	1993
Roger Mugford	CAV Acton	1956	1997
Mumtaz Mukadam	Rists Accrington	1973	1999
Clarence Evans Mulrain		1968	1980
Tim Munns	Lucas Service UK	1966	1998
Audrey E Munt	Aerospace Willesden	1960	1985
M Murphy (O'Brien)	Electrical Shaftmoor Lane, Gt Hampton St	1979	1992
Ian Murry	Lucas Marine	1979	1984
Kenneth Murray	Electrical Burnley	1958	1987
Morris Murray	Girling Bromborough	1963	1981
T J Murray	Lucas Girling	1953	1983
John Myers	CAV Acton	1945	1989
John Myring		1955	1980
H N Nabbs	Aerospace Hemel Hempstead	1952	1983
Jonathon Nash	Girling Service West Bromwich, Lucas Shirley	1991	1995
L C Nation	Gt King St	1953	1993
Stephen Naylor	Aerospace York Rd	1964	
D Needham			
L K Neumann (Andrzan)	Formans Rd	1965	1987
L J Nevett			
Tony Neville	CAV Gillingham, CAV Rochester	1961	1984
Noel H K Newman	Aerospace Willesden	1948	1988
Peter Leslie Newman	CAV Gillingham	1963	1998
Edward S Newton	Aerospace Bradford, Aerospace Burnley	1958	1985
John Nicholds	CAV Acton, Gt King St	1968	1990
Bill Nicholls		1957	1985
Leonard Nicholls	Aerospace Burnley	1953	1987
B Nicholls	CAV Acton	1963	1992
Len Nicholson	Aerospace Victor Works, Aerospace Huyton	1952	1987
Carl D Noake	Aerospace Shaftmoor Lane	1965	1993
Norman A Noakes	Gt King St	1945	1985
John A W Noble	Gt Hampton St	1963	1984
Steven Norgrove	Aerospace Brueton House, Aerospace Shaftmoor Lane	1989	1997
John Norman	Lucas Girling	1948	1988
Len Norris	Lucas CAV	1940	1987
Michael A Norris	CAV Acton	1962	1996
Jean M Nunney	CAV Rochester, CAV Gillingham	1958	1991
Arnold (Vic) Nuttall	CAV Sudbury	1953	1983
George Nuttall	Aerospace Burnley	1941	1979
David C Oates	CAV Acton, Gt King St, College Rd	1970	1989
Jean O'Brien (Wortley)	Fradley	1977	2000
Terry O'Brien	Keighley	1963	1997
Noel O'Connor	Gt King St, Fradley	1966	1998
Ken Ocraft	Gt King St, Holford	1958	1998
Kathy and Vince O'Donnell	Aerospace Shaftmoor Lane	1974	1984
Norman Ogden		1954	
Dr Keith Oldham	Lucas Shirley	1984	1997
Vytautas Olensevicius	CAV Finchley	1962	1987
Tony Oliver	CAV Acton	1944	1987
Brian E Ollis	Electrical Shaftmoor Lane, Aerospace Shaftmoor Lane, Aerospace Brueton House	1952	1993
George Onion	CAV Acton	1951	1983
Dennis R Onslow	CAV Rochester, CAV Gillingham	1959	1999
Trevor Edward Orford	Gt King St, Holford	1966	1999
Danny O'Ryan	Girling Tyseley, Girling Service West Bromwich	1954	1998
Russel Norman Osborne	Lucas Birmingham	1962	1981
Steve O'shaughnessy	Gt King St	1975	1986
Graham Osmond	Kienzle, Cannock	1974	1984
P D O'Sullivan			
Halina Oszmianska	Gt King St	1974	1987
Bill Ottoway	Aerospace Hemel Hempstead	1954	1988
Leslie Charles Ovenden	CAV Acton	1938	1981
Martin Owen	Gt King St, Holford	1968	2003
Peter Owen	Lucas Service UK	1941	1985
P J Owen			
W Joseph Ozog	Gt King St	1958	1987
Martin Packer	Bedford	1960	1995
Brian C Pagdin	Aerospace Shaftmoor Lane	1986	1993
Tony Page	Girling Cwmbran	1967	2000
David George Pagett	Aerospace Shaftmoor Lane	1960	1993
Doreen E Pagett	Lucas Gt King St	1965	1987
Roy Painter	Aerospace Fordhouses	1970	2000
Ivan J Palmer	CAV Gillingham, CAV Rochester	1976	1998
Ron Palmer	CAV Sudbury	1950	1998
D W Palmer	Aerospace Shaftmoor Lane	1947	1987
John William Pape		1964	1998
Murray Papworth	Electrical Birmingham	1978	1987
T L Pargeter	Chester St, Gt King St	1948	1980
Kenneth G Parker	CAV Acton	1951	1970
H L Parker	Electrical Shaftmoor Lane, Aerospace Shaftmoor Lane	1947	1983
R W J Parker	Lucas Gt King St	1941	1984
Lalji Velji Parmar		1976	1985
Geoffrey Parmenter	CAV Sudbury		
Louis J Parouty	Lucas Gt King St, College Rd	1940	1989
David Richard Parsons	Girling Bromborough	1971	1983
Malcom C Parsons	Girling Cwmbran	1953	1987
Mike Parsons	CAV Acton, Lucas Shirley	1966	1993
Norman Partridge	Gt King St	1932	1976
Andre Pasztor	Electrical Shaftmoor Lane	1960	1986
R A J Pate	CAV Acton	1973	1999
Dhruv Patel	CAV Acton, CAV Gillingham	1978	1998
Alan Patston		1981	1990
R H C Pattison			
Lawrence Dipple Payne	Lucas Gt King St, Lucas Shirley	1944	1986
Maurice Bryan Payne	Girling Cwmbran	1950	1989
Phil Payne	Girling Cwmbran	1957	1991
Ronald Payne		1952	1991
H G Payne	CAV Rochester, CAV Gillingham	1955	1991
Terence Peach	CAV Finchley, CAV Gillingham	1952	1999
Harold Peake	Aerospace Shaftmoor Lane, Aerospace Marston Green, Aerospace York Rd	1953	1981
Alison Pearce (Grogan)	Rists Accrington	1981	1999
Reginald Pearce	Lucas Gt King St	1961	1987
R Pearce	CAV Gillingham	1969	1996
Bill Peard	Girling Cwmbran	1949	1978
David Pearse	Aerospace Hemel Hempstead	1975	2002
Sir Brian Pearse	Lucas Corporate	1994	1997
John Pedder	Gt King St, Holford	1976	2001
Ivy Peglar (Meakin)	Gt King St, Holford	1964	1997
John C Pell	Lucas Service UK	1964	1977
Pierre Henri Peltret	CAV Acton	1958	1992
Joseph Penny	Gt Hampton St	1947	1988
Thomas John Peploe	Girling Cwmbran	1957	1986
David Peplow	Gt Hampton St	1970	1998
Trevor A Perkins	Girling Service West Bromwich, Gt Hampton St	1972	1999
Tom Perrins	Lucas Birmingham	1954	1980
John Perry	Lucas Industrial Equipment, CAV Buckingham	1965	1980

Name	Location	From	To
Colin Peters	Aerospace Shaftmoor Lane, College Rd	1959	1998
Ronald Pugh	Aerospace Shirley	1962	1978
John Peters	Formans Rd	1973	1989
Brian Phillips	CAV Acton	1967	1997
Lionel John Phillips	Girling Cwmbran	1963	1993
Norman E Phillips	Aerospace Shaftmoor Lane, Aerospace Victor Works	1939	1982
Peter Phillips	Gt King St	1956	1988
Ron Phillips	CAV Concord Rd	1968	1999
Trevor Phillips	CAV Rochester, CAV Gillingham	1954	1996
R G Phillips	Glasgow	1944	1982
Windsor John Philpin	Lucas Birmingham	1935	1977
R S W Philpott	Lucas Gt King St	1959	1988
John Pickering	Rists Newcastle, Aerospace Honiley	1962	1985
Cedric A Pickin	Rists Newcastle	1979	1997
Jim Pielow	Girling Overseas Ops	1961	1991
Laura Pierce (Bent)	Gt King St	1948	1987
E A Piggott	CAV Acton	1945	1959
I Pikelis	Electrical Shaftmoor Lane	1955	1986
P R G Pitman	Lucas World Service	1948	1991
Reginald T Pitt	Aerospace Shaftmoor Lane	1948	1986
M A Pittaway	Aerospace Shaftmoor Lane	1951	1984
Stuart Platt	Rists Newcastle	1960	1999
Albert A Pledger	Aerospace Shaftmoor Lane	1951	1983
Philip Pocknell	Aerospace Hemel Hempstead	1985	1999
Leonard Pooley	CAV Acton, Haddenham	1954	1980
David F Pope	Aerospace Huyton	1973	1993
Dennis Pope	CAV Gillingham	1978	1999
Randall Porter	CAV Rochester, CAV Gillingham	1975	2001
John Postans	Gt King St, Witney	1964	1984
Joyce Poulter	CAV Gillingham, CAV Rochester	1947	1979
David E Powell	CAV Acton	1955	1985
David Powell	CAV Acton, Lucas Park St	1954	1969
H W Powell	Girling Bromborough	1964	1982
Victor Power	Aerospace Victor Works	1955	1988
Wallace J Prangley	Girling Cwmbran, Girling Pontypool	1948	1983
Jeffrey Pratt	Girling Cwmbran, Girling Pontypool		
C J Preston	Lucas East West	1943	1989
Brian Price	Gt King St	1950	1988
D Brian Price	Girling Cwmbran	1957	1986
Derrick Price	Fradley	1970	2000
Joan Price (Knight)	Brockworth Gloucester		1980
Ken Price	Electrical Shaftmoor Lane, Electrical Australia	1943	1980
Raymond W Price	Formans Rd, Electrical Shaftmoor Lane, Gt King St	1934	1981
G T Price	Aerospace Fordhouses	1953	1996
Eric Pritchard	Electrical Shaftmoor Lane, Electrical Australia	1950	1972
Ian D Privett	Gt King St	1968	1992
Steve Prosser	Aerospace Coventry	1979	1989
David Vivian Pugh	Girling Pontypool	1984	1999
David Edward Purchase	Lucas Gt King St, Rists Newcastle	1966	1992
Anthony Purkiss	Aerospace Hemel Hempstead	1960	2001
H M Pynor			
E F Quinton			
C T Quinton	Lucas Shaftmoor Lane	1947	1980
Aziz Ahmed Qureshi	CAV Acton	1973	1987
Kenneth Radburn	Lucas Gt King St	1960	1987
E J Rainbird	Gt Hampton St, Lucas Burnley	1952	1988
Michael and Barbara Rainsbury (Hammond)			1975
Peter Ralph	CAV Sudbury, CAV Ipswich	1976	1982
Bertie Rampersad		1969	1995
Sarah Wootton-Ramsay	Apprentice	1980	1986
Graham Randle	Aerospace York Rd	1965	1991
William Allan Rankin	CAV Service UK	1956	1990
John A Raper	Lucas Girling	1955	1988
Ken Ratcliffe	CAV Acton	1964	1989
Tim Ratcliffe	Lucas Birmingham	1985	1995
Jon Rawlings	Girling Fen End	1995	2002
B E Raymond	CAV Sudbury	1965	1983
Jim Rayner	CAV Acton, Haddenham	1971	1999
D M Redfearn	CAV Acton, Lucas New Zealand	1959	1981
M D Reece	Girling Cwmbran	1954	1988
David William Rees	Chester St	1970	1980
William John Rees	Lucas Service UK	1972	2000
Susan Reeve	CAV Acton, Haddenham	1975	1995
Chris (Rambo) Reeves	CAV Buckingham	1978	1992
Sheila Reith	Electrical Shaftmoor Lane	1967	1988
Piaras B Renihan	CAV Overseas	1960	1989
Colin Rennals	Mere Green	1973	2003
Harry Reynolds	Aerospace Hemel Hempstead	1938	1982
Dr Sydney Richards	Lucas Group Research Centre	1955	1992
Keith Richards	Lucas Service UK	1987	1996
Peter J Richards	CAV Sudbury	1956	1987
Philip Leonard Richardson	Rists Newcastle	1957	1997
Alan Riddington	Lucas Gt King St, Lucas Troy USA	1953	1983
Ernest Reginald Rider	Aerospace Victor Works		1982
George P Rigby	Lucas Birmingham	1972	1992
R W Rigby	Aerospace York Rd	1954	1988
F Riley	Aerospace Bradford	1966	2002
Henry Ripley	Aerospace Burnley	1977	1989
Alexander Risk	CAV Service UK	1956	1990
James Rivett	Aerospace Burnley	1972	1982
F T Rixon	Lucas Service UK	1934	1982
David Roberts	Aerospace Fordhouses	1983	1997
David W Roberts	Lucas Park St, Aerospace Bradley	1956	1968
John Roberts	Aerospace Victor Works, CAV Sudbury	1953	1987
Peter N Roberts	Aerospace Shaftmoor Lane	1963	1982
William L Roberts	Aerospace Victor Works	1953	1983
S G Roberts	CAV Acton	1948	1983
C A Robertson			
Alfred Robinson	Lucas Service UK	1953	1978
Brian F G Robinson	Aerospace Hemel Hempstead	1957	1997
G Robinson	Gt King St, Holford	1955	1996
G E Robinson	Lucas Gt King St	1940	1987
E H Robinson	CAV Hartridge	1956	1979
D A Robinson	Aerospace Hemel Hempstead	1954	1988
R Rodens			
Joaquim F G Rodrigues	CAV Acton	1977	1998
Bryan Rogers	Mere Green	1957	1992
Mike Rogers	Aerospace Shaftmoor Lane	1959	1993
Victor R Rogers	CAV Buckingham	1965	1997
Bill Rollason	Gt Hampton St	1972	2000
A Roper			
A F Rosankiewicz	CAV Acton	1950	1986
David Rose	Aerospace York Rd	1970	1997
Edna Rose	Dordrecht Rd	1972	1985
Jim Rose	Aerospace Marston Green	1973	2001
G H Rosenthal	CAV Acton	1951	1981
R S Rosier	CAV Rochester, CAV Gillingham	1951	1990
Michael Roughton	Lucas GKS, Aerospace York Rd	1964	1997
Andy Rouse	Lucas Girling, Lucas CAV	1954	1989
Frank Rousseau	Aerospace Coventry	1974	2002
Joyce Lilian Rowe	Formans Rd, Electrical Shaftmoor Lane	1960	1987
E D Rowland	Aerospace Willesden	1949	1982
Ron Rowles	Girling Cwmbran, Lucas Industrial Equipment	1962	1979
A S Rowson	Aerospace Fordhouses	1955	1998
Fred'k A Rudd	Lucas Service UK	1972	1989
Rodney Rumble	Aerospace Hemel Hempstead	1972	1992
Norman E Rundle	Lucas Defence Systems Camberly	1975	1978
Albert Rushton	Marshall Lake Rd	1969	1981
Ellen M Russell	Fradley	1972	1992
Joan I Russell	Lucas GKS	1935	1974
Robert William Russell	Aerospace Victor Works, Aerospace Huyton	1969	1994
B C Russon			
Paul Ryan	Girling Service West Bromwich, Gt Hampton St	1975	1993

Name	Location	From	To
T A Ryan	CAV Acton	1957	1996
Raymond Rymer	Formans Rd	1968	1988
F A D Sadler	Girling Tyseley		
Alan Sagar	Lucas Burnley	1944	1985
T B Sagar			
Clive Sainsbury	Lucas Shirley, Lucas Group Research Centre	1968	1999
C R Sainsbury			
Akinobu Sakashita	Lucas Kk Tokyo	1972	2001
A P Sale			
Miss Hilda M Salt	Fradley	1967	1983
L Salter	Aerospace Victor Works	1953	1988
N D Salter	Aerospace Shaftmoor Lane	1948	1983
Peter Samson	Lucas Girling	1963	1992
John Sandy	Aerospace Shaftmoor Lane	1948	1984
J N Sandys	CAV Rochester	1948	1989
Kenneth A Saunders	Aerospace Fordhouses	1963	1992
Ralph Saunders	CAV Gillingham	1973	1996
Derek Savage	Girling Cwmbran, Lucas Troy USA	1965	2000
Brian N Savin	Fradley	1973	1981
Peter N Sawyer	Aerospace Hemel Hempstead	1954	1991
M G Sayles	Aerospace Bradford	1953	1991
Paul Scase	Gt King St, Gt Hampton St	1950	1990
George Schanzer	Girling Cwmbran	1955	1987
Mr Ray Scott	Electrical Shaftmoor Lane	1947	1985
Peter F Scott	Lucas CAV, CAV Bryce	1967	1987
Thomas Scott	Electrical Burnley	1944	1970
N Scullin	Girling Tyseley	1955	1978
Howard Sedgwick	Electrical Burnley	1961	1995
L E Selby	Lucas GKS, Aerospace Liverpool	1939	1998
John Setchfield	Lucas Park St, Lucas Panama	1964	1983
Norman Sewell	Lucas CAV, CAV Gillingham	1965	1999
David Shackley	Lucas Corporate Shirley	1958	1995
Akram Shahin	Lucas GKS	1964	2000
John Joseph Sharpe	CAV Acton	1972	2004
Ray Sharpe	Aerospace Bradford	1975	1994
Charles Sharpston	CAV Acton, CAV Overseas	1955	1965
H A Sharram	Girling Cwmbran, Girling Bromborough	1947	1981
John Robert Shaw	CAV Acton	1949	1980
P J Shaw			
Mary Shears	Electrical Birmingham	1969	1995
Kenneth Sheminant	CAV Acton	1954	1989
Richard and Daphne Shepheard	CAV Rochester, CAV Gillingham	1955	1993
Keith Shepherd	Lucas Burnley, Aerospace Burnley	1962	1995
Ronald Sheraton	CAV Acton, CAV Gillingham	1967	1986
Walter Sherwood	Aerospace Hemel Hempstead	1953	1988
E R Sheward	Gt King St, Electrical Shaftmoor Lane	1935	1980
Fred J Shillingford		1956	1981
Denis Shilston	Gt King St	1951	1988
Anthony Shires	Mere Green, College Rd	1968	2001
John Shorthouse	Lucas Birmingham	1963	2000
Peter T Shortland	CAV Rochester, CAV Gillingham	1952	1990
David Siddall	Lucas Burnley	1965	1980
Terry Silcock	CAV Concord Rd	1958	1991
Gordon Silverson	Girling Cwmbran	1947	1981
Brian Sim	Aerospace Wood Top	1957	1988
Bob Simpkin	Lucas Group Research Centre	1979	1997
Brian Simpson	Aerospace Shaftmoor Lane	1956	1988
John Simpson		1961	2001
Ken Simpson	CAV Acton	1942	1985
Lord Simpson	Lucas Corporate	1994	1996
Mary Simpson	Aerospace Wood Top	1957	1974
G Simpson Simpson-Jones CBE		1957	1980
Gerald R Sims	Girling Tyseley, Girling Pontypool	1958	1990
J Sinclair	Formans Rd	1933	1980
John Samuel Singleton	CAV Acton	1939	1984
Barrie Skinner	CAV Acton	1966	1999
Robert T J Skinner	CAV Acton, Aerospace Shaftmoor Lane	1944	1983
Leslie William Skipp	CAV Acton	1947	1986
Alan Slater	Formans Rd	1976	1989
Peter Slater	Aerospace Fordhouses		
Barry Smith	Lucas Service UK	1963	1998
Bob Smith	Aerospace Hemel Hempstead	1958	1991
Gordon J Smith	Gt King St	1942	1985
Gwendoline Smith (Moore)	Aerospace Shaftmoor Lane	1939	1979
John (Jack) Smith	Gt Hampton St, Cannock	1939	1976
Ken Smith	Gt Hampton St, Lucas Electrical	1943	1982
Norman Smith	Aerospace Shaftmoor Lane	1949	1984
Raymond Smith	Aerospace Coventry	1951	1980
Roger V F Smith	Gt King St	1965	1998
Stuart Smith	Girling Cwmbran	1968	2003
Terence Smith	CAV Acton	1956	1998
Terry Smith	Lucas Girling, Girling Overseas Ops	1956	1997
Tony Smith	CAV Acton	1966	1990
Vaughan Smith	Girling Cwmbran	1961	1991
D A Smith	Girling Fen End	1989	1998
S L Smith			
J G Smith	Lucas Group Research Centre	1961	1997
D A Smith			
Aubrey Smith	Aerospace Shaftmoor Lane	1952	1982
Clive Smith	CAV Rochester, CAV Gillingham	1954	1997
E S Smith	Formans Rd	1958	1981
Graham Smith	Lucas Service UK	1961	1999
John Smith	Lucas Birmingham	1960	1991
M F Smith	Rists Newcastle	1963	1998
R J Smith			
Ronald Henry Smith	Gt Hampton St	1959	1991
Colin Smith	Aerospace Shaftmoor Lane	1958	1984
S W Smith	Gt Hampton St, Gt King St	1946	1981
Victor Smith	Gt Hampton St	1969	1998
R H (Dick) Snewin	Gt King St, Gt Hampton St	1983	1989
Tom Snook	Girling Cwmbran, Girling Pontypool	1964	1988
Jan J Sokolowski	CAV Acton	1950	1984
John Alfred Solanky	Lucas Gt King St, Lucas Group Research Centre	1965	2001
Barrie Sollars	CAV Gillingham	1962	1996
Phil Jones	Aerospace Luton	1983	1993
Stanislaw Sosnowski	CAV Acton	1953	1984
Dennis Southall		1979	2002
C C Sparey	Lucas Service UK	1963	1986
M Spayne	Haddenham	1959	1983
David J Speed	CAV Acton, CAV Bryce	1962	2000
Jean Spencer		1948	1984
R N Spencer	Girling Cwmbran	1980	1996
Steve Spiller	Holford	1965	1993
Hugh D Spottiswoode	Lucas Park St, Lucas Gt King St	1950	1983
S Spragg			
Douglas R Squire	CAV Acton, CAV Service UK	1955	1988
Ken Stafford	Gt Hampton St, Girling Overseas Ops	1949	1986
Bill Stanley	Aerospace Hemel Hempstead	1953	1992
Mrs Brenda Stanley	CAV Rochester, CAV Gillingham	1988	1999
Mr R J Stanton	Aerospace Shaftmoor Lane	1953	1983
T Starkey	Aerospace Huyton	1955	1988
Frank Starr	Aerospace Bradford	1948	1990
Raymond Stead	CAV Acton	1970	1982
Beresford (Beck) Stevens	Aerospace York Rd	1954	1990
Chris and Jim Stevens	Lucas Gt King St, Lucas Hilver, Holford	1956	1998
J W Stevens			
Eric William Stevens	Aerospace Victor Works	1958	1981
John Stewart-Wilson	Aerospace Hemel Hempstead	1980	2000

Name	Location	From	To
A Stidder	Lucas Service UK	1970	1998
Stanley John Still	Lucas Service UK	1959	1999
Aston Stockwell	CAV Acton, Aerospace Rotax	1940	1977
D Stojakovic	Electrical Shaftmoor Lane	1967	1986
T L Stokes	Aerospace Hemel Hempstead	1960	1987
Haydn John Stone	Girling Cwmbran	1972	1999
Sydney B Stonehouse	Lucas Gt King St, Lucas Aerospace	1959	1993
Derek Storey	Tylers Green Penn	1946	1995
Jesse Strange	Aerospace Hemel Hempstead	1954	1981
Hans Hoeneck	Lucas Girling		
Ian Strangward	Lucas Electrical	1982	1988
Ken Strangward	Lucas Aerospace, Lucas Girling	1947	1990
Simon Strothers	Aerospace Fordhouses	1984	1997
Derek Summers	CAV Sudbury	1975	1996
Elsie Irene Sutton		1946	1979
Reg Sutton	Aerospace Hemel Hempstead	1989	1992
A B Sutton	CAV Rochester, CAV Gillingham	1949	1986
Ronald Leslie Frank Swain	CAV Gillingham	1977	1999
Trevor A Swain	Electrical Burnley	1961	1988
Steven Swann	Lucas Service UK	1977	1993
Richard Swasbrook	CAV Acton	1974	1999
R Tabony	Gt Hampton St	1963	1990
Joyce Tadman	Marshall Lake Rd	1965	1981
Louis Andrew Takkos	CAV Acton	1975	1998
Mohamed Ali Talib	Electrical Shaftmoor Lane	1967	1999
Bill Taplin		1961	1983
Michael Leslie Tassel	CAV Rochester, CAV Gillingham	1963	2001
Herbert Tattersall	Lucas Burnley	1946	1980
Alan Taylor	Formans Rd	1957	1989
Brian 'Pope' Taylor	Gt King St	1976	1988
Florence Taylor	Formans Rd, Lucas Aerospace	1969	1982
Lillian Taylor	Gt King St	1973	1986
Ronald J Taylor	Gt King St, Gt Hampton St	1950	1982
Tony Taylor	CAV Acton, CAV Sudbury	1954	1986
H V Taylor	CAV Acton	1962	1979
P Taylor	Aerospace Hemel Hempstead	1965	1988
Peter Templeton	Girling Fen End	1985	1993
John Thickens	Lucas Gt King St	1976	1993
Alan E Thirkell	CAV Acton, CAV Gillingham	1960	1991
David Thomas	Lucas Aerospace	1969	1996
Malcolm Thomas	Girling Cwmbran	1963	1994
Tom Thomas	Marshall Lake Rd	1973	1987
C A Thomas	Electrical Shaftmoor Lane	1953	1987
Alan Thompson	Aerospace Wood Top, Aerospace Hargherclough	1943	1982
Brian Thompson	Aerospace Hargherclough	1963	1988
Maurice Thompson	Formans Rd	1954	1982
Neil Thompson	Rists Accrington	1992	1997
D N Thompson	Chester St, Electrical Shaftmoor Lane	1947	1981
T V Thompson	Girling Bromborough, Rists Newcastle	1960	1990
L J Thomsen	CAV Acton	1941	1985
John Thomson	Lucas Service UK	1942	1990
Bert (Buster) Thorlby	CAV Gillingham, CAV Rochester	1948	1987
Alan T Thorp	Lucas Electrical, Lucas TVS	1943	1988
Barry Thorp	Lucas Service UK, Kienzle	1984	1994
Peter Thorpe	Lucas Electrical, Lucas Aerospace	1960	2000
Brian J Tidmarsh	CAV Acton, Aerospace Coventry	1959	2000
Michael John Tipping	Aerospace Coventry	1971	1999
J Tipton	Aerospace York Rd	1969	2001
A G Tofield	CAV Finchley	1964	1982
Glyn Tomkins	Lucas Group Research Centre	1973	1996
D S Tongue			
Alan Tooze	Gt King St	1960	1988
Alan Toplis	Gt King St, Lucas World Service	1964	1980
E W Townsend	CAV Acton	-	1975
Ronald Tracey	CAV Acton	1948	1987
Jim Trafford	CAV Acton, CAV Gillingham	1965	1999
Beryl Train (Gleed)	Girling Tyseley	1940	1955
Arthur Trengrouse	Gt King St	1964	1987
Dereck Tribe	Lucas Aerospace	1960	1995
Eric George Tricker	CAV Sudbury	1959	1992
P B Tromans	Aerospace Shaftmoor Lane	1948	1984
Howard F J Trott	Girling Pontypool	1979	2001
George Trubshaw	Aerospace Fordhouses	1939	1978
Colin Tuby	Electrical Shaftmoor Lane	1967	1994
Pat Tuck	CAV Acton, CAV Gillingham	1962	1998
Wally Tuck	Aerospace Hemel Hempstead	1957	1992
Kieran Tucker	Aerospace Hemel Hempstead	1958	1995
John Tudor	Gt King St	1948	1989
J F Tufnell	Electrical Shaftmoor Lane	1933	1973
Desmond Tunks	CAV Hartridge	1966	1990
S Tunn	CAV Borehamwood	1942	
David J Turner	Lucas Gt King St	1952	1988
Eddie Turner	Gt King St	1965	1998
George Bernard Turner	Gt King St, CAV Sudbury	1964	1989
Michael Hamilton Turner	CAV Finchley		1987
D J Turner	CAV Acton	1959	1991
J R Tweedale			
Terry Twigger	Lucas Aerospace	1977	1993
John Umpleby	Electrical Burnley	1970	2003
K S Valentine	Park Royal	1977	1992
David and Maureen Vaughan	Gt Hampton St	1970	1996
Keith Vaughan	Girling Cwmbran, Girling Pontypool	1968	1993
Bob and Hilary Vernon	Gt Hampton St, Lucas Service UK	1966	2000
Peter Vincent	Gt King St, Lucas Shirley	1966	2000
George Vine	CAV Acton, CAV Gillingham	1940	1985
Jack Vine	CAV Rochester, CAV Gillingham	1965	1987
Edward Peter Viner	Aerospace York Rd	1980	2002
David A Vinson	CAV Acton, CAV Gillingham	1960	2004
Donald Stanley Voice	Lucas Birmingham	1972	1988
W B Vowles	Girling Cwmbran, Girling Bromborough	1947	1989
John Waby	Aerospace Huyton	1960	1993
Mr Andrew Waddell	Fradley	1958	1984
Victor Wadsworth	Gt King St, Holford	1963	2000
Ronald Waghorn	CAV Rochester	1949	1983
David Robert Waine	College Rd	1960	1992
John R Wakefield	CAV Acton	1957	2002
Arthur Walford	Formans Rd	1962	1987
David Walker	Lucas Service UK	1966	1998
John Walker	Gt King St, Electrical Shaftmoor Lane	1937	1974
Roger Arthur Walker	Aerospace Hemel Hempstead, Aerospace Rotax	1963	2002
Margaret Wall	Mere Green	1968	2000
Sheila Wall	Mere Green	1967	1996
Tom Wall	Aerospace Fordhouses	1962	1992
Douglas Wallace	CAV Sudbury	1963	1997
J S Waller	Girling Fen End	1984	1995
W A V Wallington			
Rita Wallis	CAV Acton	1948	1987
David John Walmsley	Electrical Eastern Avenue Burnley	1966	2000
Anthony Walsh	Aerospace Bradford	1969	1997
John Walsh	CAV Acton	1960	1994
Kieran M Walsh	Lucas Gt King St	1984	1988
Cyril George Walton	Chesterton	1967	1987
Mr T J Walton	CAV Finchley	1955	1990
Clement Wang	CAV Acton	1956	1994
Barry Ward	Aerospace Marston Green	1960	1993
John J Ward	CAV Rochester, CAV Gillingham	1954	1988
Kevin Ward	Aerospace Wood Top	1954	1988

Name	Location(s)	From	To
Robert W Ward	Formans Rd, Lucas Service UK	1967	2001
Val and John Ward	Gt King St, Mere Green	1954	1999
K A Ward	Gt King St, Lucas CAV	1940	
Andy Warn	Lucas Service UK	1980	1999
Ivy Warr	Gt King St	1968	1975
Arthur Warrilow	Fradley	1962	1991
Mr WGF and Mrs K Waters	Lucas CAV	1963	1983
Alan Watkins	Lucas Group Research Centre, Formans Rd, Lucas Aerospace	1962	1989
L J Watkins	Lucas CAV, Haddenham	1967	1998
Geoff Watkinson	CAV Service UK	1954	1988
Mrs A M Watson (Walker)	Gt King St, Gt Hampton St	1953	1991
A A Watson	Fradley	1970	1991
J A Watts	Fradley, Gt Hampton St	1940	1981
Agnes Weaver	Aerospace Shaftmoor Lane	1948	1976
Roy Webb	Lucas Service UK	1950	1992
G A Webb	Lucas Aerospace	1956	1990
C A Webb			
Douglas Wells		1951	1988
Harold E Wells	CAV Acton	1961	1981
Maurice Wells	Lucas Electrical, Formans Rd	1948	1988
G Welsh	Aerospace Victor Works, Aerospace Huyton	1957	1990
Gary John Werrett	Girling Cwmbran	1963	1994
John G W West	Gt King St, Electrical Shaftmoor Lane	1957	1987
Peter West	Lucas Burnley	1953	1982
Gordon Westwell	Gt King St	1957	1986
Bill L Westwood	Formans Rd, Cannock	1955	1987
T A Westwood	Lucas Service UK, Gt Hampton St	1949	1983
Joseph Whalley	Aerospace Wood Top	1943	1980
David Whatley	Aerospace Shaftmoor Lane	1961	2001
Norma Wheat	Rists Newcastle	1976	1999
K J Wheeler	Girling Cwmbran		
Patricia Whelan	Chester St, Gt King St	1969	1987
Mike Whick	Lucas Girling, Lucas Service UK	1965	2000
Anthony J H While	Aerospace Shaftmoor Lane	1979	1991
Janet Lynne While	Mere Green	1983	2000
Brian White	CAV Acton	1952	1995
Harry F White	Aerospace Victor Works, Aerospace Huyton	1952	1983
Ian White	Lucas Engineering & Systems	1968	1995
Roy White	CAV Rochester, CAV Gillingham	1955	1986
Cyril Whitehead	Cambridge	1959	1997
Ken R Whitehouse	Lucas GKS, Lucas Shirley	1960	1995
J Whitehouse	Gt Hampton St, Lucas Brueton House	1973	2001
M Whiteoak		1953	1992
Elsie Whiteside	CAV Rochester, CAV Gillingham	1969	1986
George Whiteside	Aerospace Burnley	1956	1987
Mrs Freda Norris	CAV Rochester, CAV Gillingham	1969	1987
Doreen Whitmore (Chatwin)	Lucas GKS	1961	1986
Frederick Whitmore	Lucas GKS	1968	1998
Ron Whitney	CAV Acton	1943	1988
M J Whittingham	Gt Hampton St	1952	1990
Christopher Whittle	Aerospace Hemel Hempstead	1968	1986
Robert Whitworth	Lucas Service UK	1967	1999
Len Whyley	Electrical Shaftmoor Lane, College Rd	1940	1980
E M Wickfield	Electrical Shaftmoor Lane	1968	1986
F Wilcock	Aerospace Hargherclough, Aerospace Wood Top	1956	1985
Donovan Wilde	Aerospace Shaftmoor Lane, Lucas Brueton House	1948	1990
Mrs Bernice Wilkes	Fradley	1976	1997
Fred Wilkins	CAV Rochester, CAV Gillingham	1949	1989
David Wilkinson	Aerospace Bradford	1957	1997
Laurence Wilkinson	Formans Rd	1963	1980
Norman Willett	Lucas Birmingham	1978	1989
Samuel David Willetts	Aerospace Shaftmoor Lane	1965	1988
Alan Williams	Lucas Burnley	1967	1991
Bernard John Williams	Aerospace Shaftmoor Lane, Electrical Shaftmoor Lane, Aerospace Fordhouses	1956	1993
Carey (Bill) Williams	Lucas Girling	1941	1982
Ian J Williams	Lucas Burnley	1959	1992
John D Williams	Aerospace Hemel Hempstead, Aerospace York Rd	1953	1988
John Richard Williams	Electrical Shaftmoor Lane, Lucas GKS	1955	1989
Kay Williams	Girling Cwmbran	1962	1986
Norman Williams	Girling Pontypool	1963	2003
Richard Williams	CAV Rochester, CAV Gillingham	1967	1999
Ron Williams	Lucas Service UK	1966	1998
Walter Edward Williams	Girling Cwmbran, Fradley	1951	1988
A C Williams	Gt King St, Fradley	1958	1989
F W Williams	Girling Cwmbran	1946	1985
A Williams	Lucas Group Research Centre	1953	1988
David C Williams	Aerospace Hemel Hempstead	1957	1992
Andrew Willis	Lucas GKS, Lucas Brueton House	1970	1997
G Willis	Aerospace Victor Works	1965	1993
Mike Wills	Aerospace Hemel Hempstead	1986	2002
Alfred Wilson	Lucas Aerospace	1939	1977
Edward G Wilson	Formans Rd	1962	1980
Peter Wilson	CAV Rochester, CAV Gillingham	1967	1993
Barrie Windsor	Rists Newcastle	1969	1999
Bernard Winfield	Aerospace Burnley	1961	1988
John Winfield	Gt King St	1967	1987
M K Wing	CAV Acton, CAV Overseas	1954	1993
James W Wisdom	Aerospace Wood Top, Gt King St	1951	1980
Mike Wise	Gt Hampton St, Lucas Electrical	1965	1982
Arthur Withe	Aerospace Victor Works	1960	1988
Doug Witt	CAV Acton	1947	1984
Kieron Witt	Lucas CAV	1977	1981
Helen Wollerton (Watson)	Lucas Aerospace	1976	1987
Alan Wood	Lucas Service UK, Kienzle	1950	1991
Barry Wood	Gt King St	1942	1988
Brian Wood	Formans Rd	1936	1980
C J Phillip Wood	Gt King St, Chester St	1948	1986
Colin Wood	Aerospace Fordhouses	1957	1988
Dorothy M Wood	Lucas Electrical	1940	1975
Peter Wood	Aerospace York Rd	1953	1990
D G Woodhouse	CAV Finchley	1956	1991
Hugh Wood	CAV Acton	1951	1986
L J Woodman	CAV Acton	1941	1981
Ivor Woods	Lucas GKS	1946	1982
V Woodward	Shaftmoor Lane	1959	1997
M C Woodward	Lucas Electrical, Lucas Corporate Shirley	1962	1997
Norman S Wray	CAV Rochester	1952	1981
Joan Wright	Gt Hampton St	1961	1988
John Leonard Wright	CAV Acton, CAV Rochester	1938	1975
Kenneth Ronald Wright	Aerospace Fordhouses	1982	1994
Maurice Wright	Lucas Group Research Centre	1954	1987
Stephen Wright	Lucas GKS	1979	1986
William J Wright	Formans Rd	1966	1983
J Wright	Aerospace Wood Top	1954	1980
Phil M Writer	CAV Acton	1973	1984
A C Wyatt	CAV Acton, CAV Rochester	1948	1981
G Wyles	Aerospace Fordhouses	1969	1989
Clifford Yates	Aerospace Willesden, Aerospace Hemel Hempstead	1940	1982
Malcolm Yates	Lucas Electrical, Lucas Girling, Lucas CAV	1943	1987
William Young	Lucas GKS	1948	1979
Jim Zigel	Lucas Aerospace, Lucas USA	1987	1999